AGEE:

Selected
Literary Documents

AGEE:

Selected
Literary Documents

edited by
Victor A. Kramer

The Whitston Publishing Company
Troy, New York
1996

Copyright 1996
Victor A. Kramer

Library of Congress Catalog Card Number 95-62174

ISBN 0-87875-465-2

Printed in the United States of America

This Book is dedicated
to
the memory of
Patricia Anne Bailey

Contents

Preface

Items in this collection of literary documents have been selected to represent James Agee's many kinds of writing. They range from his earliest moments of aspiration to the late 1940s when, as mature writer, he had demonstrated he could produce literary work within a wide variety of modes. This selection of documents spans over twenty-five years in Agee's career and demonstrates his movement as a writer who first mastered conventional prose, as well as dramatic and poetic forms, and then went on to develop distinctive methods of writing based on an intensely felt awareness of the need to observe and "honor" reality, a task which he felt was especially difficult during the final years of his life even though he had achieved considerable success as a professional writer.

An acquaintance of Agee's remarked to me in 1970 that whenever Agee was asked to designate his profession he would never answer "poet," or "novelist," or "journalist," or "critic," or "screen-play writer"—all of which he was. Instead, Agee simply replied that he was a "writer." Such simplicity says much about him as a person, and it also indicates how he went about his job as writer throughout a very productive, yet diverse career. Agee's varied production is, however, more of a piece than some commentators have suspected because always informing his precise style are strong moral convictions and his concern with accuracy of observation. His definite moral concern (reflected in the preciseness of observation) informs all the published work, and it is such a concern which unites all of these ungathered pieces, too.

This volume consists of some early, some unsigned, and even some unfinished documents; yet it probably is true that as much, or more, energy and enthusiasm went into these diverse writings as went into the extremely revealing letters which Agee wrote to Father James Harold Flye over the same thirty year period. It is in the same spirit of respect with which Father Flye edited Agee's revealing correspondence that these writings are gathered. Each piece stands as a separate performance, yet when read together all these documents reveal much about Agee's interests, and, as a writer, his development toward the kinds of accomplishments which punctuated his career. Cumulatively, these ungathered pieces help us to understand the published work. This collection is the natural outgrowth of my study of Agee during the past two decades.

This book consists of fifty separate pieces, most of which have been before unavailable even to the most dedicated reader. Only through careful use of bibliographies can Agee's unsigned book reviews be identified, or his juvenilia located. In addition to the poetry, fiction, and drama which appeared only in student publications, *The Phillips Exeter Monthly* and the *Harvard Advocate*, and the unsigned book reviews from *Time* magazine, which have been heretofore inaccessible and are now selected here, other revealing material remains in manuscript. It is safe to assume that few of Agee's admirers will have had time to seek out all these materials and thus this selection will assist readers to appreciate Agee's total literary output.

This book includes several items which have not been available (except in my doctoral dissertation) as well as some which, while posthumously edited, appeared in limited academic publication. (For example, my editions of the early poem, "Pygmalion," the complete "Work" chapter for *Famous Men*, and "1928 Story" were published between 1968 and 1976.) Other unpublished data and information remains in manuscript. Those materials are, however, of limited value to someone seeking knowledge about Agee's development as a writer.

Since *James Agee: Selected Journalism*, edited by Paul Ashdown, is now available in a companion volume published by the University of Tennessee Press, the focus here is placed on the literary career, and while this gathering is not a complete edition of ungathered or unpublished literary materials, it is an attempt to provide the most significant materials which seem of most importance for understanding this writer's progression from an ambitious beginner to accomplished writer who could, as he once wrote to Father Flye, turn on the valve like a water faucet and write. Because these various poems, sketches, dramas, reviews, statements, and stories include the polished and the fragmented, they must be read with this in mind. All these materials reflect Agee as a craftsman of language *and* as an observer of his culture. The range of material clearly also demonstrates how the career progressed. Agee's earliest writings were preparation for someone who had the gift of writing; his journalism and speculative work of mid-career provides a foundation for the later often autobiographical accomplishments in fiction and in screenplay writing.

This gathering reminds us that Agee was seldom satisfied with his accomplishments, and therefore much of what he wrote became a conscious step away from earlier accomplishments. His frequent experimentation allowed him to begin many projects with a fresh eye, and to build on what was already done. By reading each of these pieces as indication of steps in the development toward the major fictional work, we appreciate Agee's struggle to be a good writer, and we also see the relationship of his continuing struggle toward the successes of his best known mature writing. This collection should assist readers in seeing the continuity of the total career.

The materials which have been selected for this volume include the majority of Agee's significant ungathered and unpublished literary writing which promises to be of value for scholars who seek to understand the development of his career as a writer. While still other pieces and fragments do remain ungathered in issues of *The Phillips Exeter Monthly*, or the *Harvard Advocate*, or *Time*, and remain in manuscript at the Harry Ransom Humanities Research Center of the University of Texas, I have included here the best of the available materials I consider to be necessary to give a broad picture of Agee's developing literary career.

Materials in two other categories remain to be published in the future. Agee's correspondence with persons such as Robert Fitzgerald, Dwight Macdonald, and Walker Evans, for example, will eventually make a significant volume which will provide more information about the complexity of a writer who provided such a poignant picture of himself in his letters to Father Flye. Film materials, especially screenplays, might also be edited in the future.

Victor A. Kramer
1986-1991

Acknowledgments

The unpublished materials and previously edited manuscripts incorporated here are drawn from the James Agee papers now owned by the Harry Ransom Humanities Research Center of The University of Texas at Austin and are used with proper notification of intent to quote.

Acknowledgment is made to the editors of the *Mississippi Quarterly* where "Pygmalion" first appeared, and to the *Texas Quarterly* where "The Complete 'Work' Chapter of *Let Us Now Praise Famous Men*," as well as the three 1940s poems, "1928 Story," and the two selections from unused manuscripts for *A Death in the Family* were originally published.

Appreciation is also extended to the editors of the *Journal of Popular Culture* and the *Southern Humanities Review* for permission to incorporate materials which first appeared in articles for those journals.

Acknowledgments are also extended to the editors of *The Southern Review* and to the Mercer University Press for permission to adapt materials for the introduction which are drawn from published articles.

Permission also has been provided by The Phillips Exeter Academy, the *Harvard Advocate*, *Time* magazine, and the James Agee Trust.

"Pygmalion" first reproduced in *The Mississippi Quarterly*, Vol. 29, pp. 191-96. Reprinted by permission of the James Agee Trust. ©The James Agee Trust.

"The Complete 'Work Chapter' of *Let Us Now Praise Famous Men*" first reproduced in *Texas Quarterly*, Vol. 15, pp. 27-48. Reprinted by permission of the James Agee Trust. ©The James Agee Trust.

From "Notes . . . on the magazine under discussion . . ." first reproduced in *Journal of Popular Culture*, Vol. 5, pp. 755-66.

Reprinted by permission of the James Agee Trust. ©The James Agee Trust.

Selections from "Scientists and Tramps" first reproduced in *Southern Humanities Review*, Vol. 7, pp. 357-64. Reprinted by permission of the James Agee Trust. ©The James Agee Trust.

"James Agee By Himself" first reproduced in *Esquire*, Vol. 60, pp. 149 & 289. Reprinted by permission of the James Agee Trust. ©The James Agee Trust.

Textual Information

Many of the documents included in this collection are gathered from things Agee himself saw into print. But of the diverse categories of pieces selected for this book Agee saw published only the pieces which appeared in *The Phillips Exeter Monthly*, the *Harvard Advocate*, and book reviews for *Time*.

One short essay of the 1940s was apparently left in manuscript; it was published posthumously in *Esquire*, as "James Agee by Himself." All the remaining materials in this book are edited from James Agee manuscripts at the Harry Ransom Humanities Research Center at the University of Texas at Austin. Some of this material appeared in my doctoral dissertation in 1966, and has been used by Agee scholars in subsequent research since then.

When possible the pieces included here are based on a complete manuscript or typescript. Sometimes only a pencil manuscript exists and often only one manuscript copy remains. This is the case with the typescript for "Pygmalion" and the carbon copy typescripts for the unused *Time* articles which have been chosen for inclusion.

With the remaining materials, autograph manuscripts have been transcribed or a typescript has been used which necessitated very slight editing. Always the procedure has been to transcribe these materials word for word with no editorial emendation, unless clarity demands it. All emendations are placed in brackets. This procedure was easily effected with manuscripts which apparently were substantially complete. Thus no serious problems were presented in editing a piece such as "1928 Story," based on pencil holographs which were apparently fairly close to finished.

Other materials, not finished, such as unpublished verse and the selections chosen from "Scientists and Tramps," were edited from pencil manuscripts or from typescript which included variants. Some deletions were made in these cases. The manuscript for "Notes and Suggestions on the Magazine" or the unused *Time* magazine stories were left in a draft state. In such cases I considered it my job as editor to transcribe as accurately as possible what had been written, while some selection, and thus slight omissions, were sometimes necessary. Ellipses marks are mine. The same is true for the editorial procedures for the fictional materials excluded from what became Agee's final (posthumous) work, the "Dream Sequence" and "Surprise" chapters for *A Death in the Family*.

V. A. K.
1986

Introduction:
The Possibilities of Writing Well

While he was often called a born writer, James Agee frequently expressed doubts about the possibilities of writing well, especially within a society where the human spirit he so respected seemed to be frequently ignored. Significant doubts already manifested themselves within his earliest writing, the exploratory and sometimes satirical pieces written at Phillips Exeter, Harvard, and during the earlier years of the nineteen-thirties, some of which is included in this book. This selection of literary documents, in fact, is designed to reflect Agee's life-long attempt to find ways best to use language to honor the world he loved.

Over a period of three decades Agee kept experimenting. Perhaps because he remained so aware of the need to write well, yet also aware of the ever-present difficulties inherent in any use of language, some of his best "performances" would not be written at all; these were accompanied by gestures within conversations for which no draft copy could be made. Agee's concern about language and the problems of accurately using language also clearly contributed to his sustained interest in film and criticism. Concerns about language, culture, and the responsibilities of all users of language are therefore a fundamental unifying pattern throughout his diverse writing, a body of work often critical of modern civilization, but at the same time a unique body of work which reflects his skill as artist, and also his desire to be a great writer.

This collection of documents appears in slightly different form than originally conceived. As first planned, it was to have included more unfinished or draft material which indirectly provided documentation of Agee's development as a writer. The 1934 essay "Reflections on *Permit Me Voyage*"; his rough draft for the short story "Before God and This Company"; notebook entries about plans for editing and writing which grew out of the work for *Let Us Now Praise Famous Men*; his draft for "Whenever a Critic," a story about changing from film critic to screenplay writer; Agee's letter to his friend and editor Archibald MacLeish about collecting films for preservation in the Library of Congress; and other work including poems, a short story about the Civil War, and quotations as extensive as I should like to have drawn from his projected screenplay for Charlie Chaplin will not be found here. On the other hand, it has proved possible to include in this collection more finished but not generally available selections from Agee's 1940s work first edited by me for *The Texas Quarterly*. Although they are more polished, these materials provide similar insight into Agee's continuing development as writer-critic, and particularly his fascination with language. It should also be noted that, in the absence of the complete draft of "Notes on the magazine under discussion . . ." and of certain materials from his projected screenplay for Charlie Chaplin, adaptations from my own earlier articles dealing with both projects are provided as an appendix. Thus, their resonance is added to that of the many other documents here brought together for the convenience of those seeking fuller acquaintance with James Agee.

Agee's early awareness of problems of language, a skepticism perhaps reinforced by his admiration of I. A. Richards, one of his teachers at Harvard, in interaction with a life and work in New York City, combined to generate a significant body of writing. But as we see from the diversity of this collection, his was a wide range of work which was ultimately unfinishable. We remember that in *Let Us Now Praise Famous Men* (1941) he insisted all work is a "cheated ruin," but the thing through which anyone stays alive. To an important degree Agee's career as a professional writer in New York was both livelihood and ruin; yet it also provided stimulation and reward. We know he was already aware in the nineteen-thirties that his continued work for *Fortune* seemed to be a trap. His insistence that he had to be free of such regular obligations strengthened his conviction that he had to pursue "his own writing"; yet if we look at the career as a whole the fact is the writing he did as journalist led to many other experimental and literary projects. Finally Agee's poetry, journalism, criticism, autobiography, and fiction blend together. It is for such reasons that two unused *Time* magazine articles are included here for they demonstrate that the journalistic work, cultural analysis, and storytelling did all fuse.

Agee's concern about the difficulties of using language, and his skepticism about reflecting the world as observed through writing, ultimately combined to lead him beyond conventional uses of form in poetry, reportage, or fiction. His mastery of conventions, however, was always the starting point. The documents of this collection are proof of the diversity of Agee's skill and of his accomplishments as writer. Together they document moments in his development as a writer, experimenting as he grows, frequently seeking other ways to reflect upon and imagine the world he loved.

Agee's earliest writing done at Phillips Exeter and Harvard demonstrates he could produce traditional poetry and prose, but it is clear that quite early, and throughout the nineteen-forties, he continued to feel a need for developing other modes of writing. This accounts for the mixture of tradition and rebellion in both *Permit Me Voyage* (1934), and in an analytical mock-review by him about his first book which still remains in manuscript. Such self-criticism suggests early that he wanted to push on to other things.

Similar facts account for both the fun and failure of the long poem, "John Carter," which was then in process, and the accomplishment of, and frustration about, much of the writing done for *Fortune* magazine in the nineteen-thirties. Agee wrote to Dwight Macdonald about his projected long poem, "John Carter," what he dreamed would be "a complete appraisal of contemporary civilization and a study of the Problem of Evil." He wanted to give contemporary language variety and vitality, and to create a poetry which would hold a modern reader's attention. A light tone, he hoped, would maintain interest, enforce serious passages, and also allow acceptance of his moral and religious intention. Yet he also indicated doubts to Macdonald as he pondered what he called his "cockey narrative poem." He wrote: "On the whole, a flop, but I'm fool enough to have faith in the idea: vaguely—that I can take a somewhat bawdy situation, fit to characters common to Chaucer & to Mid-western 'Realistic' novels—and make something of it." What is important is that "John Carter," now included in *The Collected Poems*, is as ambitious as *Famous Men*, but only two sections (about forty pages) were completed. It is a fine example of Agee's dreams, skill, and experimentation. So also are many of the other pieces included in this selection of literary documents.

The mock-review, "Reflections on *Permit Me Voyage*," alluded to above demonstrates that Agee felt his first book was an apprentice exercise and that its accomplishments were things of the past. A few years later in 1935, he would again write to his friend, Dwight Macdonald, to say he was enjoying Henry James's *The American*, but his qualifying remarks reveal his fundamental attitude during these years:

> I can imagine that I w[oul]d equally enjoy and have to finish anything James ever wrote that I once started, on the other hand am not so dead sure I will start anymore. Possibly more sense in reading less-good contemporaries who by hook, crook or otherwise open up a little more of future: though meanwhile name me 5 who do.

His own elaborate "Plans for Work," written during the following year as he was hoping to leave *Fortune* magazine, accompanied a Guggenheim application in October 1937. Those "Plans" must have seemed to the selection committee far too concerned with methods which might "open up the future." Included was his elaborate outline for some forty-seven separate proposed projects. Predictably, no fellowship appeared. Agee explained how he planned to do various pieces of fiction, notes on photography, music, theater, and revues. Five of his proposals were suggestions for ordinary fiction; yet significantly, he also wished to write serious stories "whose whole intention is the direct communication of the intensity of common experience."

Much of what he actually accomplished in the nineteen-thirties and forties, as this collection illustrates, is an extension of his fascination with the complexity of ordinary emotion and consciousness. He knew that there were many critical projects waiting to be done, and many stories to be imagined which might grow from careful observations. Why not write, he had suggested, a "new type of 'horror' story" about the horror "that can come of objects and their relationships"? Such "stories," not traditional fiction, could communicate the intensity of common experience, and would concentrate "on what the senses receive and the memory and context does with it." Such proposals are the logical outgrowth of what Agee had observed as early as "They That Sow . . .," an autobiographical story written while at Harvard. Also, his "Plans" are steps in his progression toward *Famous Men* and, as we see from the various manuscript and typescript "notes" included in this collection, he continued in the forties to devise elaborate plans for the analysis of culture.

(He could also—as we might observe from the fragment of a short story, "All Through the Night," transcribed for my dissertation from a pencil manuscript, yet excluded from this collection—focus on materials which were totally imaginary but which were probably stimulated by World War II.)

Once *Permit Me Voyage* had appeared in 1934 Agee began seeking other ways to perfect his writing. His "Lyric," "From now on kill America out of her mind," published in 1937, might be read as a set of instructions for the better work of the years which followed. That speaker suggests little is to be achieved from thinking in abstractions associated with nation. To think of individuals and "the land / Mutually shapen as a child" is better. Another poem of those years, "Summer Evening," is based on specific memories. It clearly evokes an ordinary evening in a small town. Such writing signals Agee's imaginative return to the quiet which he associated with his own childhood as stimulation for his writing. His beautifully evocative poem "Sunday: Outskirts of Knoxville, Tenn." is another example of his "new" type of writing with a concentration on specifics such as later would become the focus of the masterwork *Let Us Now Praise Famous Men*. Other experiments, like the sketch written in the spring of 1936, "Knoxville: Summer of 1915," which Agee described as an unconventional short story; his analysis of Brooklyn, rejected for publication by *Fortune* in 1939; and still other work occupying him—the unfinished draft of a short story, "Before God and this Company," which remains unpublished is a further example—prepared Agee for writing about his experiences with the farm families he came to know in Alabama during the summer of 1936.

Agee's awareness of the difficulties faced when confronting the obligations of writing is reflected in the "Intermission: Conversation in the Lobby" section of *Famous Men*, answers first written for questions which had been sent to writers by the *Partisan Review*. The editor, Agee's friend, Dwight Macdonald, had returned Agee's answers with the curt comment: "No publisher is under any obligation to publish an attack upon himself." These answers to the *Partisan Review* questionnaire reveal much both about the method of *Let Us Now Praise Famous Men*, and the impact of conventional thinking upon Agee at this stage in his literary career. Asked if war came, should a writer use his abilities to attack the enemy, Agee seemed perplexed, and replied, in his opinion he had always been "at war with the enemy." The text for *Famous Men* is part of that battle, and much other writing composed during those same years is also part of that battle.

During the years when the tenant book was being finished Agee worked as a book reviewer at *Time* magazine. He wrote scores of reviews and the tone of those reviews ties in with Agee's developing theories about how an artist must be a good observer of reality. Those theories merit attention. As early as 1937, Agee had speculated how he might handle the diverse material for *Famous Men*: "Any given body of experience is sufficiently complex and ramified to require . . . more than one mode of reproduction: it is likely that this one will require many, including some that will extend writing and observing methods . . . the job is perhaps chiefly a skeptical study of the nature of reality and of the false nature of re-creation and of communication." The word "skeptical" is at the heart of Agee's declared procedure which led to the text of *Famous Men*. His *Time* book reviews seem to have been written with a similar attitude in mind. The many books he chose to review also indicate his personal interests and reveal the writers for whom Agee had an affection, such as Joyce.

Predictably, when *Famous Men* appeared, just as America was entering the Second World War, no one was particularly interested either in tenant farming or in Agee's experiments in communication. His method of reporting the "unimagined" in *Famous Men*, in gestation for years, included the total experience—biography, how the book was set into type, guilt, facts, and imagination. Agee's insistence on being present throughout *Famous Men* in fact violated all accepted criteria for journalism and for documentaries. Any close analysis of his text would reveal how he systematically voiced questions about communication. There is hardly a page in the book where Agee does not imply the difficulty of what was attempted. He insisted, however, that much could be implied about his Alabama experience, and by implication any experience if a writer constantly acknowledged the difficulty of reporting the truth and worked constantly to achieve it.

Agee knew *Famous Men*, as published, was only a beginning. His excluded "work" chapter, included here, demonstrates the success of his expansion of some of that material. Also, his autograph unpublished *Famous Men* notebook entries, not included here, make it clear that Agee seriously thought about using the techniques developed for *Famous Men* in analogous projects. In a sense his film criticism became his extended cultural analysis, along with all the other projects—written and dreamed—reflected in these documents. The various selections included in this volume in which Agee analyzes his personal relationship to the culture, and, later, where he distances himself from that same culture, document how he kept seeking ways to analyze what was observed. Both "Notes and Suggestions on the magazine under discussion . . ." and his Chaplin screenplay, from which only a few selections are included as an appendix to this book, show this. Through the nineteen-forties, Agee's writing was most frequently about, or for, the movies. His book reviewing and film-criticism can be viewed as an extension of methods developed for *Famous Men*, procedures for the revelation of culture as observed through the manifestation of particular facets of society. Also, during the nineteen-forties Agee became increasingly aware of the complexity of the individual's struggle within modern society. His awareness manifested itself in many ways—in journalism when he wrote feature stories for *Time*; as overt commentary ("Dedication Day," "Scientists and Tramps," and "A Mother's Tale"); and, more importantly, in the movement by Agee, the artist, toward both historical and autobiographical writing.

New materials in each of these categories are provided in this collection. The "1928 Story," probably written about 1948, is a good example of the successful combination of Agee's critical attitude toward society which was working in harmony with his deepening autobiographical impulse. The same is true of other materials included in this collection, but excluded by editors from *A Death in the Family*. The same might also be said of a story, "All Through the Night," which appeared in my dissertation, and which should be studied in conjunction with Agee's love of and adaptation of Stephen Crane.

Another group of materials, verse, chosen for this book, is of a private nature. These are draft poems which reflect Agee's doubts about society and about being a writer within a society which is unthinking. These late nineteen-forties poems also have a value in that they reveal a side of the writer—sometimes depressed and sad—who could nevertheless move forward from such feelings by means of his use of words. The same might be said of the elaborate notes for the screenplay "Scientists and Tramps" written for Charlie Chaplin—imagined as a sardonic commentary about society after the Ultimate Bomb.

Agee's personal convictions about the difficulty of acting as an individual were clearly intensified by the horrors of the Second World War and the use of the atomic bomb. In his opinion the war, and much of the cynicism connected with it, had been too easily accepted by many. The fact that he sketched an outline of a screenplay about an imagined society "After the Bomb" is not well known; that draft helps us to understand other things he wrote about individualism. (Agee's most succinct treatment of the demise of individualism is "Dedication Day, a rough sketch for a motion picture," a piece which satirized the dedication of a monument designed to commemorate the discovery of the atom's destructive power, and is as well a parody of a news story.) The selected draft materials for the screenplay "After the Bomb," called "Scientists and Tramps," and designed for Charlie Chaplin's tramp, included as an appendix here, provide new insights about Agee, the culture, and what he considered to be the problems of individualism.

The partly autobiographical "1928 Story" also seems to grow out of thinking both about the difficulty of living in the late nineteen-forties and the difficulty of writing about those depressing years. This story closely resembles later autobiographical fiction. It catches the spontaneity and enthusiasm of an earlier time in Agee's life and corroborates significant facts about him as a mature writer. As the first sustained attempt since *Famous Men* to recreate a mood from his own life, "1928 Story" demonstrates that Agee could catch the beauty of earlier times. As the story opens Irvine, a professional writer, listens to old records which remind him of his earlier years when the same music had been heard in an altogether different atmosphere. He longs for the clarity of those moments as remembered, and then in the making of the short story, he recreates some of that earlier time. "1928 Story" helps us to appreciate all the later accomplishments of Agee, and to understand his continued doubts and wonder about what any writer sets out to accomplish. This story, like *The Morning Watch* (1951), is, therefore, a step toward *A Death in the Family*, which was also begun in the late nineteen-forties. "1928 Story" shows how Agee learned to focus on the particularities of his own life, yet build art through that focus. "Dream Sequence," the true introduction to Agee's last book, works the same way. Thus, just as *Famous Men* grew out of Agee's work for *Fortune* and his desire to reflect the truth as he saw it, the final autobiographical writing was, to some degree, the result of personal frustration which Agee experienced during years which were his most successful as a journalist, but were also years when he remained somewhat dubious about his ability to reflect the complexity of his own world.

Agee's career followed few predictable patterns. Certainly his varied writing was hardly the production he dreamt as a young man. It is safe to assume that he probably even felt his literary "career" was largely a failure: but it is also certain there was no failure of integrity, or accomplishment. We may wish that Agee had written more, but we would do well to remember that on many occasions he himself insisted that there is no separation between an aesthetic and a moral sense. The many experiments reflected in the pieces of this collection document this fact. These pieces provide evidence that Agee put his whole heart and mind into whatever job he pursued.

Agee was a writer. As such, he produced an enormous range of material. He was a poet who did not seek to pursue a conventional poetic career, yet we might say that all of his subsequent writings reflect his poetic ability. He was a journalist who sometimes felt the job of journalism was constricting, but in all his work his eye for detail and the need for careful analysis, not just reporting, informs the writing. He was a critic, but always a gentle one who could usually find something good to say about the books and films he criticized, and this quality, too, permeates everything that he wrote. Above all, he was a story teller, and through his gifts as writer he could imagine stories which speak to a wide audience. Agee's gifts as a writer allowed him to do many different kinds of things. The many pieces gathered here, sometimes early and sometimes unfinished, sometimes confessional and sometimes analytical, provide evidence about the continuity of his literary accomplishments, a writer who, while he perhaps began more projects than could ever be finished, has given us more insights, analysis, and pleasure that many a writer less ambitious, reflective, and honest.

Agee has often been referred to as a religious writer, and in fact it is his intense reverence for God's world and his concern for how best to reflect the beauty of that world—seen, remembered, analyzed, misrepresented, loved, imagined, celebrated—that is at the heart of all these varied documents. Seen as the continuing attempts by Agee to honor a world which he loved, they document the development of a writer who was never completely satisfied with what he accomplished, while they also are the record of accomplishments as he kept looking for ways to document the world he so loved.

Victor A. Kramer
1994-1996

Part I
APPRENTICESHIP

Phillips Exeter Writing:
Prose, Drama, Poetry, and
Non-fiction
(1925-1928)

Phillips Exeter Fiction

Apprenticeship in *The Phillips Exeter Monthly*

Agee's earliest literary writing is occasionally derivative; yet the variety of the fiction, satire, poetry, and drama published in *The Phillips Exeter Monthly* from November 1925 to June 1928 demonstrates his success and foreshadows what later became help and hindrance, this writer's stubborn insistence on non-specialization. Within this earliest published work many characteristics are exhibited which seem distinctly destined to be Agee's, most especially careful observation, wit, and irony—frequently about those caught in a middle-class life. All the apprentice work chosen for inclusion here demonstrates a young writer's ability to write about the world as observed and his ability to suggest a reality apprehended just below the surface. The story "Knoxton High" which satirizes small-town provincialism is clearly based on memories of a year spent in Knoxville in 1924-1925. It is a humorous experiment.

Other early tightly written stories which have Tennessee settings are more somber. For example, "The Circle," which may have been influenced by Sherwood Anderson, is about a young man trapped because of his father's death. It demonstrates Agee's definite skill in observing details. "Bound For the Promised Land" uses the specifics of a funeral as focus; its concentration looks forward to *A Death in the Family*. Still other early work reflects Agee's wide reading and his knowledge of classical literature.

These Phillips Exeter materials reveal the young writer's skill in documenting emotion. Occasionally the writing seems to be so based on other literature that the models appear to get in the way, yet Agee already at this time aims to suggest the complexity of actuality. Sometimes his attempts at poetry tend toward the abstract, yet they are usually carefully executed, and some poems successfully objectify the loss which he realized his family had sustained with the death of his own father. Early poems are also important as indicators of thematic concerns to be developed later. "Ebb Tide" is a good example; its speaker is aware that he is left alone, while also aware that the cyclical nature of all creation makes that separation only temporary. This same theme is later developed in *Famous Men* and in the major fictional work.

The most important of Agee's four dramas written at Exeter is called *Menalcas*. It is a competent one-act play modeled on Greek drama; thematically, the plot is related to another early dramatic piece, a play set in the Tennessee mountains entitled *Any Seventh Son* in which a family curse plagues the seventh son, born monstrous, the child of a seventh son. In the classical adaptation, *Menalcas*, the hero begets an idiot son by his daughter; and chorus, gods, and nature call for the sacrifice of the child. While it is contrived in plot, the sparse language is successful; the chorus approximates the quality of classical verse; a tragic tone is sustained. Still another play, *Catched*, is a quiet rendition of the theme of the rejected child, this time accomplished in language of the mountaineers of Tennessee. It is also of interest that the family name of one of these imagined mountaineers is "Gudger": the same name which recurs for one of the families in *Let Us Now Praise Famous Men*. Themes of rejection and loss, especially in the opening section of the tenant book, can be related to this early drama. The fact that Agee, as an aspiring writer, attempted to handle the theme of the rejected child so variously is an early indication of one of his continuing interests.

His sketch, "Extracts from the Diary of a Disagreeable Young Man," and his review of *Elmer Gantry* reveal still other sides of the young writer which were to turn up later—the Agee dissatisfied both with himself and with what he considered to be worn out conventions.

"The Circle"

I

As he descended the stairs, Edgar resented, as he had every morning these six years past, the glaring reproduction, in stained glass, of heaped grapes, and pears, and bananas. Through this garish window of the seventies filtered the light which saved the hall from blackness. When he opened the "living-room" door, his father instantly rose and lumbered toward him. He was a heavy man, a mass of comfortable convexities, and when he walked he seemed to be moving on casters. (Edgar, as a child, had described him as "rounded off at the corners.") His rusty-black suit bagged at the knees and seat; his large face expanded in a damp smile, and with repeated wrappings of his forehead he exuded pinguid pleasantries.

"Well, how's young Dan'l Webster this mornin'? Feelin' fine after last night's festivities?"

"Pretty good," dully.

"You better set down, my boy; you look peaked. It's an awful hot day! Got some grass cuttin' to do," he gasped. And he laid on Edgar's shoulders plump eager hands.

"No, I'm all right." His father's showy affection was a continual source of annoyance. As he crossed the room, and leaned upon a hard-knobbed horse-hair excrescence, he felt proud eyes boring into his neck. In his mind's eye he could see Mr. Butler's fat fingers working into his tight vest as he swelled with pride.

He turned. Yes, they were.

"Well, how's Aunt Selina this mornin?"

"Havin' her breakfast, dear boy. It's right late now, most ten, but—oh, my. I didn't mean—'course you stay in bed now long as you want . . . I . . [. .]" He lapsed into silence, as he noticed Edgar's look of bored exasperation. It had worried him before.

Now, nervously fingering a heavy watch chain, he dared: "Edgar, I was real proud of you last night. You, you done well, son. I been talkin' with your Aunt Selina about—about you goin' to college, and I reckon if I keep at her you'll go." He fumbled, brought forth a slip of paper. "Here's—uh—I wanted to make you a little present—sort of—It's just somethin' I been saving up from cuttin' grass. You might use it for spending money next year." He handed the paper to Edgar. It was a check for forty dollars. Edgar was amazed, and vaguely ashamed. "Thanks, pa," he gulped, "I'm—much obliged—uh—I appreciate this," he ended stiffly. He was, he persuaded himself, grateful, *truly* grateful to his father. Yet he could not bring himself to admire this fat, stupid man. He knew it to be a boy's smug duty to "stand up for his dad," but in his he could find nothing to stand up for. Mr. Butler's constant "dear boys," his heavy, pawing hands, bothered Edgar. He knew that he owed everything to his father; he'd read and heard that all his life. Now he was disgusted with himself because, despite his realization of his father's sacrifice, he did not love him for his gift. He could see that his father was disappointed, hurt. Mr. Butler was moving toward him—he must get away, somehow.

"I guess I'll go in and see Aunt Selina." He tried to nod pleasantly, and left quickly.

For fifteen minutes he read to his aunt, a shrunken, mute shadow. His reading was stopped as she shoved his elbow. He looked an inquiry, and she wrote upon a little pad, "Tell your father I want him. Come about mortgages."

He found Mr. Butler in the hammock. The father went in immediately and Edgar took his place.

Aunt Selina was endlessly fussing about her business affairs. Edgar's father would be with her for hours, sometimes, patiently repeating every misunderstood point. It was inconceivably difficult to bring within her comprehension the simplest facts. As the years had passed, her disposition had become worse, for her brain was bloated with egotism, which would never allow her to admit that her failing ears had not heard rightly. She had developed a growing suspicion of Edgar and Mr. Butler, her only relatives.

Often after these numerous racking business interviews Mr. Butler would stride quickly from the house, lips silently moving, fat, frantic fingers tugging at the heavy watch chain—desperate, yet usually a phlegmatic man.

The house, which had once been LaFollette's pride, was still the largest dwelling in town; when occasion demanded, it was still referred to in the LaFollette *Banner* as "The Butler Mansion." But in recent years it had fallen into bad repair, and its broken, ivy-fringed, attic windows seemed to glower haggardly at Kirby Street. It was a conglomeration of every possible architectural monstrosity, fallen into decay. Only the lawn which separated it from the street relieved the gloom. Edgar's particular hobby was gardening, and he had rather over-peppered the broad lawn with small round beds of flowers.

For six years since the death of his mother Edgar had lived there, and his intense hatred of the place was alleviated only by his assurance that ultimately he would escape.

There was a grating of wheels on bricks, and, looking across the lawn, he saw Catherine Meade bounce past in her buggy. He lit a cigarette and arranged the cushions.

Next fall he would go to the State University to study law. He himself had no money, but Aunt Selina would one day be proud to say that she had given him his start. Why, only last night he had made his mark. As valedictorian of his High School class he had been conspicuously the success of the evening. He had a flair for oratorical effect, and he had succeeded in holding his provincial audience to close attention. The speech, although nothing remarkable, was really worthy of a bigger town than LaFollette, and it had been delivered with restraint and a certain dignity.

This morning Edgar had become rather worried with the realization of a long summer in attendance upon his aunt, but the worry was only momentary, for as he settled comfortably in the hammock, a wave of invincible optimism swept these disconcerting thoughts from his mind. He lay, watching the silhouetted leaves move lazily about him. Life seemed marvelously easy to conquer. He would be an "honor man" at college, study law, and practise in LaFollette. Before long, through recognition of his undeniable ability, he would be elected legislator. Then in quick succession, he would become a senator, a governor. . . . who could tell? He was far above the average dub, he told himself. He looked upon the loafers about the horse-trough and pool-hall in mingled pity and contempt. What clods they were! Most of them had never been through High School. Certainly none of them could feel on equal footing with Catherine Meade. They'd never read poetry, you could bet. They couldn't appreciate the greatness of such poems as "Invictis" or "Psalm of Life."

He lit a cigarette and settled more comfortably. Three months of enduring Aunt Selina and—yet, he couldn't look at it otherwise—his father—a brilliant college career, and success and fame, with a fine, sweet girl like Catherine for his inspiration. She was a wonderful girl, he told himself. She liked to hear him talk of the future,—and incidentally, of himself. He liked her better—so much better than other girls he knew. When in her company his own relatives seemed incredibly drab. Such a stupid man his father was, with his great pawing hands, and his incoherent attempts to be affectionate! Tiresome. Edgar could see him now; his loose-fitting rusty suit, the watch-chain swinging; tufts of brown hair in his ears, with flecks of lather adhering from a morning's shave. He could never appreciate such a girl. And his Aunt Selina. He could not imagine her as young and pretty, this tremulous old woman, as he saw her now, blinking drearily and hopelessly. Never could she have inspired him. No one, in fact, except Catherine understood him, truly appreciated his ability.

Soon his troubles would be over. He had been made much of for that address; when his career was really begun, what honors would not be accorded him! People about him were so stupid. Men turning bald; they would never accomplish anything. Women moving slowly down the sidewalks, faces blank; they could never know the meaning of a love such as was his for Catherine. There was nothing heroic, nothing noble, in their lives. With Catherine as an inspiration he would soon conquer this brainless world.

It was wonderful to have a Big Future crowding before him; wonderful to be so smart.

II

Two months passed uneventfully. Edgar spent part of each day with his Aunt Selina, reading, carrying on a difficult conversation, occasionally skirting the rather precarious ground of college tuition, which the old lady skillfully avoided.

This had, for awhile, bothered Edgar. His father, however, had promised to "use his influence" in time, and Edgar had in this, as in all other things, taken no initiative. It was a fault which he found in his father, also.

(Once, earlier in the summer, he had begun a diary. Fol-

lowing Catherine's advice it was to be a diary of "impressions."
Faithfully he had manufactured impressions and recorded
them—for a week.)

Sometimes Edgar took Catherine Meade to the movies.
More often they sat in the swing in her yard.

On a certain evening in August they had left the Rex
Movie Palace, and had walked out beyond Kirby Street to the
Broken Boat, a favorite trysting place for LaFollette couples.
They had spoken of the movie, of love, of the stars, of love, of
correspondence schools, of love. Always they mentioned love
impersonally, and between it and themselves they put the abyss
of their shyness. Edgar spoke at length of his favorite theme—
himself; Catherine murmured that she would miss him in his
brilliant years at the State University.

He had swallowed uncertainly, fished for her hand, and
suddenly mumbled an oblique proposal of marriage. And they
had sat together, whispering, seeming to share a wonderful secret, until the town clock started them into normality.

They arrived, in silence, at Catherine's gate. Edgar hesi-
tated. Should he take her to the door? He wanted to say something big, noble—something that would leave a beautiful im-
pression of his manliness.

Quite suddenly she threw her arms about him, and kissed
him. Edgar was bewildered. He murmured, "Wha . . . what?"
Took her in his arms, and whispered, "Gosh, Catherine, you're
so lovely. C-Couldn't we g-get married before I go?"

"I—come and see me tomorrow night."

"All right," Edgar swallowed; both were silent for some
moments. Finally he spoke: "Well . . . I—I s'pose I be goin'.
Pa'll be in bed by now." He moved from one foot to the other,
nervously; his hands fumbled. "Well . . . thank you for a
pleasant evenin'."

Catherine extended her hand formally. "Good night,
Edgar." She ran lightly up the gravel path.

He started. "Uh . . . wait! Can't I kiss ya again?" And he
found himself walking down the street. He hadn't even taken
her hand; had scarcely noticed it. What a silly ending to a glorious evening! What a fool he was! She must be laughing at him
by now. Could he *never* do the right thing? How could she care
for him? Did she really? The questions boiled through his
brain. He became a little calmer. Catherine had told him to return the next evening. Evidently, then, she was thinking of

marrying him soon. After all, maybe he hadn't appeared so ridiculous. Lots of things he had said were fine, noble. His father was in bed now, snoring, probably. It was revolting. Yet he could not help pitying his father.

Mr. Butler was so foolishly fond of him; he had such terrible difficulties with Aunt Selina. Why, just the atmosphere of the house—the thought of the tremulous, hopeless old woman, with her twitching hands, was dreadful.

He turned up the path, which divided his smooth, well-kept lawns. He was surprised to see lights in one wing of the house. They should, usually, have been out an hour before. He looked about, and noticed the auto at the curb. He had seen it, subconsciously, and thought it to be his father's Ford, which was often left there. But it was not. It looked like—why, it was Dr. Scar's car! He walked on, more quickly. Probably Aunt Selina had had a relapse. He opened the front door quickly. The gas fixture in the hall was turned on full; the imitation crystal ornaments, fly-specked, swung slowly to and fro. Through half-parted curtains he saw a heavy form, standing near the "center table." His father, of course. The form turned and approached him. Something about the air of Dr. Scar made Edgar stand rooted to the carpet.

"Edgar, your father died of apoplexy half an hour ago." A pause. "He is on the sofa." He paused uncomfortably, realized the futility of consolation, took his bag from the marble-topped table, his hat from the grotesquely ornate rack, and walked past Edgar into the night. Edgar was vaguely conscious of a sheet-covered bulk in the next room of his father's coat and vest, heaped on the floor. But he did not move.

"Father," Edgar's voice was thin and weak. "Your father died of apoplexy half an hour ago." He started. Half an hour ago he had been happier than ever in his life; he had been in heaven. He began trembling violently, his hands striking together repeatedly. In his head was a terrific roaring—pounding. Blood surged through his eyeballs; they felt as if they were being pushed from their sockets. Mechanically, guided subconsciously, he climbed the stairs. . . .

III

The evening after the funeral he brought in the supper he had cooked, and ate with Aunt Selina, who had been unable to attend the burial. When he sat down she produced the little pad, and wrote in her jagged hand: "Was the funeral pretty?"

He made an indefinite movement with his head.

She pursed her lips, and began the absorption of a badly prepared meal. Her tumbler fell with a crash, and she emitted little inarticulate murmurs of distress. Edgar picked up the fragments and threw them from the kitchen door. When he came back she had appropriated his own, and was taking little gulps, then throwing her head back, letting it run down.

Edgar looked at her with disgust. Without a word he took another tumbler from the closet.

After supper he took the dishes to the kitchen, and was rinsing them in cold water when he was interrupted by a loud rap. Aunt Selina. He hurried in. She shoved to him a heavy volume of "Spencer's Synthetic Philosophy" with the familiar expression—pleading with him, and simultaneously daring him to refuse.

"Aunt Selina, wait, please, till I wash the dishes."

She did not understand at first. When she finally grasped the idea, a terribly hurt expression clouded her face. With an air of martyrdom—her eyes filling with tears—she made a wavering gesture toward the kitchen door, and her long, nervous, blue-veined hands fell in her black alpaca lap.

Edgar was intensely exasperated. "No," he said, purposely ill-concealing his feeling—"No—I'll read!" And he snatched the book from her hands. She was in tears, but he tried not to notice it. He continued his reading, with the feeling that he had been cruel—should apologize. But he did not. It spoiled what would have been at best a deadly evening.

His head was aching, but he read for two hours. He felt a tug at his arm, and his Aunt Selina pushed the pad under his nose: "What time is it?" With a rather weak attempt at a kind smile he drew out his watch. "Nine-thirty." She nodded wisely. "Shall I go on?" he asked. An imperative nod.

Ten minutes later came another silent command from his importunate companion. "Light the gas in the bathroom, and open my bed." He performed the duties. When he came down, she had risen from her chair and was stooping for a shawl which had slipped from her knees. Edgar ran to pick it up; then took her arm and urgently assisted her to the bathroom. When she got there, she wrote upon the pad and gave Edgar another note. Her bleared little eyes held an angry glance.

"Do you think I'm too weak to climb stairs alone?"

Edgar was astounded. It seemed as if all his efforts were useless. He walked into his room, and slammed the door.

As he sat upon the edge of his bed, his head in his hands, the first realization of what the future held in store for him flashed into his brain.

The idea of college now was out of the question. He must stay in LaFollette—must care for his Aunt Selina, week after week, month after month, year after year. She was not really old—sixty-eight. She might live to be a hundred. She was practically helpless without an attendant; he was her only relative. Long acquaintance with her penuriousness drove from Edgar all hope of hiring a nurse. Yet she was one of the richest people in town. He felt that he could not speak to Catherine now—could not speak of their promise. Why, she would not speak to him now. His bright future—to grow old, gray, in care of his terrible old Aunt. To have held Catherine in his arms so few hours before—whispering in her ears his brilliant expectations—the thought was unendurable. Thoughts of his egotism increased the torture. Before he had looked down upon everyone in the town, had told himself that such a mind as his needed a more intellectual atmosphere for its expansion. Worse still, he persisted in believing this. Now he would be in this town, with no friends, but the pool-hall sports—the intellectual ciphers. All his life he would have to speak to no one but inferiors.

He rocked to and fro in agony. Years, years would pass, and he would be lower in the scale at the end than now—a middle-aged small-town grass-cutter.

The realizations whirled boiling through his head—a continuous cycle. He sat there for hours. When the clock in the hall struck thrice he turned off the gas, took off his coat and shoes, and fell, exhausted, upon his bed.

IV

The next morning Edgar, by feigning a headache, found a few hours of freedom from his aunt, and thought despairingly of Catherine. Twice he was on the point of going to her house; finally he decided to write her. He wrote her this letter:

"*My dear Catherine*:

"Since Monday night I have done a great deal of thinking, and I have come to the decision that our love must stop. I feel since my great blow that I should be unable to provide adequate means for our support, and that, at any rate till later, our love must stop.

"As you can probably discern, my career has been warped by my father's decease, and college is for the present out of the question. I must stay with my aunt now, for I see nothing else I can do. I won't even have a job and be a typical business man, but must stay with my aunt.

"I am sure you understand that it is necessary for us to see no more of each other. So I write you this farewell letter to explain just how matters stand. To know you has given me much happiness. I can say truthfully that you have been my only intellectual companion. You have brought me out as no one else has and I still like to feel that we were above the common 'hoypolloy'—together on another sphere, as it were.

"So I write you this farewell letter.

"Very sincerely yours,

"EDGAR SLOAN BUTLER."

When he had read it over, he attempted to cry, and was surprised to find that his ecstatic self-pity was beyond tears. He read the letter again, and quite cold-bloodedly dabbed at it with spit-moistened fingers. He considered a post-script lachrymosely explanatory of damp spots, but decided that to make these so obvious would be bad taste.

Then he sealed and sent the note.

Hotly and tearfully Catherine responded, and declared anew her passion, and her intention of marrying him regardless of his circumstances.

After reading her letter over, she tore it up, put on her hat, and appeared ten minutes later in her father's office.

Catherine's ideas of the good she was doing Edgar by her subsequent actions were probably vague; her only clear feeling was that she was doing as Patricia Young, resourceful heroine of "Hearts Aflame," would have done for her man.

Consequently, Edgar received next day this offer of a position as a real estate agent. A conference with J. J. Meade, president, was suggested.

Edgar was waiting, uncomfortably and disconsolately waiting, in one of the crackling wicker chairs in Meade's outer office. He was annoyed by the greasy and splintery floor, and by the sandy-haired and superior stenographer. This person attempted conversation; and it was conversation not tinged with adulation. He seemed to have forgotten Edgar's recent prominence as an orator; perhaps he had never heard the address. The thought struck him that even in so small a town there were hundreds to whom his name meant nothing.

He shifted on the edge of the chair; it sagged and sounded. He made repeated attempts to make this cipher see his place; but he would not. Thus it had been—and would be—with everyone he had known, except Catherine. He began to wonder about her . . .

He was ushered into The Presence. He had never before realized just what Mr. Meade looked like. He had always been a mere shadow beyond Catherine.

But he saw now, with disconcerting clearness, a well-fed man, with spare hair, ice-smooth, bad teeth, rimless and chained spectacles, a disinfected breath, and white socks.

"Well," clearly snapped Meade.

Edgar faltered, and seemed to have lost his former assurance; occasionally, however, he drew himself together, and his replies were tinged with condescension.

He had a miserable ten minutes, omitting stilted fragments of the speech he had prepared, declaring that it would really be impossible for him to "accept the position" because of "unlooked for domestic circumstances." Having delivered such a sentence, he stood looking as if he might be asked to give synonyms for every word. He was intensely uncomfortable in this man's presence, and, subconsciously, he acknowledged him superior, but his apparent discomfort was that of a noble who finds himself forced to be protected by his slave.

When, finally, he left, without the position, both he and Meade were much relieved.

He silently complimented himself upon his ability to "soft-soap" men.

He was never offered another position on salary.

VI

On the next Saturday night Catherine went to the movies with Mark Watson, and until midnight Edgar read to his aunt. The next morning he gasped through their first conference about her land-holdings; that afternoon he cut the grass. Catherine passed in Joe Dugen's Ford; on the porch sat his aunt, a shrunken shawled figure. . . .

VII

Fifteen years passed. LaFollette in general changed but little; Aunt Selina and Edgar changed much.

Edgar's aunt had gradually become more and more helpless. Now she was absolutely dependent upon him—unable to
walk, almost stone deaf. She seemed to shrink each year; became
a mere ghost of a woman; her skin was dry and opaque, like vel-
lum. Sometimes it seemed that she must fall into dust, but the
old woman clung tenaciously to life, which had dealt with her so
cruelly. Through her yellowed, flat little eyes there shone a
deathless spirit.

Edgar himself was 33, and looked 40. Fifteen years of almost constant attendance upon his aunt had wrought marked
changes. He had never become accustomed to the routine; had
never been able to adjust himself. As time had passed he had
become more and more nervous and irritable. Every duty was
performed with cumulative exasperation. No small part of this
was anger at himself. He wished that he had gone away fifteen
years before. Everything then would have turned out beautifully. He often wondered what had made him stay. Certainly he
had not because of affection. But he knew that it was because he
had waited for things to "work themselves out," and they had
done it in the simplest way. The realization maddened him.

Worst of all, there was no one to talk to. Edgar's outcrop-
ping egotism did not encourage companionship. There was no
one to whom he could confide his thoughts—no one to give
sympathy. There was, always, upon his face, a strangely tight
look. His bitter reflections preyed upon his mind continuously,
seeking some outlet and finding none.

He had an usually difficult morning. As he chopped
wood that afternoon in late summer, incidents which had been
peculiarly maddening flashed through Edgar's mind. He
stopped for a moment to wipe sweat from his forehead, and returned to his work, striking savagely. Once he looked up: he saw
Catherine Fallas pass with her husband, Maxon Mason, in his
Buick touring car. Since the night of his father's death, Edgar
had shunned Catherine, had dreaded meeting her.

On the few occasions they had talked, he had blundered,
stammered, mumbled like a scared schoolboy. Nothing was
ever said of their evening in the boat. He continued blindly to
mangle the refractory blocks of wood. He had a job later cutting
grass, then would come an interminable evening with the
ghostly old woman in the chair. How many more years in that
dark, depressing house? . . .

(April 1926)

"Revival"

He became uncomfortable. The air of the place was heavy, sticky, filled with the penetrating odors of sweat, tobacco, bad whiskey, and perfume. A hymn was sung, a hymn, long and earnest, a hymn full of heart throbs. People began to get worked up. Men and doubtful looking women poured in from the streaming night, and sat steaming beside radiators. The Rev. Victor Moody arose and spoke. He became eulogistic of the Glorious Old Flag, of the saving grace of Jesus, of prostitutes turned pure. As he progressed, his voice became tinged with something suspiciously like enthusiasm. When he spoke of the evils of the dance, he became wickedly graphic. He spoke not too guardedly of "Eating Soup in the Devil's Hash-House," and the young man squirmed uneasily. The boy began to understand the methods of salvation. The idea was to arouse the basest emotions of the audience—then, at the psychological moment, to turn on the spiggot of Cheap Piety. Indeed, that was what the evangelist was doing now. When he saw the flushed faces of the young men in the front row, he began with long, breathy gasps, to sell his pious wares. A youngish woman, her face powdered to a lime-white, her waist a jagged, slight and furiously crimson flame, struggled to her feet and made a disgusting confession. Sobs and ejaculations arose from the room; a man in a tight coat caught and kissed the girl, slobbering, "We're both saved together! Hallelujah!" A coy, fat dressmaker struggled and fought toward the front; then came a dessicated little man, then a greasy bartender. All were weeping, gasping, crying out thanks for their salvation. The revivalist stood very still, with a benign smile lighting his perspiring countenance; then, at the right moment, he ordered the dish pans to be passed among the congregation. God's earthly agents must live. The boy grew more and more disgusted. He looked at his friend for sympathy; his friend wasn't there. He searched, and caught a glimpse of him kissing Rev. Moody's hand.

(May, 1926)

"Knoxton High"

Education in Knoxton, Tennessee, is by no means what it used to be. Along with Real Estate, the Ku Klux Klan, religion, population and bootlegging, it has boomed, and its boom is likely to be more enduring than any other—except, perhaps, that of bootlegging. Up to that stirring time when conflicting epidemics of patriotism and flat-footedness swept our land, the education of Knoxton's youth had been carried on in segregated and miserably cramped firetraps. In these the plaster was often cracked; and no maps in the possession of the school board recognized the existence of Lithuania. Besides, two of the schools had dark halls, and there was complaint that in all of them the windows were set too invitingly low to encourage attentiveness.

A large, large fund had been appropriated for the erection of an auditorium, a War Memorial; but to the consternation of the townspeople it developed that Chattanooga had by several days anticipated this plan, and were even now demolishing mansions and making an impressively deep hole.

What, now, to do with the money? All the Methodists as one offered the suggestion that an elaborate plagiarism on Westminster Abbey be constructed, nominally under Methodist sanction, but, let it be understood, to be the "Common Rendezvous for Prayer for all, uh, yes, All Denominations." An eminent Baptist led his flock to endorse ardently such breadth of mind until he discovered that there was really little probability of his becoming pastor; whereupon he rounded up his flock, and snatched all but a few materialistic lambs from the clutches of those "unscrupulous, ungentlemanly, and unchristian money grabbers," the Methodists.

At the end of the season Knoxton had led the Appalachian League; they almost were to build a Memorial Baseball Park. But for long "Gink" Ford, their star pitcher, had threatened to leave them, and indeed this very winter was hopefully subjecting himself to workouts in Florida; and Johnny Clunk, who had played short stop with an accuracy almost holy, was known to be doing erratic things with cocaine. Then Greeneville bought Eddie Wales, who had framed his keystone game in the World's Series; and Knoxton voted down the Ball Park.

Then, for no known reason (certainly the teachers had nothing to do with it) everybody in town was suddenly glaring at everybody else; the city enlightened and re-enlightened itself concerning the sequestration of the High Schools, the old-fashioned system of education, the dimness of the corridors; concerning the startling fact that Catholics had complete power to educate their young, and the fact oddly like unto it; that it would be a good, broadminded gesture on the part of the Protestants if We invited the Catholics to mingle with Our Children, and perhaps if we were to pass an ordinance suggesting that denominational High Schools be abolished.

And so it was that, despite noisy opposition from the Catholics, and despite smouldering opposition (but silent) from the admirers of dim corridors, it was decided to build a great Knoxton Memorial High School.

II

Completed, the Knoxton Memorial High School was a sight to warm the hearts of all Boosters of progressive Educational Methods. It was equipped with a City School Superintendent, imported from astounding success in Chicago (Knoxton offered him a slightly more astounding salary for coming); a Principal from Toledo, who was, nevertheless, a staunch Methodist, music lover and Fundamentalist; windows which were, to a prohibitive height, of opaque wired glass; Astolat drinking cups, to be discarded after a single use; two English teachers (female) who understood the literary connotation regarding the chastely titled Cups and thought it lovely; one French teacher (male) who likewise understood it, swore with an orotund mellowness, and privately drank from the faucet; an Auditorium (oftener useful as a Study Hall); and a great number of chronically stolen 400-watt bulbs. The Faculty consisted of the assembled migrated flocks from the extinct schools (with the exception of two German teachers who, unfortunately, were not linguistically limber), and of perhaps a dozen Young Things from U. T. and the State Normal.

Out in front, to remind one that it was Knoxton *Memorial* High, was a Doughboy statue of heroic proportions. The Doughboy struggled through one singularly unimposing strand of bronze-painted barbed wire. Knoxton had been in doubt over the selection of this statue, some preferring a Winged Victory as more congruent with the marble High School columns, but the ringing virility of the following advertisement saved the day for the Doughboy:

"IT WAS HELL,
BUDDY

Yes, sir, nothing but that will quite express what you feel about the Great War, old scout. But now that it's all over, you want some lasting Memorial in your Home, which will keep before the eyes of the Wife and Kiddies what you suffered for Democracy, what Bit you did to lick the Dirty Hun. Don't you want to keep that memory fresh before the Kiddies? Won't you be proud to hear them lisp to envious little schoolmates, "*My* Dad helped win it!"? Then, buddy, the thing that you need is a genuine Doughboy Statue, executed by a blind Doughboy, who gave his sight for us. Popular size, 16 in.; also with socket in head for bulb; also makes beautiful Memorial or Park Adornment. See handsome catalogue.

DOUGHBOY STATUE MFG. CO.
BOX C
Corinth, Neb."

III

Knoxton High was endowed with all the most modern improvements. The auditorium boasted genuine theatre seats and a dubious capacity of 2500. The toilets had a five-foot wainscoating of white tile, upon which poetically inclined youths found it most difficult to write. There was a library, branch of the Lawson McGhee Library, likewise memorial; and the librarian could show you most promptly the twelve copies of Silas Marner, the History of the World War, Vanity Fair, Elsie Venner, Halleck's English Literature, and a 1906 bound volume of *Life*. But at mention of Sinclair Lewis she looked shocked, and it is recorded that, when asked to excavate a copy of "Ethan Frome," the woman asked what he had written, then hunted in vain. In the basement was a large and glistening kitchen, in which damsels taking the advanced course in Domestic Science, opened pineapple cans, and on the pineapple squirted little dinky designs in youthful cheese. These "salads" were sold to the discriminating at ten cents each, along with the somewhat more substantial, if less aesthetic, dishes of stew and potatoes and pie, prepared, by the way, by stalwart middle-aged Domestic Science teachers, whose experience in cooking was broad and conducive to economy. It was, however, rather a placid ignorance, coupled with the fact that he had never partaken of the D. S. fruit than (as the Student Body avowed) a helluva sense of humor, that moved Principal Elmans to remark that it was nice for the lads to feast on the delectable dishes prepared by the fair fingers of their, uh, heh-heh, I might say loved ones. There was a salon for girls' gymnastics and for aesthetic dancing; there was an excellent basketball court; there were two laboratories splinterey with broken test-tubes; and there were, of course, a great number of most up-to-date classrooms—all this vast variety nestled under one great roof. And half a block away, above a fire department, a whole room, some 12 x 15 feet, was devoted to the High School orchestra, which annually perpetuated the names of the immortals, Chaminayde, Beezet, Saint-Saenz and Victor Herbert. In the corridors stood startling statues of Apollo (well dressed), Pocahontas, the Winged Victory and Abraham Lincoln. On the walls hung pictures of Aurora, General Grant, Whittier, Abraham Lincoln, Washington Crossing the Delaware, and General Knox. And everywhere in class-rooms were constant foot-prints on the sands. In Latin rooms Julius Caesar, an unrobed goddess, and a Latin crossword puzzle stared at each other impersonally. In the English classroom were pictures of good and great men, gentle men, whose works and, apparently, heads, were to be a perpetual inspiration for Youth. In fact, everything seemed to be quite renovated and modernized and improved to the utmost. Except, perhaps, the teacher's salaries.

IV

In the autumn of 1924, The Southern School Supply was clamorous with green clerks, brave with crackling textbooks, smelling of glue, hotly fetid with the woven breaths of a jam of bored students. Here were three days of tremendous industry, a sort of conglomerate swan-song of utlity clerks, of the books that are to be sold and stolen, of the excited proprietor. Tomorrow, and for another year, the sales would be limited to gritty erasers, library paste, Papini's Life of Christ, Theme Pads, and No. 6H pencils.

(In a back street a little man modest before school Superintendents quietly laid his annual nest-egg as his exhaustive collection of Latin translations, biology notebooks and well-drawn maps became bare shelves. Tomorrow, and for another year, his days would be sleepy with grazing through yellow-backed novels of Sudermann or Gautier, with the begrudging sale of these volumes, the reading unfinished, with addressing affectionate sarcasm at his tobacco-colored wife and at his snuff-colored dog).

There came a day when Advisers advised rattlingly, when young gentlemen and young ladies galloped unceasingly between Miss Cinnorgham in Room 2 and Mr. Hendricks in Room 19B, charged back to perspiring Advisers for repetition of advice; when an enterprising young girl sold to some seventy-one freshmen fake tickets to their seats in the Auditorium at fifty cents each; when, in the gravel court, boys stood in line for hours, awaiting, apparently in vain, the distribution of R. O. T. C. uniforms.

Of all the School Year, that day was the most universally exhausting.

V

The largest room in the building was known as was variously expedient as the Auditorium, Assembly Hall, Study Hall, or Chapel. There were, perhaps, 2200 seats, which accommodated 2500 people. They were built like, they resembled, they were as uncomfortable as, regular theatre seats; but on each was a special hinged arm, about the size, shape, and stability of a beaver's tail, which was to be a desk when the room assumed the title of Study Hall. The walls were of pockmarked plaster, painted a dusty cream color, with a rash of white initials in guarded corners. There were two pictures, one (purely allegorical) depicting Education, a tall and lovely goddess surrounded by cypresses, quadrants, papyrus rolls and intense-browed bare youths; the other of Aurora, her chariot riding clouds wild as a ripped feather bed, as a belch on a winter morning. The stage was hung with green, shining cloths, presented by the Dramatic Club to conceal some interesting and ineradicable attempts at artistic self-expression which had been made once during a rehearsal. They were of use occasionally, irregularly twisted and irregularly hung, to represent "a woodland" in Shakespearian comedy or the tall timber surrounding "Jack Van Puyster's camp in the Rockies; late p.m." The green was in clever contrast to the lush velvet curtains of royal blue. Bold above the stage, in large brown letters, blared: "Ye Shall Know The Truth, And the Truth Shall Make Ye Free."

It was in this room on a September morning, that over two thousand souls, young and old, were drawn together by a common bond and in a common interest: Education. Such was the opening sentiment expressed by Principal Elmans before he deserted the golden oak rostrum in favor of the Reverend Mr. C. Claverly Bicket, A.B., D.D., Ll.d., Ph.d. (The degrees were from U.T., Zeither Seminary, Balthazar College, and the Entwistle Baptist University). Reverend Mr. Bicket buttoned his coat, unbuttoned his coat, smoothed his hair, displayed Rooseveltian but synthetic teeth, and advised God somewhat as follows:

Oh, God, that it afforded the Rev. Mr. Bicket great pleasure to be here this morning, standing up there in the sunlight radiating from so many fresh young faces, eager for Knowledge, clean, pure faces, faces backed by clean, pure thoughts, faces of Young America; O God, these were the Parents of the Coming Generation, yes, the Fathers and Mothers of the Future Generation, might they look upon each other with loving eyes, but in the good sense of the word, Lord; O Lord, might this coming year lead them closer not only to Latin lessons and Readin', Ritin' and Rithmetic', but to Thee, for it was Thee alone that uh Who counted Lord, and Lord might they realize that before it was too late. And O Lord, that the Superintendent, the Principal, and every teacher might be inspired with a holy zeal for teaching, and might this in every way be the most successful and Sanctified year in the history of K. H. S. A-men.

The Rev. Mr. Bicket's cornet soloist had very kindly consented to accompany his pastor, and now led the assembled multitude in "Shall we Gather at the River." This was followed by the K. H. S. Football Song, which had been quite easily adapted from the Cherokee College Shuffle by the substitution of Knoxton-High for Cher-o-kee. Through invincible popular demand, the cornetist played "What'll I do," and, at the advice of his pastor, closed with "Brighten the Corner Where You Are." The Superintendent, in a short and encouraging speech, advised the Student Body to go into this Game of Education with all the Vim and Pep that it showed on the Football Diamond. He confided to his captives that that was all School was, anyway, just a great, big Game, and that By Jingo we were all going into it together, teachers and all, heads up, tails over the dashboard, weren't we? That would be all for today.

VI

School had begun.

Helene Mundy sat in scant glamourous pajamas, swathed in a peculiarly unglamorous bathrobe. Quo usque tandem . . . what's usque. whaddluh-dooooodledoodloodooo . . to what lenth . . . where be the bon-bon box . . . ouch! Damn' chair. Catilina, that's easy. A sticky sound; Cicero through a screen of sugar . . . to what lenth than. O Cattyline, to abuse our patience . . . Quam diu . . . whaddluhdooo-oh, Charley . . . what—Charley, you . . . *Quam diu etiam furor iste tuus nos. . .* what's furor. . . . oh, I wish Charley was in my Cicero section . . . oh . . . *iste tuus nos eludet?* Doodle-de-doo . . . oh, damn this stuff. Wish Ma'd go out, I'd call up Charley. . . .

Evelyn Neibert arched over a history text-book, painstakingly copying out "Suggestive Questions." How are the pyramids proof of a high civileyezation? That was a splendid talk Superintendent Sherwood gave this morning. . . . School just a big game. . . . "Yes Ma I'm coming. Ma I really *can't*—I'm awful'—dreadfully sorry, I *can't* pay so much attention to you now I've started teaching. Please! I'll be in in about a half-hour. I got—I must be alone and try to concentrate when I'm making out a lesson." Goodness! T'morra, uh, to-morr-roe, sh'd meet her first real classes. She was to have the chance—to be given the privilege—of teaching Ancient and Mediaeval History—of making it interesting, and vivid, and alive. Not just lists of dates, silly notes'n' everything . . . make everything seem— almost like a movie—graphic, sort of. But—how green she was! Her body was tying itself into one great knot at the dread of tomorrow. She copied out the next question: "From the map (p. 11) locate Egypt, The Nile R. Gizch, Memphis, Thebes." Let's see; I'll tell them where Alexandria was later to be . . . Try to make it thrilling—idea of new civileyezation springin' up—Oh, it's going to be wonderful to teach! Ray Moffett, the football coach, hustled the "boys" out the back door: "Sorry's hell boys, but Hog-Eye Elmans is makin' a call—no-sir, fer nine months now I got to be healthy an' dry! Jeze! Lucky I hadn't took a swig when he rung. Well—Sorry boys I gotta make tracks. So long." His bulk reeled through the creaking dimness; he was opening the front door; "Oh—eve-nin' Mister Elmans, mighty sorry to of kep ya waiting. Now won't you sit down over here!" "Want to invite you over to Chapel tomorra to give a little fight-talk—fine thing for the School to work up a good Spirit right at the start." "You bet, Doctor Elmans, I'll be right there. 'N' I'm of a mind to add just a little about general Health—you know—sanitation, carryin' flasks, draggin'—smoking cigarettes an' all. 'S' murderous. 'S' absolutely murderous!"

School had begun.

(April 1927)

"Jenkinsville"

From Jenkinsville, Tennessee, sprawl two sagging railroads, writhing among the rocky hills like the trail left by a snail. Every night the Dixie Flyer shrieks through at sixty miles an hour, leaving only stirred grass, an oily-smelling, speed-sucked vacuum, and vague longing in a few restless souls.

Jenkinsville has a White Way. It is a hundred yards long, and it leads from the depot straight to the Court House. It is lighted at regular intervals by very new, very chaste, street lamps, and it has been carelessly splashed with asphalt, which lies along the street's centre like a tattered and wrinkled ribbon. At the Court House, however, all improvements end in a dusty loop, well shaded, and frequented by mountaineers, hounds, sows, and other animals.

The Court House, which put the town on the map, has a box-like simplicity from ground to gutter-pipe, where it blazes forth in bilious monstrosities of slate and wrought-iron.

The Depot can scarcely be said to hold up its end of the White Way. It is scabrous and barnlike, painted an uncertain yellow. An ambiguous, chalk-smeared bulletin hangs awry, a ticket-agent is not present; but three negro boys and one hen examine cigarette stubs and peanut shells. They radiate an air of mild dejection.

The New York Store sells Jaz Bo's—All the Rage on Broadway—to the Sheiks, and Dotty Dimple hats to the girls. It is very dark, painfully narrow; its proprietor affects a collar tie during working hours, and is privileged thereby to "put a little edge" on his prices. Occasionally a pinched country mother confides her meteorological opinions to the clerk, and that "damn overstock o' patten' leather Button's" is diminished by a pair. Otherwise, the reason for the existence of the New York Store is seldom guessed at and never known.

There are two Grocery Stores. Andrews', a dim welter of spitting loafers and hen-crates and limp lettuce and cats, substituted for air the fetor of ancient eggs and myriad mice, is patronized by most of the villagers. When Angus Smeed started the General Supply Store, he was ambitious; he made his interior light and airy; he adopted the motto, "The Best Is None too Good," and endeavored to live up to it. But he failed, as shall be seen.

Most of the stores were originally frame houses. To convert them into stores, the fronts were torn out, gnarled plate-glass was installed, and a sign was put up. A few buildings, however, are more ambitious. The General Supply Store is covered with squares of crumpled tin, hopefully painted granite-gray; the Farmers' Bank has a Gothic doorway in beaver-board, and the Post Office blithely masquerades as a Greek temple.

Fitch Avenue, a wabbly crescent from the Court House through the Residential District to the Depot, has since the Dixie Highway's coming fallen into decay. It is really a continuation of Main Street. Two blocks contain its aristocracy; then it dwindles to the bay-windows and scrolls of the eighties, and hides its face at the splatter of whitewashed shacks, belonging to the section hands, near the railroad.

Jenkinsville has a Baptist Church, a Methodist Church, a Presbyterian Church, and a Convent School. In the hills, a short distance from the outskirts, is a Primitive Baptist Church; in Niggertown is a church Baptist in name and Voodooistic in practice. And there is a movie theatre.

(December 1926)

"Jenkinsville II"

I

Jake Slade

In Traveller's Garage there emerges from oily dimness a skinny, vealy little man, his hair piled pads under a network of sweat-greased leather straps. His sharp pale nose and sharp pale eyes suggest an anaemic downishness which his speech confirms.

But across one sallow cheek is a red, mad scar. A course thread of horror, of cruelty, seems to have been pulled too tightly through his face, to have gathered the flesh into raw puckers of pain.

As a boy, Jake had hung about the Garage, day and night. And, as all such boys, in and out of fiction, seem to do, he at last landed a job. Now he is known to every resident motorist for miles around, and in the spring and autumn, when the Florida-bound autoists ape the wild geese, they make a point of stopping at Traveller's, of joking with him, of chanting, with infinite ritualistic boredom, the praises of the Great God Auto. Even in their boasting of deeds done in His Name are they reverent, and at Jake's limited praise do shyly flush. They have found favor with the High Priest.

But the scar:

When the war came, Jake quite casually enlisted. Just as casually he stood in the nave of "Notre Dame," (when it was vibrant with glorious music); he watched the Folies Bergers; and he drove groan-racked ambulances through mud.

He returned to Jenkinsville with three stolen army shirts, a medal, (valueless, since the inscription was in Latin), a broadened and cynical knowledge of woman, and the scar. This was his complete knowledge of French: "voolay-voo coochay avec moy," "pum de tairs, maim'selle," "oy-oy," "bon jour, manure," and "jay tayme." Also, he knew that he had entered Paris at 9:17 P.M., and had left at 8:23 P.M. next night, that the Ef-feel Tower is the highest structure on earth, and that all French women are prostitutes.

And that he was one of Pershing's crusaders.

II
Emerson Davis

As a young man, very poor, Emerson had married Aline Tate; they had gone to New York, where he was to become the author of the Great American Novel. For a year he knew happiness.

But Aline's mother, upon hearing that her daughter was "expectin'," insisted in tear-splotched letters that the poor dear lamb come home for proper care. So together they journeyed to Jenkinsville, quietly smiling. (It was such a little thing to do—to humor Mama this way—and Mama might not last forever.)

Emerson never saw New York again:

Racked with pleurisy, his wife was delivered of a son. Through seven months, she struggled toward health, and, at the brink of convalescence, died.

Aline's mother was puffily, tearily, black-crepely beseechingly; Emerson stayed awhile. Aline's sister was aging, sad-eyed, and physically like Aline; Emerson married her.

As the years went by, their dullness was jabbed by spasmodic moments of unrest. He grew to hate Mary. The mere shell of Aline; and he detested Mrs. Tate. But the grit ground deeper into the white soft tissue of his soul; and gradually he was squeezed dry of ambition.

Once, at forty, there came rebellion, with the idea of writing his own life into a novel. He completed three chapters.

Now he works in a Chain Shoe Store, of which Jenkinsville is inordinately proud.

III
Seigbert Pearson

Proprietor of the Friendship Pool Hall, was a typical village roué. He had no opposition in trade now. Once a man had started up his "Billiard Parlors, Ladies and Gents" across the street from Pearson. But Sig had been tactful. The admission of Ladies, he realized, stuck in the craw of every preacher in town; Sig made haste to ally himself with Virtue. For a week he kept his shutters pulled modestly down, and his patrons were liberally tongued only in the back room. In a few weeks the rival had gone.

Now Sig's joint flourished—flourished so admirably, indeed, that Sig saw fit to hire a helper, and was able to go to Knoxville quite frequently, for a lil' week-end. In the Pool Hall, he accompanied the announcement of such an excursion with an elbow and a leer. (When he mentioned it to his wife, he discarded the leer and the elbow.) Upon his return, on the noon train Monday, he was invariably very cross, very sickish, very sleepy. Sig drooled a little when he slept, and when half drunk he never bothered to take off his shoes. Accordingly, after he had flopped upon their splintery veneered double bed, his wife would lift his damp, ponderous head, would roll aside his sausage-like legs, and would lay funny papers beneath him. She did enough washing for other folks without doing up bed linen every day in the week'n.' Sunday too. She was a bleached, work-worn, solicitous woman, with moist flat eyes and a mouth so nervously sprawling over her jumbled teeth that she seemed always on the verge of tears. Of late her neurosis had taken an intensely religious turn. It was she who shouted loudest, sang the shrillest, repented the most vehemently at every revival. After many of these hysterical religious debauches she was unable to get around. Upon such an occasion Sig would prepare breakfast—a greasy, peculiarly savory mess of fried pork, potatoes and green beans—and would tidy up the two rooms they had over the Pool Hall. Late in the morning he would slouch down into the room below murmuring that the Old Lady'd got one of her nervous spells. And from immersion in some "juicy one" he would move ponderously upward, flinging back, with a gleam of gold teeth: "Reckon I'll go up'n see how there doin.'" He was held a kind husband, a patient father.

It was the life his wife led made him go on a spree sometimes.

(January 1927)

"Bound for the Promised Land"

"Clean up out heah, muh babies," wheezed Mrs. Rucker, and she trailed after her guests, an importantly heart-broken woman. Gently she closed the door on the segment of the parlor. The daughters looked hard at the door, as if to see through it, and strained to shred from the rustle and mumble beyond it a single phrase. Useless.

"Well—if we huh yup we can git in for some of it," whispered Mayme. "You clean up da table, I'll wrench da plates."

"I'll wrench 'em."

"Yeah. You got on yoh pahty dress. Not much does you wren 'em, Rosaline."

"'Taint agonna huht muh dress. You'd git yer haid all full a kinks."

Mayme teeterd on the memory of two torrid hours beneath grease and hot irons. She spred a "Well" on her tongue, and reflectively chewed.

"Pap . . . Pappy wouldn' want ye to thoo way foh bits . . . like nothin' tall . . . Sides, I can put on a aphun."

"Well . . . I wouldn' let ye if it wasn't foh Pappy."

Rosaline dove into a great crisp apron, and shoved the sleeves of her party dress above her large jointed elbows. She had bought some dye at the five-and-ten; a long struggle had ended in compromise, and the dress had emerged a bedraggled gray. When she bent over the dishpan, platoons of bluish polka dots stood at attention across her shoulders. Both girls had long anticipated new dresses for this occasion but when the really necessary expenses had been met, there was just enough left to buy each patent-leather pumps and blue ribbons to bind about their foreheads. Nevertheless, the shoes bravely squeaked, and each bore her ribbon like a laurel toward which she had striven throughout those lean seven years.

Rosaline plunged her brown arms into the water and hummed into the steam.

"Boun'foh de Promis' Land."

 . . . . . .

By the closed parlor door stood Mayme. One hand clamped a platter against her hip. The other stuffed to her mouth a lavender-frosted cupcake. She could hear breathing, and the creak of unusual shoes. She glanced back at the jungle of chickenbones, swimming, ice-cream, faded flowers. A tear dropped into the arid bones heaped upon the platter. A thrust of the cupcakes stifled a sob.

Together they began to dry the dishes. They could hear Reverend Sampson's voice, as if through a telephone; a jumbled metallic snarl.

The cinders in the back-yard crunched. Someone banged the screen door.

Rosaline opened it. "What does you want, cullud boy?"

"Wants to see da lady a da house."

"Wheah you come fum?"

"Up to college . . . Wuk fuh Doc Pinckney."

"Come in an' set down. I'll get huh when sober with."

He humped over in the crackling chair, his eyes on the lift of their skirts as they came and went with the dishes.

 . . . . . .

"Keep on settin' yuh," whispered Rosaline. "Be thew foh long."

Under cover of a hymn the two girls stole in, and stood behind their mother. They were amazed at the beauty of the room, which was banked high with flowers. Some of the flowers were donated, but many more, as the girls well know . . . Along the wall glided Mr. Johnson, carrying folding chairs, which he noiselessly shoved beneath them.

The hymn was finished.

There was a long silence. Upward into the hot sweet dusk strained the lily flames. The shades were drawn, and eyes shone like bits of china. The men were lunged forward in their chairs, round heels hunched between shoulders. Between their knees dangled their hands, knotty fingers interlaced. Beneath puckered foreheads the white eyes stared, straight before them, hard and fearfully.

 . . . . . .

Outside, wagon wheels ground past. A baby cried. Somebody was shingling a roof, and a postman's whistle sounded near at hand.   The mid-summer sun blazed down on the whirling earth, the sun, among the blinded stars.

.   .   .   .   .   .

Rosaline caught herself gazing at the little valley in which was embedded her mother's spine. Down that channel coursed a rivulet of sweat. Mayme caught herself examining the white horns of corset which butted at the transparent fabric of her mother's dress. Above it, the coffee colored flesh puffed out beneath a film of crepe.

Horror-stricken, sick with shame, the sisters stared at each other, and each achieved a sob.

.   .   .   .   .

At last the undertaker rose. Drawing fresh white gloves over his large, coffin shaped hands, he spoke:

"Mohnahs who desiah a las view a da Remains will now advance."

There, in the rosewood coffin, he lay. His hands were folded upon the glistening shirtfront. The head lay upon a white satin pillow. It might have been carved from a lump of mahogany, and polished, polished. That head was all the austerity of death.

Gazing upon it for the last time Mr. Johnson permitted himself an ingrowing smile. His mental fingers lingered almost sensuously upon each minute beauty of his handiwork.

Gazing upon it for the last time, the mourners (fine food and religious fervor suspended within them), the mourners realized as never before what a fine man Leopold Rucker had been; a true leader of the community.

Gazing upon it for the last time, Reverend Sampson spread above it his spidery hands, and said, "He is not dead, but sleeping."

Gazing upon it for the last time, Mayme and Rosaline recalled past moments of objection to their unnecessarily intensified poverty, and wildly wept.

Gazing upon it for the last time, Mrs. Rucker was supremely happy. Now, at last, the goal achieved, the goal toward which he had striven these seven years. She saw that head sunk in sour pillows, netted with green shadow, motionless from day to day, from year to year. She saw those eyes wide, bright, nailed to the vision of his glorious death. In shadowy processional the self-denials of seven years swept past.

And now this head, with beauty, splendor, to surround it. His neighbors gathered to witness this glorious commencement. The sacrifices became still more shadowy . . . became cobwebs . . . became the dark air of the room. Down through the gloom swooped the face of Mr. Rucker himself. His hand caressed her shoulder, and he smiled.

She looked up. Mr. Johnson withdrew his hand, and his eyes said, "You must look no longer." He rose to his gaunt height, and arched above the coffin, making large vague movements. His black bulk dominated the room, and even the mourners felt pride in Mr. Johnson. An assistant handed him screws.

Rosaline leaned over and whispered; Mrs. Rucker rustled from the room. The young man was standing near the dining room door, wiping his fingers on his pants. "What does you want, cullud boy," whispered Mrs. Rucker. The young man swallowed. "Who, me? I don't want nothin. It's Doc Pinckney. He sent me down." "Aw righ . . . what Doc Pinckney 'mand?" "I wuks foh 'im up to Science hall, an' he says had you got a man in do house can hep wi da diggin'." "Says which?" "Say he thought tover, an' thought mabby if you was so po' as you has to sell da body, he wonduhed has you got a boy cud hep wif da diggin—you know—diggin' 'im up—he cud give youns some extry pay." "Yuh—you tell Doctuh Pinckney thankyuhsah, but we ain't go no man in da house." "Aurightm." He ran down the back steps, whistling as he ran, "Boun' foh da Promis' Land." The women returned to the parlor.

The pall bearers lifted their burden. The door opened, and a knife of sunlight cut the room in two. On the hearse the plumes stirred in the stale summer air. A telegraph boy sped past; a negro lolled on the opposite corner, twirling his cap.

The sleek horses stamped. Carriage-wheels began to grind.

(January 1928)

"A Sentimental Journey"

I

Mrs. Lula Green arranged little Ella among the jumble of bundles in the seat opposite, crouched against the rubbed plush, and, the heel of her hand jammed against her teeth, stared out the window. The tangle and swirl of tracks slipped away with a sharp rattle of steel. The train roared past the flickering windows of trackside tenements, past a spatter of bungalows with garages of tin and front yards of red clay; at last settled into the long swaying, creaking lunge of journeying in the open country. Without enthusiasm she saw trees, cows, fields, houses, pivoting about each most distant landmark. When she tired of this, there was always the faithful companion track, whose, parallel bends swam with beautiful constancy, just above the window-sill. Or, again, there were the telephone wires, rising and falling, strutting up a high bank, or sinking below the level even of the friendly track, just when you least expected it. She was grateful to the track for its consistency, to the wires for their temperament. Between them they made life beautiful; they diverted her mind.

For nearly an hour she sat thus: then, opening her purse, she dabbed at her nose with a pinkish-gray powder-puff—and her eye fell on the letter.

Immediately the thoughts which had for so long circled above her descended and fastened their talons, their beaks, in her brain. Their wings beat her eyes into blindness. All her senses were bent toward the savage agony within her.

Only a few hours, and she'd be there. Back home—back under the power of her mother and her great-aunt. Fragments of the letter fluttered about, assembled into a terrifying demonstration of what she had to face . . . Mamma hadn't come to the funeral, but surely she could understand that, couldn't she, with

Aunt Etta to see to and all? Oh yes, she could understand only too well. And she'd been down with the grippe, and couldn't have written any sooner, but dear, she knew how close she was to her in her bereavement, didn't she? And the Lord giveth and the Lord hath taken away—and that should be an eternal comfort to her, poor dear. But now that it was all over, Lula must feel free to make her home with momma just as long as she wanted, and everything she'd said when she ran off and married Alvin was forgiven and forgotten. . . .

Yes, she was free, now, to come home and be the grateful slave to Aunt Etta. Free, to crawl meekly back and be forgiven. . . . She knew the brand of forgiveness to expect—forgiveness in a voice stained with triumph, cruelty. She saw the trap ahead of her; she saw her mother and aunt waiting, like two great cats. Always she would be in their power, scrambling between the hypocrisy of one and the blistering hatred of the other. And there was no way out; she had to give Ella a home.

And worst of all, she hadn't even loved Alvin. All her life with him . . . his death under any circumstances but these would have been a relief. No, she hadn't the comforting memory of his love. From the very first, it was her pride, her disinclination to obey her mother and aunt, which had driven her to marry him. Since she could remember she had fought against their smugly guiding hands. . . .

In short, every important turning-point in her life, up to the present, had been governed by her pride, and now a factor new to her, necessity, was turning her backward, forcing her full against the consequences which she had given no thought. An insect caught in a pitcher-plant is happier; at the worst, he did not himself set the spikes which imprison him.

During the week since the funeral these thoughts had torn at her brain until, now, it was a little better than an insensate pulp. Even now, she was not capable, as before, of realizing her plight with any great intensity of pain; rather her brain ached dully, and thoughts worked through as steam bubbles and puffs in boiling oatmeal.

The rhythmic noises and movements of the train were doing their part in kneading her brain into utter blankness. As time passed, her muscles, her nerves—finally her mind itself, gave in to fatigue and to the oppressive monotony in the cradling movement of a train. She retained only a symbol, as it were, of her life; a long, bare corridor, whose four walls, gleam-

ing beneath a hard and shadowless light, drew down, at the end,
to an utter blank.

.   .   .   .   .   .

II

As if through misty water she noticed that Ella was attack-
ing the child in the next seat. Rising, she took Ella by the
shoulders—

For a moment the movement of her muscles, the action
of her mind, hung suspended, as a smile burned into her soul.

Recovering, she swung Ella round, and said, "Hungry?"
The child nodded. With unsure fingers she fumbled at the
strings about the "Dolly Dainty" box, and laid out the hard-boiled
eggs, the limp jelly sandwiches, and what salt and pepper was
not already widely distributed throughout the lunch.

As they ate, she glanced covertly across the back of the
seat, seeking out the man who had smiled. Seeing him, she was
convinced that she had found her savior.

Yes—this—this man and she had been *born* for each
other! With a feeling almost of delighted recognition she gazed
at him, utterly oblivious of any impropriety in the boldness of
her act. She decided that his taste in neckties was abominable,
and was wondering how she might tell him so without hurting
his feelings when she noticed that in shaving that morning he
had cut his cheek. Poor thing—he must have been in a dreadful
hurry. Alvin wouldn't have bothered to shave, at such a time.
He'd been a dirty slob pretty near from the first week they'd been
married, it seemed. How on earth she'd ever happened to *marry*
him, *that* was more than *she* could see. But on the heels of this
came the explanatory thought—that she married Alvin so that
she might be on this train, at this moment. For that matter, that
explained Ella's existence. Ella was really some good, after all—it
was Ella who'd first drawn her attention to Quinn—Quinn must
be his name; no other'd suit him as well.

"Do you want some water, dearie?" Lord God, s'pose he
got up and left while she was gone! Couldn't take any chances
on a thing like that. Oh, but he wouldn't—

"Don't spill so—here. Let me wipe your dress."

"Everything they'd ever done, all their lives, had led up to
their being on this train, siting [sic] facing each other. When you
thought of that, it was absurd to think he'd leave, now. No—he
was hers, and she was his, and he was going to stay on that train

as long as she did. Maybe—maybe they'd *never* leave the train!
Anyway, they'd go on through Portersville—maybe she'd get a
glimpse of her home, from the back—mamma hanging out
clothes—Be wonderful to holler at her—to cuss her out, at the
top of her lungs! Thought she'd get *her* back there, huh? Chain
her down to Aunt Etta? Well, she guessed not! Thought she'd
have her right where she could yell all she wanted about how
crazy she was to marry Alvin—and she couldn't talk back for
Ella's sake? No, that was the time she fooled mamma!

Pity not to see the look on her face, though, when she
heard she was gypped—heard she was married again. Maybe
she'd ask Quinn to get out at Portersville, and stop over a train,
just so they *could* tell her to her face—

"Hello, mamma. (And she'd have to kiss her.) How's
Aunt Etta?"

"I knew you'd—Why, who—"

"I want you to meet my husband, mamma, we were
married—married by the conductor. His name's Quinn . . . and
I'm awfly sorry, but we can't even stay to supper because we're
off on our honeymoon you see."

Oh, it'd be *swell*. But maybe, wouldn't it be even sweller
to swell, sweller, swellest, maybe to just to see her hanging out
clothes, or—yes, hanging out clothes? As they went by on the
train, see mamma hanging up sudsy underclothes.

Oh well plenty of time to figure that out. Right now, you
couldn't beat just sitting there, sort of sagging in the seat, and
looking at him—not even saying a thing, just looking and smiling at him. Funny, the way he got red; what did *he* care, if there
were people around? But then, of course, men were always sort
of scared, maybe. Alvin'd blushed like that, when they'd got on
the train right after the wedding. Well—she'd never have to
think of all that again, now. There wouldn't be mamma and
Aunt Etta bringing it up and throwing it in your face every five
minutes. Not that she didn't know, now, that she *had* been a
fool to marry him—but it was admitting it at home that hurt.
Damn 'em—she'd never even have married him if they hadn't
kept nagging at her—

Oh well . . . she was through worrying now—she could
just sit back and take life easy and—

What was his idea, picking up a paper and reading, like he
didn't even know her? She had a good mind to tell him what
she thought of that—no though—best way was to act like she

didn't care—look out the window, or play with Ella, or—there; she had him worried now, all right . . . oh, go on—read your darn paper, then. . . .

Clicketyclunk-ty-clicktyclunk, click-etyclunk-ty-click-ty-clunk—that next pole'd come before she'd done three—clickety clunk-ty-click-tyclunk, oh yeah, it *would* go up a bank . . . Must not be more than couple of hours out of Portersville—not that she had to worry about Portersville? . . . There was the whistle for some place or other—clicketyclunk-ty-clicktyclunk, click—start slowing down the clicketys, in a minute now, clicket—

What in *time* was Quinn up to *now*?

"Where you think *you're* goin'," she said, jacosely. Well, you don't have to take off yer *hat* to talk, like you never *saw* me before."

"I—'scuse *me, I* ain't seen you before, lady."

Conscious of suffused faces about him he blushed.

She drew closer and whispered, with a touch of anxiety, "Say, Quinn, what's wrong with you today, anyhow? Crazy, or somethin'?"

Behind her rang out a loud, metallic laugh, followed by a horse whisper: "Hear *that*? She asks him is he *crazy*!"

The train stopped. Snatching at his bundles, at his clothes, she followed Quinn from the train, whispering loudly, "What you think yer *doin'*, huh? What ya think yer *doin'* . . . *Huh*? And, as she felt the gravel underfoot: "Aw, Quinn, *don't* run off like this Quinn. . . . Aw, *Quinn* . . . Who ya lookin' for like that . . . here I . . ." A woman hurried up, looked at her in a puzzled way, and kissed the man. Lula tasted blood in her mouth; all that she saw swam in a milk-blue haze. She flung herself against the woman and a knotted rope of profanity dragged from her mouth. The train began to slide past, the windows crowded with glutinous grins—and seeing Ella's face flattened against one pane, she grabbed Quinn by the shoulders and said in a painsoaked voice, "Oh, Quinn, I'd never a thought. . . ." And sprang on to the train.

.   .   .   .   .   .

Throughout the rest of the journey she sat as she had at first, the heel of her hand jammed against her teeth, her eyes now on the fields, on the wires and poles, or on the companion track. At first it was supremely painful because of the thought of Quinn to observe how smoothly and faithfully they kept their parallel course;—but as time passed, they grew to mean all she had wished Quinn to be; they symbolized the constancy she so needed now, and in her way she was happy watching them and hearing the rhythmic hammering of the rails. Occasionally she glanced over at little Ella, who was reading "A Barrel Full o' Fun," with evident delight. Her brain was like a field of grain; a million chaotic thoughts, which shifted and assumed new significance as each mood blew over them. Now, however, no change of mood brought back the old dread of returning to her mother and Aunt Etta; she looked upon all that almost without emotion, save for an untroubled, almost a smiling contempt. When, at last, they were among the splattering of bungalows with garages of tin and yards of red clay, she wiped Ella's nose, and gathered their belongings. When they swung beneath Liberty Hill, the house appeared, and, to her delight, she saw mamma hanging out clothes. The train rattled along the tracks; drew to a stop. Taking little Ella by one moist paw, she descended to the platform.

She rang the bell and heard the floor creak. The door opened. The house smelled of cabbage and medicine.

"Hello, mamma." (And she had to kiss her.) "How's Aunt Etta?"

"I knew you'd come. Why what's—"

"I want you to meet my husband, mamma, we were married—married by the conductor. His name's Quinn . . . and I'm awfly sorry, but we can't even stay to supper because we're off on our honeymoon you see!"

(March 1928)

Phillips Exeter Drama

"Catched"

A Play in Three Scenes

The Characters:

Ed Winters

Maw Felts

Mag Felts

Pop Felts

Sam Hayden *the Stranger*

Liza Gudger

Time: The Present. Late afternoon.

SCENE ONE

(The simple interior of a log cabin in the Tennessee Mountains. A small kitchen stove is in the left, set rather far back. Two or three chairs, with seats of woven hickory, are around it; another is at the table. In rear center a door opens on to a clearing. There are, also, two windows, small square ones. Upon their sills are climbing vines and plants, potted in tin cans. Another door, (closed), leads to a room on the right. A hound is dozing beside the stove.)

As the curtain rises there is heard, from far off-stage, the *clump* of an axe, beating time to the cracked voice of a woman:

Ah'm jest a *married-gal*,

An' ah *wish* that ah could *die*;

Ah'm jest a *mar*-ried *gal*;

Set by the cradle an *cry*.

Mag Felts, a fresh-looking girl of fifteen, is standing before a mirror at right of stage, listening. At the conclusion she mutters:

That'l be Annie out thar . . . a won't ketch *me* adoin that. . . .

Ed Winters, a huge, rawboned fellow, slouches in from rear door and stands behind her. Excepting a great wen on one temple, he is a rather good looking brute.

Ed—Howdy, sugar-foot.

Mag—Howdy, Edmund. *(She does not turn.)*

Ed—Don't you Edmund *me*. Say it right, now.

Mag—*(Turning)* Howdy, Ed.

Ed—That's more like it. Jest come in f'm plowin'.

Mag—Yer?

Ed—Doan' be so uppish thar, sweetheart. Air ye in a mood fer kissin' this evenin'?

Mag—I ain't a-saying.

Ed—Reckon I'll find out, then.

(He starts toward her.)

Mag—Don't ye tetch me, Ed Winters.

Ed—Why not?

Mag—Jest keep yer hands offen me, that's all, er you'll find out.

Ed—Who's a-goin' to say anythin' about it? Huh?

Mag—*(Coquettishly)* I hain't a-sayin' if ye cain't guess.

Ed—'Tain't Hen Cook, is it?

Mag—No.

Ed—'Tain't Al?

Mag—No.

Ed—*(After a pause.)* Looky hyar! That feller f'm town hain't been a-hangin' roun' here, has he?

Mag—I hain't a-sayin'.

Ed—Le' me see ary one roun' you, an I'll whup hell out-en' 'um. Now, kiss me.

Mag—Ed, you be keerful what you do. *(She kisses him.)*

Ed—Say, Mag, I got somethin' mighty pertickler to ast ye.

Mag—Yer?

Ed—Kin I carry ye to the box-supper Cheusday evenin'?

Mag—Yer—naw—I hain't a-sayin' yet.

Ed—Ye'll come, a'right. So long, honey, I'm a-goin' to feed my hogs. *(He goes out. After a short pause Maw enters. Maw shuffles, exhausted, to a chair by the stove. She is barefooted; her skirt is torn, and there are deep lines in her thin, sagging face. She fans herself with her apron, as she talks.)*

Mag—Kin I he'p ye, Maw?

Maw—They ain't nothin' to be done jest now, I reckon, honey . . . I jest put the kittle on to bile, and come in fer a breathin' spell. *(A pause.)* Phew! Shore is a briler of a day!

Mag—Shore is. *(She is silent for a moment, and seems to be gathering courage.)* Say, Maw.

Maw—(*Not turning*) Yes, Mag.

Mag—Maw, I'm . . . I'm afeared if—Ed Winters . . . (*Maw looks at her*) . . . I'm afeared he's a-goin' to make me marry him.

Maw—Well strikes me it's about time; Great gal fifteen years old. . . . But—why air ye afeared?

Mag—I—I do' know! I—Hit's like this-yer . . .

Maw—Has he ast ye?

Mag—Not—not yit, but . . . he's—he's a—

(*Liza Gudger enters. A typical mountain woman of her age; she is 40, and looks like 60. She is clad in a filthy flannel blouse, a skirt that is a black rag, and large broken men's shoes. She lays aside her poke bonnet, and as she speaks she brushes back her straggling gray hair.*)

Liza—Thought I'd come in and set with ye awhile, Miz Felts.

Maw—Pull ye up a cheer. (*She does not rise.*)

(*Mag quickly draws a chair toward Liza, then goes and leans against table.*)

Liza—(*As she sits down*) I'm obleeged to ye, Mag. Lord, Miz Felts, what a big gal she's a-gettin' to be, hain't she?

Maw—Yer, Mag's right smart of a young lady, now— lively's a lizard, too. Brang yer own snuff?

Liza—Yer, I brung my own. (*She produces a snuff box, and takes a twig from her mouth.*) Shore is a hot day.

Maw—Shore is.

Mag—(*In a faint, echoing treble*) Shore is.

Liza—(*As she dips snuff.*) Reckin' Mister Felts is a-workin' at the still, hain't he?

Maw—He does right smart of work thar. To-day he's gone a-huntin'.

Mag—He orght to be back soon, Maw.

Liza—Oh, that does put me in mind. Have ye heared about this feller f'm town, come up here?

Maw—Naw. What's he up herefer?

Liza—Claims he's up on a huntin' trip, as Abel heared.

Maw—I reckon' I better warn Pop.

Liza—The fellers down at the sawmill air on the lookout fer dirty work.

Mag—What's he like, Miz Gudger?

Liza—(*laughing loudly and raucously*) Good Lord, Miz Felts, you better be a-watchin' that gal o' yores!

Maw—(*also laughs*) Mag, shorely yer not aimin' to get

this feller on yer string, air uye? *(Mag blushes sullenly and is silent)* Mag Felts, you quit that sullin' er I'll smack ye good. You think yer too big fer me to handle, do ye? Do ye?

Mag—Naw—I don't. I was jest a-wonderin' what—

Liza—*(jocularly)* Why Mag, I thought you was a-goin' purty steady with Ed Winters. Feller *is* purty tall on looks, I hear. Reckin' Ed better look fer another gal. *(more seriously, to Maw)* I might a thought them two would be settn' a date, by now.

Maw—Reckin' they'll set their own, Liza. I was a-tellin' Mag jest now she orta been married months ago.

(Liza emits a breathy "Well, well," and is quiet. There is a long, ruminative silence. The two older women are enjoying one of their rare moments of relaxation, and they are profoundly and mutely grateful. Mag, on the other hand, being young, is a little restless. Only the squeaking of Liza's chair as she rocks monotonously is heard. Liza dips snuff mechanically; from far off in the woods comes the sound of a shot. Finally Liza breaks the silence with—)

Lord, how time does fly . . . Air ye havin' trouble with them shootin' pains, Miz Felts?

Maw—Yer. . . . Sometime I feel thur most a-killin' me, Liza. *(She pauses, and when she again speaks her voice is shaky)* Oh, Miz Gudger . . . I . . . I'm jest a run-down machine, now—on the downward track! *(She sobs.)*

Liza—Thar, thar Miz Felts. Don't feel so down-hearted.

Maw—*(brokenly)*—I'm jest a—a old ooman, Liza.

Liza—*(soothingly)* Thar! Now, ye hain't hardly old at all.

Maw—Mag, go off an' see if the soaps a-bilin! Tote it off if hit's ready to cool. *(Mag goes out. Maw looks after her, then turns to Liza.)* Ye know, Liza, that gal says to me—these few minutes ago—she says she's afeared of Ed Winters!

Liza—*(leaning forward, eyes beady.)* Why—why Miz Felts! But—why?

Maw—That's what I cain't figger out. *(a puzzled pause, then her face lights up)* I'low, I know what! That gal's jest shif'-less. Jest plain shif'less. She's a-skeered o' plain, honest to Jesus work! I know *now* why she begged to go to school . . . I tell ye, Liza Gudger, if she don't make up to Ed, I'll wear that gal out!

(Mag enters, and the two women sit in confused silence.)

Liza—Have ye heard the news?

Mag—What?

Liza—Annie Martin's expectin'.

Maw—Shore enough! Well, the Lord giver'er better luck than she had *last* year! Annie's a good, hard-working gal. . . suthin' *you* might take to heart, Mag.

Mag—What do you mean, Maw?

Maw—Never you mind what I mean. Did ye take that soap off?

Mag—Yes'm.

Liza—*(Rising, and putting on her poke bonnet)* Well, I must be movin' along, Miz Felts. Good bye, Mag, Good-bye, Miz Felts.

Maw—I reckin I'll walk a spell with ye. *(She puts on a poke-bonnet, and they go out. Turning at the door, she says)* Mag, see to the house. *(They disappear.)*

(Mag draws a chair to the table and sits, head in hands. From far off-stage comes a faint, long-drawn "whooop . . . whooop . . . whooop-ee!" She sobs suddenly, and begins to speak.) Mag—That'll be Ed out yander, feedin' 'is hogs. . . . Oh, Lordy-Lord! *(She looks about, her eyes damp, and addresses the sleepy hound beside the stove.)* S-pose—s'pose *you* was in my fix, Tubby: what would ye do, . . . what *could* ye do, if ye had to get married? Oh, I know Ed's a good spry feller,—bettern' most aroun' here, but . . . if—if I marry, I'll be . . . in ten year . . . I'll be a old ooman, like Maw! I—I wanta stay purty! *(She crys out loudly, and clatters across the floor to the mirror. She looks at herself, and "primps" as she talks.)* I am a good-lookin' gal, an' it ain't right fer *any gal*—to get old so quick! *(The hound trots out.)* Warshin' an' a-plowin' an' a-feedin' stock—luk what hit's done to Maw! Scourin' an' shoppin' wood—while Ed sets up an' spits at a bush—I hain't a-goin' to git catched! *(She is talking more and more rapidly. Her hands are twisting, her cheeks blazing.)* Luk at Annie Martin! Seventeen year old, and gettin' yaller teeth an' shootin' pains! One brat dead and another un on the way! Ed'll have me bearin' kids—oncet a year, reg'lar as clock-work *(She laughs sharply)*—til I'm nothin' but a saggy old 'ooman! I'm *damned* if I get catched!

(There is excited talking just outside and a groan. Mag quickly composes herself, and runs to the door. The Stranger, enters, leaning heavily on Pop and Maw Felts. Ed follows them in; he has, evidently, met them on the way. The Stranger is short, and thickly built. Altho not good looking, he has about him the smoothness, the suggestion of an easy "line" of a travel-

ling salesman. Pop puts a gun beside the door.)

Maw—Mag, you git a pan of water hot. Hurry now. *(Mag runs out.)* Howdy, Ed. Pull up a cheer thar, Pop Felts! Nothin' wrong with *yore* legs.

(They ease the Stranger into a chair.)

Pop—*(whose personality is that of the "houn' dawg".)—* Ye see, Maw—hit warn't no fault of mine. I was a-huntin'—jest a-drawin' a bead on a squirrel, and jest as I shot—somethin' went wrong with the gun.

Maw—You mean somethin' went wrong with *you*, Pop Felts. Le' me smell yer breath. *(Bus)* Mm-hm, I reckoned so. I can tell ye stranger, yer can be glad ye come out alive, with that ole houn' full.

Stranger—Oh—he couldn't help it—I don't think it's really hurt me—much.

Maw—*(after a short pause)*—Oh! Air *you* the feller up on a huntin' trip?

Stranger—Why, yeah—I suppose so.

Pop—Yeh—he was a-huntin' too, when I—when the gun went off. I brung 'im home; *jest* thought I better.

Maw—Well, I reckon you better of thunk so! He's a-goin' to stay here 'til he wants to leave. *(Mag comes in, and sets a pan on the stove.)*

Mag—Here it is, Maw.

Maw—A'right. Now, Mag, you tear up a old shirt. *(Mag glances at Stranger, then at Ed, and goes into the room at the right.)*

Pop—Ed, do you aim to carry Mag to the box-supper?

Ed—I reckon I do. *(To S.)* How long air you a-goin' to be here?

S.—I don't know. It all depends—

Ed—Yeh—hit all *dee*pends, don't it. *Good* evenin' Maw Felts. *(Goes out.)*

Pop—Now, Maw, reckon what's come over Ed?

Maw—Shet up, Pop Felts. *(Mag comes in from right with rags.)* Mag, yore sweetheart jest went out.

Mag—Ain't no sweetheart of mine. *(Maw glares at her, but keeps a baleful silence.)* *(To Stranger)* Air ye hurt bad, Mister?

S.—Nope, I think not very bad. I—I hope not. *(He directs at Mag a calculating stare.)*

Mag—*(a little fluttered)* Well—I hope hit ain't a-goin' to—

Maw—Mag, you quit a-pesterin' Mister, Mister—uh—

Stranger—Mister Hayden. Sam H. Hayden. *(He bgins, from force of habit)*: I represent the Peerless Kidney Kure—well—*(he chuckles)*—I guess I won't bother you with that! You see, my business is travelin'. Yessir, travelin' drummer. 'Fact, this is the first vacation I've took—taken in my time—

Pop—Whar does yore work take ye?

S.—*(carelessly)* Oh, I go all over the state; sometimes into Georgia an' Alabama. Headquarters is at Knoxville. *(He pauses, to allow that point to "sink in".)* And I'll tell ya: I get more sales off of you folks in the country than anywhere else. *(Maw almost beams upon him.)* Yes-sir, I was sayin' just last week, when I was in Knoxvul—fella says to me—

Mag—*(interrupting)* Was you in Knoxvul jest last *week*?

Sam—You bet, Sister, and it's a great old town. You wanta come down sometime.

Maw—Mag, that water orght to be hot now. *(Mag takes the pan from the stove.)* Now, Mister Hayden, ef you'll jest pull up yore britches leg a little—

Sam—*(releasing a groan, and looking for its effect on Mag)* I—I don't know if I can get that pulled up . . . kinda sore. . . .

Pop—*(Taking out a bowie knife)* I'll jest take an' cut this yer . . . roun' here . . . like that-ar. *(There is the sound of tearing cloth. Pop is sitting so as to half hide the operation from the audience.)* Thar ye air. *(Sam grunts with evident pain.)*

Maw—Now, Mag, you hold the pan under his leg. I'll warch it of, so's we can see what we'ere a-doin'. *(She slops the water on. There is a rather long silence. Pop is much interested. He takes a huge "chaw" of tobacco, and occasionally spits upon the stove. At last Maw straightens, and points an accusing finger.)* Thar—look, Pop Felts, what ye done!

Pop—Mist' Hayden, yer know I'm right tore up about this-yer, but—look, Maw—I don't think there's ary a shot in 'im. *(He is closely examining the wound.)* 'Pears like hit's jest tore up the fat meat a little.

Maw—*(Bending over)*—Pop, you said right oncet. *(To Sam.)* Well, Mister Hayden, I'll jest slap some grease on this-yer and tie'er up. Mag, you git some grease. *(Mag scrapes a big spoon in a dirty skillet on the side table, and gives it to Maw.*

Maw quickly ties up the wound, straightens, and says) Thar! Now, can yer walk?

Sam—I'—I'm afraid not . . . well. *(He rises apparently with great pain, and glances at Mag. He limps about painfully, and sits again.)* Nope—that's pretty bad.

Maw—Well, ye can stay here 'till hit's healed up good.

Sam—Oh! why—Thanks a lot!

Maw—Ye can sleep in here. *(She indicates door at right.)* Mag, you sleep out on the bed here.

Mag—Yes'm.

Maw—You scrape up some snack, Mag. I'm a-goin' to the sprang. *(She goes out. Mag goes to the sidetable, takes a large pot and sets it on the stove.)*

Mag—I'll jest heat up these beans, Pop—Mister Hayden, would ye keer for some bacon and coffee?

Sam—Now, Sister, don't go to any trouble on *my* account. Anything.

Mag—*(giggles a little)* Well, I'll fry some, anyhow. *(She works about the stove as she talks.)* Air ye a-goin' back to Knoxvul soon?

Sam—N—uh—yeah, I guess I will, soon's I leave here.

Mag—Lordy—wish't *I* could see town! Is Knoxville right good-sized?

Sam—You bet. But you oughta see Cincinnatti! [sic]

Pop—Never heard of hit!

Sam—I was there once, for a couple uh weeks. Oughta see.

Pop—Well, I al-ways thought I'd ruther live in the hills as in town; can't tell what kind of devil-*ment* the youngun's gits in.

Sam—*Oh,* now—I do' know; yuh see—

Pop—*(who has been looking through the door)*—Here comes yore Maw, Mag you'd ought ter git the snack on.

Mag—Mister Hayden, will ye come over to the table now? *(She notices that he rises with apparent pain, and, after a pause says)* Maybe you need he'pin over. *(Mag takes Sam by the arm, and helps him to the table chair. Maw appears, and stands framed in the door in surprised silence as)*

The Curtain Falls

SCENE TWO

(At about nine in the morning, two days after Scene I. Inside the cabin. As the curtain rises, Pop is sitting near the door; his thoughts are evidently far away. Mag enters from the room at the right, and crosses to the mirror.)

Mag—Howdy, Pop.

Pop—You been a-fixin' that feller's bed?

Mag—*(at mirror)* Yer. Whar is he, Pop?

Pop—Don't worry yourself about Stranger. Heh, heh . . .

Mag—Aw, shet up, you.

Pop—Strikes me you're a-spendin' pow'ful time at that mirror to-day.

Mag—*(abstractedly)* Yer?

Pop—Reckon as how Ed may be a-comin' over?

Mag—Don't make nary diff'unce to me. *(She moves across to stove.)* Don't keer . . . let 'im come.

Pop—Thought ye was a-goin' purty steady with Ed.

Mag—Well, I hain't no more. *(a pause)* So jest shet up about it.

Pop—*(meekly)* Why Mag, I hain't done nary a thing, but—but Ed's a mighty spry feller. Ye cain't do much better nor stick to Ed.

Mag—*(in a burst of pent-up sincerity)* I know that, Pop— Ed's—Ed's a awful nice feller, but—but . . .

Pop—Ye hain't stuck on *this* feller, air ye?

Mag—*(Half to herself)* Ed's a better lookin' man, but— Pop ye cain't understand; I'm *skeered* to marry Ed—skeered to marry any-one—in these hills! Oh, Pop . . . I wish't ye could see what I mean! Listen: how old is Maw?

Pop—*(puzzled)* 'See . . . , your Maw's a *old* woman; she must be round thirty-year old.

Mag—That's jest what I mean! Maw was a right purty gal, warn't she?

Pop—Reckin she was, er I wouldn't 'a'choosed her. Heh, heh—

Mag—*(breaking in)* Now luk at her! Why Pop, Maw's not a *old* ooman, she's jest wore out! You ree-collect that ooman come to the Mission at Pelham? How old do ye reckin *she* was? Forty year old, an' she didn't look half the ages of Maw. *She* was from *town (a thought flashes across her face as she repeats, and a husky voice)* town. That's what 'tis, Pop: A hill gal ain't got a chanct, an' *I* ain't a-goin' to marry Ed!

Pop—Well, what *do* ye aim to do? *Every* gal in the hills gets married—'cept some lone gals that's—ruint. Ye know Maw won't let ye stay here.

Mag—I—I do' know. Oh, Lordy; they ain't no chanct fer me . . . everythin' comes to the gals in town. . . . unless—*(her face lights up, and she seems unconscious of Pop)*—unless I git to town. I . . . Pop!

Pop—What's got in you, Mag?

Mag—Pop! Will ye swear not to tell Maw?

Pop—What would I want ter tell yer Maw fer? That ooman 'ud snatch me bald-headed, every chanct.

Mag—I know *my* chanct, Pop!

Pop—How—

Mag—This feller from town—Mister Hayden! What—Whar is he—Pop?

Pop—Say Mag—Mag, looky h—

(Maw comes in, and Sam limps after her. Pop and Mag sit in stupefied silence.)

Maw—Mag, I want yer to do that churnin' now.

Mag—Yes'm, Maw. *(She goes out)*

Maw—Now, Mister Hayden, I got right smart of work to do now. Ef you'll jest set in hyar Mag'll keep ye comp'ny.

S—*(sitting)*—Thanks. *(Maw takes hoe from behind the door and goes out.) (There is a silence.)*

Pop—Stra-uh—Mist. Hayden, hev ya got some terbacker?

Sam—You bet. *(He produces a sack.)*

Pop—I' ain't got no pipe handy; reckin I jest chaw mine. *(He takes a bite from a plug in his pocket.)* All-ways *did* like a chaw better nor a pipe, nohow.

Sam—Yeh, chewin's pretty good, but—cigarettes fer mine. *(A pause.)* Mighty pretty country you got here.

Pop—Yer; I s'pose 'tis, for them that's not used to it. I al-ways did say, thet—*(Mag appears outside. She is carrying two pails which she empties into a churn outside the door as she speaks. Neither Pop nor Sam move to help her.)*

Mag—Howdy, Mist' Hayden.

Sam—Howdy kid—uh—Miss Mag.

Mag—I'm a-comin' in to keep ye company whilst I churn. *(She lifts churn aside, and draws a chair near the Stranger.)*

Pop—I always *did* say, that—that—

Mag—Pop, ain't ye ever goin' to work on yore st—*(looks nervously at Sam)* on the branch?

Pop—Now, 'tell the truth, I ain't feelin' uncommon spry, today. Always *did—(Mag transfixes him with a dagger-like glance. He goes on, weakly.)* Always did—*say* that—*(he squirms under her gaze)*—that—exercise would liven a man up. *(He goes slowly out.)*

Mag—*(not too shyly)*—Right pretty mornin'.

Sam—Yes, 'tis a pretty mornin'. Mighty pretty country you got here.

Mag—Do ye think so?

Sam—Sure I do. Mighty pretty.

Mag—*(in a wavering voice)* 'Tain't so purty when ye have to live here.

S—What's the matter, Sis?

Mag—Oh, they ain't nothin' to do here. They ain't nary a soul around, an' the gals jest work and work! I get awfully sick of it.

Sam—Ain't you got some sweetie her, Hon? Fer instance, this young feller that was here last night?

Mag—Ed? Oh, I been a-goin' right smart with Ed, but—but he—

Sam—He what, Sister? *(He is patting her arm in a doubtfully fraternal way.)*

Mag—Oh!—he's—he hain't *smooth*! He's jest big, an' tough—an' he wouldn't think nothin' of workin' his ooman to death. *(She sobs.)*

Sam—There, there, little kid *(Taking advantage of her apparent grief, he passes his arm about her shoulders.) Now,* now, now, now, why do you worry about Ed?

Mag—*(in a tearful voice, just tinged with flirtatiousness).* I—I don't when *you're* here.

Sam—*(laughs)* You're a cute little devil! Kiss me, Hon. *(She kisses him, and he begins to "pet" her.)* You're an awful—

Mag—*(snugging against him.)* Oh, I'm—I feel so good! When will ye take me away?

Sam—*(quite dumbfounded) Away?* What—

Mag—When'll ye take me to town? When—

Sam—*Well* now, uh, *sister—Mag—*that all—you know, you're an awful pretty little devil, do yuh know it?

Mag—*(giggles)*—Aw, ye ole lover-liar. Oh Sam—I'm glad hit's a'goin' to be!

Sam—*(weakly)* Yeh. . . . Kiss papa, honey. *(She kisses him again. There is a pause. The Stranger looks doubtfully at the dark head snuggled against his shirt; he isn't quite sure of his ground.)* Mag—honey—you ain't serious about us gettin' married, are you?

Mag—*(in an abstracted voice)*—Huh?

Sam—I say: You don't think I can really marry you, do you, hon?

Mag—Why, what *air* ye aimin' at, Sam?. . . . What . . . *(she moves from him.)*

Sam—*(a trifle uneasily, but with a slippery smile)* You see, I couldn't carry you off to town, kid; it—couldn't be done, me a travelin' man and all. *(Mag is silent.)* Now, honey, don't get mad . . . uh . . . we needn't let that come between us, Huh? . . . *(Mag looks straight out; after a thoughtful silence, she says, firmly)* No.

Sam—*Course* not! Course not! That's a good kid. *(He leans toward her, and is about to rest a hand upon her shoulder when Liza Gudger enters. They do not see her at first, and she has successfully disguised her interested stare when Mag senses her presence and turns nervously.)*

Liza—*(unctuously)* Well, *good* mornin' Mag. *(She levels a hostile but curious glance at Hayden.)*

Mag—'Mornin' Miz Gudger. Miz Gudger, meet Mist' Hayden; Mist' Hayden, shake hands with Miz Gudger.

Liza—Right pleased to meet ye, Mister Hayden. *(They merely nod.)*

Mag—*(Spoken together)* Pull ye up a cheer, Miz Gudger.

Liza—No, honey. *(Come to see yer Maw. Reckon whar she is. She sits down, despite her refusal.)*

Mag—Down in the tater patch, I reckon.

Liza—Might of thorght you'd 'a'-been a'workin' this time o'day, Mag, but I see ye got comp'ny.

Mag—I *am* a-workin'—been churnin' here. *(indicates churn).* Pop went an' shot Mister Hayden right in the leg Satti-day evenin'. He's a-goin' to stay with us till hit's healed up.

Liza—Yer, I heared about that f'm Ed Winters. Ed. 'peared to be right int'rested.

Mag—*(uncomfortably)* What you mean?

Liza—*(ignoring her)* Lord: way he tuk on 'th'is Pop, you'd 'a' thought he'd done the shootin' his own self! You could 'a' briled bacon on that feller, he was that hot! *(She takes a dip of snuff, rubbing it around her gums with great gusto. There is an uncomfortable silence. Liza rises.)* Well, I must be a-

movin' along, Mag. Mighty proud to've seen ye, Mister Hayden.
*(She ties on her poke-bonnet, and walks off crab-wise, talking
over her shoulder.)* I'm a-comin' by fer yer Maw to-morry night
to go to the box-supper at Har'son's Chapel. *(She stops at the
door and turns.)* Ed. Winters *claims* he's a'goin' to carry ye thar.
(The curtain begins to descend.) Is that true? *(Mag is struggling
for words, and Liza disappears as*
The Curtain Falls

SCENE THREE
*(The next day, late in the afternoon. Same setting. Mag is
finishing buttoning a clean pink calico dress as the curtain rises.
She goes to the mirror, and begins smoothing and patting her
hair. Sam comes in from the clearing, and stands beside her.
His limp is almost imperceptible.)*
Sam—Hello, honey.
Mag—Howdy, Sam. *(There is in her voice an even hard-
ness.)*
Sam—What're you dressin' up for?
Mag—The box-supper's to-night, 'course.
Sam—You're not goin' with *Ed* after—what happened
last night, are yuh?
Mag—Ye know Ed wouldn't—have me, if—he knowed it,
Sam. Yore a-goin' to carry me to this-yer box-supper.
Sam—Why, honey, *I* can't—
Mag—Don't yer "honey" me, Sam Hayden. Ye think ye
was a-foolin' *me* with yer "honeys" an' "kids?" Do ye?
Sam—Listen h—
Mag—Don't ye know I jest *used* ye? Do ye think fer a
minute I *keer* a straw fer ye? I—I wouldn't never of—done it—
if . . . *Now* ye *got* to carry me outa these hills! Yer *got* to carry me
to town! I hain't a-goin' to stay here an' git married, and rot! I
hain't—
Sam—Listen *here*. Damn you! Do you think I'm goin' to
marry yuh? D'yuh think just because I've fooled around here
with yuh, I mean to take yuh *back* with me? *(He has driven her
before him, word by word.)* You little fool; you're crazy.
Mag—*(crying)* Why, ye *got* to! Ye cain't—*cain't*—leave
me here!
Sam—*(More kindly)* Now, look here kid: I'd like to do
the right thing by yuh. Now, cool off, and git ready for the box-

supper. *(She glances hopefully.)* Naw—I mean, Ed'll take you. *I won't.*

Mag—*(wheeling suddenly, in a rage).* You know damn well Ed wouldn't *tetch* me! I knowed it, too. I might 'a' knowed I couldn't count on ye to get me out of this . . . *(she sobs convulsively)* . . . I was a-feered o' that last night, but I knowed— *knowed* that Ed, ner *nary* a man—would *tetch* me if I was ruint! You pore fool, that's why ye had the least chanct! That's why I come in last night, arter everyone'd gone to bed! *Now* le's see who'll try to marry me!

(Maw and Liza Gudger enter, just then. Liza is clad in her best; Maw Felts is still in her working clothes.)

Maw—Mag Felts, what *air* ye a-takin' on so fer? We heared ye way down the road, an' come a-runnin'!

Mag—*(shrilly)* I reckin' they's a-plenty fer me to take on fer! I reckin—

Maw—Mag Felts, shet up. Have ye got yer box fixed?

Mag—I hain't a-goin' to need no box! *I*—

Maw—*(slaps her)* *I'll* learn ye to talk foolish! Pull yerself up, thar. Ed's a-comin' soon.

Mag—I hain't—Ed won't take me to no box-supper!

Maw and Liza—Why not?

Mag—Luk at this dirty houn' here! *(She points to Sam, who is cringing in a chair.)* Hit's because—'cause he—Oh, Maw, I'm ruint, I'm ruint!

Maw—*(with a deadly evenness)* Is that true, Stranger?

Mag—*(Breaks in)* Yare, that's true! Ye cain't back out! Ye—

Liza—I suspicioned somethin' yesterday—

(Pop enters. He is carrying a jug, and he is clean-shirted and collarless.)

Pop—What you a'rarin' around at, old ooman?

Maw—You shet up, Pop Felts. Mag, you—*(Mag sits down, and buries her head in her arms.)*

Pop—What's wrong with Stranger? He's a-lookin' awful squeamish.

Maw—Git down yore shot-gun, Pop Felts; yore a'goin' to take another shot at Stranger.

Pop—What you a-sayin' Maw?

Maw—Mag here claims he *ruint* her.

Pop—Ruint? Why Mag, you told me *yi*sterday mornin'— said—

Maw—Pop Felts, load yore gun.

Sam—*(jumping up)* Look here! I—*(He runs for the door, into the arms of Ed.)*

Ed—*Well!* Whar the hell ye thenk *yore* goin'?

Liza—Brang 'im back in here, Ed. *(Ed shoves him to the center of the room.)*

Ed—Mag, air ye ready to come along? Why, whut air ye a-cryin' fer?

Maw—Mag's got plenty to cry fer, Ed. She hain't a-goin' to no box-supper with ye.

Pop—Ye won't want ter marry Mag no more. Hain't no-body'll want to.

Liza—*I* suspicioned somethin'; I come here yesterday mornin'—

Ed—Looky here. *(To Sam) You* got suthin' to do with this-yer! You spill all of hit! *(Sam is silent, and a little dazed.)*

Pop—Mag told me—

Maw—Ed, this feller—ruint Mag.

Ed—*(after amazed silence)* Yuh—yuh damn pole-cat! Yuh—yuh— *(He steps forward suddenly, and hits Sam with all his strength. Sam reels to the floor, rises, moaning, and rushes from the cabin, holding both hands to a bleeding mouth.)*

Liza—*(quite beside herself with excitement)* Kill 'im, Ed, Ketch 'im!

(Ed has started after him, but at the door, he stops)

Ed—No, the damn fool hain't wuth the trouble—the boys at the mill' take keer of him. *(There is a pause, and Mag is heard, sobbing miserably.)*

Pop—I'm right tore up at all this yer . . . I've al-ways thought you an' Mag was a good pair, but *now. . . .*

Maw—*(in a consolatory tone)* Well, Ed, I oughtn't ter say sech a thing of my own gal, but she—low-down lil' woods-calf—hit served her right. She hain't wuth yer a-worryin' over. *(She pauses)* They's—they's plenty good gals'd jump at ye, Ed.

Liza—Fer instance, my Mandy . . . but *thar*—I orght not to say that.

(There is a rather long silence. A hound ambles in, and lies at Pop's feet. Ed is standing in deep thought. Muffled sobs are audible from Mag, huddled in a chair. Finally Ed steps to-ward her.)

Ed—Mag . . . Mag, hon, git up. *(Mag rises dazedly. Ed drawls heavily on)* Come hyar, sugar-foot. Ed keers fer ye jest the same; *(he folds her in his arms)* Ed likes ye—keers fer ye—no matter whut! Hon, I'm a-goin' to marry ye. We'll git married, right soon.

Pop—Ed, that's right fine of ye, but—

Ed—No, Pop, I mean every word of hit! Mag's a-goin' ter be my bride!

Liza—*(Half to herself)* Mag'll worship Ed fer this, all her days!

(The two stand in the increasing dimness, and there is in Ed's posture the suggestion of conscious and "stagey" heroism. Mag, with her head on his breast, awakes from her daze; begins to realize all that has happened, but her expression is hardly one of worship, of gratitude. There is a short silence; then, from far off-stage, comes the thud of an axe on wood, keeping time to the cracked voice of a woman:

Ah'm jest a *married gal*, An' ah *wish* thet ah could *die*;

(Here the curtain begins slowly to descend.)

Ah'm jest a *mar*-ried *gal*; Set by the cradle and cry.

As the song ends it is just above the heads of the players. Then it drops quickly.)

THE END

(February 1926)

"Any Seventh Son"

(Midnight. The "settin' room" of a little log cabin. The two walls form a triangle, with the front of the stage as its base. In the right wall are a door and two small windows. In the left is another door, leading into a bedroom. As the curtain rises, the stage is dark, with the exception of a single shaft of lamplight, which falls through the half-open bedroom door and across the middle of the room, picking out a rough table. After a pause there comes from the next room a short series of convulsive, straining gasps. Then a voice, scarcely audible.)

THE VOICE—*(soothing)* Thar, thar, honey. *(Pause)* Thar! . . . No—now keep a holt o' that sheet . . . thar, th—

(The voice is drowned out by boisterous talking, and by footsteps near the outside door. Then the door bursts open; the room is flooded with moonlight, and Jed Long lurches in, followed by his brother Jake. Jed is a gigantic man, big-boned and hairy. His brother, smaller and quieter, is a pale reflection of Jed.)

JED—*(lumbers across the bedroom door, and puts his head in.)* How's things a-comin' in hyer, Hester Bright?

THE VOICE—Git your head outer thar, Jed Long!

JED—*(With a roar of half-drunken laughter.)* No nyews is good nyews! *(He crashes one ham-like hand on Jake's shoulder.)* Heh, Jake? How 'bout it?

JAKE—*(Wincing)* Ow! Yer, I reckin' so . . . quit poundin' me, Jed! I hain't made o' san'stone!

JED—You al-ways was puny, Jake. *(He takes from the table the jug he brought in, drinks, and continues in thick-tongued garrulity.)* Warn't nary a one outen the hull seven un ye could whup me. You recolleck that time ye hooked my nyew straw hat, 'time I tuk Mandy to camp meetin', an'—an' I come over, right in the midst un it, an' beat yore face in? Do ye?

JAKE—*(a bit reluctantly)*—Yer, I do.

JED—*(laughs)* I reckin' you do! Yore mug luked like a rotten mush-melyon for moren' a week! *(He takes another drink.)*

JAKE—Does 'pear to me you might 'a' waited till the preachin' was done, though.

JED—*(scornfully)* Shucks! I warn't the man to cheat no preacher outen a show. *(Laughs.)*

JAKE—*(After a pause, with a tinge of malice)*—You never did keer much fer 'legion, Jed, but I ree-colleck one time you was pow'ful skeered, and called on the Lord.

JED—Whin was that-ar?

JAKE—'Time Hester Bright—

JED—*(starting towards him!)* I God, I'm as good a Babtis' as ary man—

JAKE—*(retreating)*—Now Jed—hyer—keep back—I didn' mean nothin'—

JED—An' a durn sight better un nor you, but I hain't . . . I—

JAKE—Ye hain't a-claimin' that ye hain't skeered o' devils, air ye?

JED—*(stopping)* Naw—I hain't. *(Morosely he takes up the jug again, and falls into an ill-humored silence.)*

JAKE—What do ye aim to call the kid? *(He jerks one thumb towards the door.)*

JED—*(immediately good-humored again)* Zeke Har'son Long. *(He begins to strut about the room.)*

JAKE—You 'pear to be mighty handy with a name fer hit, but yo're fergettin' one thing.

JED—Yare? An' what ye thenk I'm fergittin'?

JAKE—S'posin' . . . jest s'posin' this-yer turns out to be a gal?

JED—*(Stops dead, then approaches Jake menacingly)* What you mean by that-ar, Jake Long? Air ye a-hankerin' to git shot?

JAKE—Hit's a fair chanct hit'll be one.

JED—Shet yer trap, Jake Long. You know durn well hit won't don't ye?

JAKE—*(cringing)* Y-Yer . . . I was jist—

JED—Ye know hit'll be a boy, an' hit'll be a whale, too, don't ye? Don't ye? *(Not waiting for an answer)* I hain't agoin' to have no gals, a-clutterin' up the house, an' haint' a-goin' to stand fer nothin' puny, an' pious, like you, Jake *(He hiccoughs on, in drunken parental exaltation).* You watch that boy o' mine, Jake. Some day he'll whip ye with both han's behine him. He—he'll raise the best crap in this county—an' make the best blockade! Yer, by God, an 'ee'l carry off the best-lookin' gal in these hills!

JAKE—*(Looks out from door)* They's clouds a-scuddin' up, Jed—jist a bilin' up over Shake-Rag Rift. Reckin' we'll have rain.

JED—You—

(The midwife enters, and they are silent, a little awestruck. She is a shrunken, mute shadow, but in the dusky light she moves slowly, ominously. For several seconds there is silence. A cloud crosses the moon, and the room is steeped in blackness.)

JED—*(Almost sober)*—What—nyews do ye brang, Hester Bright? *(The light brightens.)*

HESTER—I brang good nyews fer ye, Jed Long—

JED—I knowed it! What'd, I tell ye, Jake? *(Darkness again.)*

HESTER—*(evenly)* An' I brang bad nyews. *(Silence)* Jed Long, ye air a seventh chile, hain't ye?

JED—*(fearfully)*—Yeh.

HESTER—Ain' this-yer is yore seventh born-ed.

JED—'See, they's Jim-Tom an' Len Tom, an' they's Elsie an' Mazie, that's dead, an' they's . . . yer, this-yer. *(Suddenly)* Oh, Lord! Lordy, Hester Bright—I never thought o' *that!*

HESTER—They's the workin' o' the devil in this yer, Jed Long, an' they's the work o' the Lord. Yore chile is a boy—the seventh son un a seventh son. He kin see what's a-goin' to come, an' he kin talk to the wild critters an' the devil. But he's twisted an' taller-colored as Mandy is herse'f now.

JED—What you mean?

HESTER—Yore boy's got little squinched-up lags, an' he's gashly pale—an' 'is back luks like hit'd been plowed an' harrered!

JED—*(towering above her)* Ahhr, ye ole turkey-buzzard, tell me that ain't true!

HESTER—*(stands up to him)* Hit is true, Jed Long.

(There is a silence. The clouds have come faster and faster since the entrance of Hester. They give the lighting the effect of a fluttering candle. After a few oppressively noiseless seconds,

wind is heard in the trees outside; a few drops of rain fall, seeming to blot all moonlight from the room.   Jake closes the outside door.)

JED—*(With intermittent grunts of mental agony)* Oh, God . . . Oh-h Lordy . . . *(He seems to uproot his great legs from his station in the center of the room; walking towards the bedroom door, he roars)* I hain't a-goin' to stand fer this-yer! *(There is a crash of thunder, and the rain begins to pour.   Jed is sillhouetted against the lamplight, framed by the bedroom door.   Above the din of thunder and pelting rain is heard his inarticulate bellow of rage and frustration.   He lurches forward, raises one huge fist.   There is a loud, horrified scream in the bedroom as*
THE CURTAIN FALLS [)]

(June 1926)

"MENALCAS"

(Outside a palace, falling into decay. Inside, a light glows. Wind, rain, the sound of a heavy sea breaking on rocks. The Chorus is silhouetted against the night sky. Wind presses their garments against their gaunt bodies. They are grouped upon a rise of ground, at the rear.)

CHORUS

Gone, gone the snap and strain of sails
    In the cold wind leaning;
Gone the taut snatch of serried oars
    In the sunlight gleaming.
Gone, the bright soaring of the ship
As through the water's grind and slip,
    With sunlight spattered,
She plunged her black and drenchéd prow
Among the toppling waves . . . and now
In the dry sand, a broken plow,
    Lies buried, shattered.

Now: The slow march of myriad waves
    From the sea's blank rim
Advances on the crumbling rocks
    Despairing, grim.
Relentlessly they smite the crags;
Wave upon wave its sorrow drags
    And on the stones,
On the black crumbled stones it flings
The sorrow's weight, and while it clings
Fast to the shuddering cliff, it sings
    Its dirge; and moans.

(Enter Menalcas.)

MENALCAS
Is this the house in which one Sorrow drags
Forth to the light another Sorrow still?
This black uncomprehending skull of stone
Holds now the softened remnants of the brain
Which thought too well to serve the progeny
Of Aeschinas; but thought not long enough,
Nor dreamed to see the strangeness in the eyes
Of children of his children, into whom
Was forced a wedge of pride for family—
A pride which deemed it impious to defile
The pure blood of the clan—a pride which now
Drives like a wedge into the riven brains
Of us who sit within these hollow halls.
Father and daughter, man and wife, we two—
Our veins a circled gutter, down which drag
The thin lees of the Blood of Aeschinas . . .
Undefiled.

CHORUS
Behold the scorpion pride
Which, in its passionate defence of self
With its own sting drains out its bitter life!

LEADER
Aeschinas, father of Glory,

CHORUS
Father of Death,

LEADER
Captain of plunging ships,

CHORUS
Of sandfilled hulks—

LEADER
Behold thy palace, set amongst the hills,
Black, black against these brown and folded fields.
See how the stones, beneath the leaning storm,
Crumbling seek once more their ancient sleep
Beneath the tangled roots.

CHORUS

Behold the heir,
Menalcas, laden with these thorny flowers,
Whose roots have clutched the bodies of his kin—
Flowers wet with the cold rain; and in each thorn
The thinned and bitter blood of Aeschinas.

MENALCAS

Weave, weave these night-blown blossoms, interlock
In cold embrace the bended stems, the thorns
Laid serpent-like among the o'erlapped leaves.
Fashion me festal wreaths; I go to fetch
A young bull for this joyful sacrifice.

LEADER

Stay but a moment.

MENALCAS

Wherefore should I stay?

CHORUS

Spill ye sour wine, salt blood,
    As libations to a God,
In thanksgiving for this gift:
    A child, of brain bereft?

A child, of brain bereft!
    In thanksgiving for this gift
As libations to a God
    Spill ye sour wine, salt blood?

While ye clenched twisted limbs
    Chanted we Cythera's hymns
With the vision of this dawn,
    Of this malformed spawn?

Of this malformed spawn!
    With the vision of this dawn
Chanted we Cythera's hymns
    While ye clenched twisted limbs?

Bare to worms, bare to winds,
    All thy kin have stretched their limbs;
Gainst the stony earth they strained;
    Into earth their bodies drained.

Into earth their bodies drained.
    Gainst the stony earth they strained.
All thy kin have stretched their limbs
    Bare to worms, bare to winds.

Thou alone, with thy wife,
    Hold the blood and the life—
Hold the power, now, to end
    With his death, or to extend
Through the seed of thy child
    The blood galled, the brain wild,
The bent limbs, the sightless stare
    Which fall as due share
Of this noble heritage
Which Aeshinas, sage
Through his life, at his death
With his dying breath
    Bequeathed.
                    A silence . . .

MENALCAS
Alone—in me alone, and in my wife,
Now drag the lowest and the bitterest dregs
Of all the unmingled blood of Aeschinas
Which filled the vessel, once, to overflowing.
In me alone . . . and . . . in this child who now
Enters the world with the o'erclouded dawn. . . .

Tonight I wandered wide the stony fields,
And gathered for my wreaths these thorned blooms;
And, weary, sought the shore, and sat beneath
The shadow of that sandfilled ship which once
Lunged at the waves, and bore away to war
My Fathers, in whose veins this thin blood coursed
Swift in the warmth and purity of newness.
I watched the silent swerving of the heavens
About the gleaming prow of brinedrenched bronze;

I watched the grinding phalanxes of water
Advance, and reel, and topple, and retreat.
The water clutched my ankles, and the heavens
Gazed down at me with myriad cold eyes.
And all the while, within my breast, I felt
A measured march of footsteps; and I know
The blood of Aeschinas drags slow within me.

But held within my wife, this newborn child
Has drawn from her our blood—and in his veins
Courses again this dreadful distillation!

LEADER

This curse can end in you.

MENALCAS

    Nay, but I cannot
Take to myself this frightful task. Shall I,
When generations past have well obeyed,
And onward sent this blood within its course—
The old curse cursing spill this hallowed blood?
Nay! For such dire impiety, the Gods—

LEADER

Surely the Gods are with thee—else wouldst thou
Alone of all thy family, be given
A brain untainted, a remarking eye?
And being thus bestowed, wouldst thou alone
Of all thy family, be left alive?
Nay, unto thee the Gods have given power
Now and forever to blot out this curse!
The Gods are with thee; rather will their wrath
Smite thee to earth if now ye fail their trust!

MENALCAS

Oh, that some heaven-sent sign might tear away
These veiling fears, and lay my duty bare!
Or, failing that, could mortal approbation—
Some sign from my dead Fathers, but be mine!
Then could I wrench away these clutching doubts
And, the deed done, live fearless, justified.
Alone, I dare not do, yet dare not fail—

My skull encompasseth conflicting seas
Which, wave upon rolling wave, lash one the other
Into a roaring fury of frustration.
                    (*He advances toward some trees.*)
On every side of me the air is filled—
Filled with dim writhing phantoms,—with the bodies—
The bodies bent, the malformed limbs of those—
Those Fathers who transfused to me their blood!
Fathers! Ye twist your arms, ye stretch your hands
Suppliant toward me. On each gnarléd cheek
Lies cold a tear, and through thy sightless eyes
Burns a strange light of pleading. And I fail thee not!
            (*Turns to east. A final dash of rain from the red sky.*)
Now the blood-tarnished bowl of all the heavens
        Drains on the sated earth its last dark dregs!
High in the heavens the Gods have set their sign.
        Hasten the wreaths; I bring the sacrifice!

CHORUS
        (*Bending the long-stemmed blooms into circles.*)
Of Aeschinas remains alone this skull
Behind whose sockets glory, like a flame
Guttering, flares and struggles, and dies out.
(*Within, the light is extinguished, Menalcas comes out, carrying a child. He walks to the highest point of land and, surrounded by the Chorus, who raise their bare arms, he extends above them his own, bearing aloft the child.*)

MENALCAS
Infinity of collapsing waters,
        Sea of my Fathers:
Brown fields and shuddering angled crags,
        Land of my Fathers:
Silently swerving eternal heavens,
        Sky of my Fathers:
World of my Fathers, and Gods of my Fathers
        omnipotent:
I salute Thee! Behold now the task thou has set me, is
        done!
And in witness behold ye this babe, new-born, new-
        slain.

Unto the Water, the Earth and the Sky, the Gods,
Life becomes Death, and its blood in libation outpours.
Thus to the heavens I left thee;
                    (*He strains the child upward.*)
On the stones and the sea do I hurl thee!
                    (*He hurls the child over the cliff.*)

CHORUS

Swaddled in sinouus grasses of the sea,
'Neath the green contemplation of her eyes,
Clasped in the flexing circle of her arms,
Thy babe has found the mother of you all;
Thy babe has found the bride of Aeschinas.

MENALCAS

My babe has found our Mother—Yet his own
But now in mute despair, on bended knees—
Knees bent at his conception, at his birth—
Pleased that he might live, with that same light
Within her eyes, which in my Father's eyes
A moment past had for his death flamed high!
And yet from out her arms I tore the babe,
And from her stricken eyes I tore my own,
And to the Gods hurled our begotten life!
Ye gods, Thy will be done! To me ye gave
First life, for which I cared naught, then a body
Malformed and evil-passioned, a fit vessel
In which to pour that frothed and sour ferment
Which is the unmingled blood of Aeschinas.
Thus did I differ little from my Fathers;
But in this body ye have deemed it meet
To plant a brain, and in that brain the hatred
Of all the needless Grief derived from Grief
Which is the heritage of Aeschinas.
Behold: With pious fear the holy task
For which Ye thus endowed me, is completed.
My duty done, I offer sacrifice.

(*With his sacrificial knife, he stabs himself; and, dying,
falls to the ground. Behind him the Chorus gathers; in rhythm
to their chant they cast over his body the half-finished garlands,
the torn blossoms.*)

CHORUS
Bare to the water,
Bare to the wind,
Unto the earth
The stilled flesh
Bestows itself.
Completed now
The circle, as
Sinking among
The stones,
Blood is
To blood restored.

Now the clan
Of Aeschinas,
Dwindled to one,
Along the earth
Deploys its limbs;
And into earth
Hollowed, is gathered;
Is clapsed within
The arms of earth
And wave and wind.
Deep into earth the stilled flesh sinks.
Deep, deep beneath the folded fields,
The blind winds, and the tumbled sea.
Above it water into water melts;
Root upon root, rock upon rock o'erhead
Clasp one the other. Grasses interlock,
And round the silent tomb waters and winds
Weave patternless their bright and binding web.

(December 1927)

Phillips Exeter Poetry

"Water"

I

Suave shadows smear across the saffron swirl
Of water, filmed with iridescent oil.
A ghoulish fish with phosphorescent eyes
Lurks in the clammy ooze among the weeds.

II

Out of the bellowing blue
Swoops a grand gale,
Churning the open sea
Into insurgent mounds—
Gone just as suddenly;
Chaos its trail.

(February 1927)

"Widow"

The children are asleep, and now I sit
Stringing flaky pop-corn, bit by bit;
Polishing the apples till they shine—
Hark! "Annie, won't you *ever* stop your whine?
Yes, Santy Claus is comin'—go to bed,
Dear"—(God, how memories pound through my head)!
And now the tinsel, and the fragile balls—
Bubbles of flashing fire among the twigs.
One drops, bursts, lies in splinters at my feet:
Brakes shriek and scrape and grind in the dark street;
The radiator bangs and the Big Ben

Alarm clock buzzes . . . "Gentlemen,
May nothing you dismay"—the carolers.
"Dismay, you blabbering idiots"—here, stop!
I've got to take things quietly, I can't
Go raving crazy now, dear God, I shan't!
More tinsel now, to decorate the tree—
There, I step back a little bit to see
The finished job. My, how they'll love all that!
(They'll dance and squeal and howl and blab and blat
And make my day a hell)—But they don't know;
They can't see what I see now—*all* I see;
The coffin lowered in the sifting snow
Only this afternoon—and now to go
Through Christmas, keeping up a silly sham
Just to make those kids upstairs forget—
Forget the thing they never understood! . . .
That branch is thick—it spoils the symmetry.
I'll get the hatchet now, and lop it off . . .
How sharp and bright it is; how cold the blade!
I draw my thumb along the edge; and think
What it could do! Oh, God forgive me that!
I can't do it—the children sleep upstairs,
And I must cook the goose, dole out their shares,
And stay with them, at least till after that. . . .
And stay . . . with them . . . till . . . The blue night is flat
Against the window panes; it stares at me
And seems to lick their lips! The back-stairs creak. . . .
I cannot stand it more; with stifled shriek
I creep to our old bedroom. I undress
And lie . . . and wait a comforting caress . . .
And your hard arms . . . and find but . . . emptiness.

(May, 1926)

"Orbs Terrae"

Earth, thou art turning, turning endlessly,
A ripening fruit upon Time's laden bough.

Swollen with ripeness, strange and poisonous fruit,
Who dared to pluck thee?
    Cooled and shrivelling now,
Drained of thy wine by greedy parasites,
How short must be your time before you drop
Silently and unnoticed, into Space?

(May 1927)

"Ebb Tide"

He's gone, he's dead; he carried away my soul
To empty space where stars sink sighing past.

And now—my life to live, a gaunt, sad life . . .
My life—it's like a little shallow pool
Left in a hollowed rock by ebbing tide;
A pool which slowly turns to bitter salt. . . .

My life . . . a tepid slowly dwindling pool,
To join—once more—the vastness of the sea.

(November 1925)

"In Preparation"

Strip off these glittering baubles—robe in white.
Kneel! On the bare floor of thy wretched cell,
Blind in the wan chill of Advent's moon,
Weave thou the carpet of thy Penitence!

(November 1925)

Phillips Exeter Non-fiction

"Extracts from the Diary of a Disagreeable Young Man"

December 1st. Alumni, the eating place. What a sordid process it is, that of filling oneself with things sprung from the filthy soil! All about me, clatter. Cabbages being absorbed greedily with loud, sucking sounds. Nauseating! Paper napkins, crumpled. Waiters spilling soup on cursing boys. Yellow and gray cravats, with foot spots. God, how long must I bear it?

December 3rd. This morning as I walked behind Dunbar Hall I saw something shining in the bright sunlight. I stooped, and found a banana peel,—once gallant, golden,—trodden into the cinders; broken. It, like my spirit, had aspired to too great things; it had been stripped from the more substantial fruit and—and crushed! Tears fall on my paper as I write these words. Oh, for sympathy! Oh, for understanding! Oh, for the wide golden vodkas on which I grew to manhood!

December 7th. This dreadful monotony of existence has, at last, been broken! Today I walked into chemistry class with my coat on hind side before. Everyone laughed, jeered. What cared I for that? I smiled faintly, proudly. I know I did because I practised it before my mirror that morning. And then—I was told to leave class! Fools! Clods! Can they not realize my passionate yearning for expression of Self? My soul beats against the bars; I struggle for air!*

*Recorder's Note: Next day he got it.

(December 1925)

"Elmer Gantry"

It is a fact provocative of cynical comment that, after a number of excellent novels have been allowed to pass (not without excited notice), Sinclair Lewis has achieved the ultimate, ecstatic ultra-superlatives through a decidedly inferior work. True, "Elmer Gantry," has been torn asunder by numerous eminent critics, not the least of whom is Billy Sunday, but that is a thing Lewis and his followers have learned to look forward to and to thrive upon. Far more sad and significant is it that no mere jacket-flap blurbs inform us that the author is the greatest satirist since Voltaire.

Enough has been shouted against the structure, the loudness and the lewdness of the novel; there remains but one comparatively untouched thunder bolt.

It seems to me that Lewis' powers as a great satirist are rapidly disintegrating. It is interesting to trace the development of these powers throughout his novels beginning with "Main Street." In this book was a certain clod-hopping strength, and an immense amount of unpleasant truth. He seemed fumbling for, and occasionally achieving, subtlety in his use of words, but a rather puerile performance was obscured by the timeliness of the book and the excellence of the title. In "Babbitt" we find a rapier-like delicacy in the handling not merely of language, but of rather unwieldly characters, which could only too easily have been grotesquely exaggerated. It is, for the most part, a mellow and broadminded, if not too kindly slam at our nation. Lewis is not ashamed to make his symbol a really lovable man. "Arrow-smith" shows the same finesse in its handling, but the book is permeated with a withering bitterness. One feels that Lewis wrote it with his lips pulled flat against his teeth. From a literary standpoint, it is his finest piece of work, although "Babbitt" has greater lasting powers. But the author has ever been careless of literary laurels; he writes primarily as the satirist; the fact that he tells a story better than most men living interests him but little. In "Arrowsmith" one feels an ever narrowing concentration that is sinister as a cat's eye. Then comes "Mantrap," an innocuous, clever little story, obviously serving merely as a "windup" for the most ambitious of the Lewis novels. "Mantrap" delighted me, not so much in itself as in its apparent indication of the loosening of Lewis' lips in a smile superbly tolerant of humanity. In combining this tolerance and his devastating cleverness lay his hope of real greatness; and this I looked forward to finding in "Elmer Gantry." I knew that its field was to be religion in America. It seems to me that here was Lewis' great opportunity. Of all the facets of our national life, none so cruelly radiates our true selves as does our religion, no theme is so tremendous and inclusive. Done as Lewis seemed capable of doing it, the book bade fair to obscure even the panorama unfolded in "Babbitt."

Lewis' mouth had shrivelled in a mummy-like smile; he dipped his pen not in ink, but alternatively in vitriol and T. N. T. The man Elmer Gantry is to me the most asinine and grotesque beast in all literature; and Gantry almost continually [is] the hub around which a galaxy of back-fence portraits revolves. Lewis evidently enjoyed himself immensely while writing the book; it boils with an indiscriminate and exuberant hatred. He almost continually employs sledge-hammer methods of driving home his points; all delicacy of writing is described, and one has the feeling that at any moment not Gantry but Mr. Sinclair Lewis himself is going to explode a most undignified and Sauk Centreish bomb of cussing. Evidently a great boil has been festering and swelling in Mr. Lewis' brain; he jubilantly squirts every last drop of its contents upon Elmer Gantry and his compatriots, and great is the relief to him. It is more charitable to say that he is spuriously and gawkily loud-mouthed as a result of mere uncontrolled kiddishness than that he has deteriorated into a sensationalist; and hopefully I think it is more true. If, as I believe, he writes with the sincere idea of showing up our civilization truly if scathingly, and of producing a widespread effect, he must already realize that he overdid "Gantry" at great expense to himself.

"Babbitt" and "Main Street" are now bywords not only among the Menckenites; they issue from the mouths of the Babbitts and Villagers Themselves, and with something of the same intelligent derision. But "Elmer Gantry" will scarcely make even the most broadminded clergymen introspective. The really vital truths are obscured beneath a manure-pile of invective which they will rightly deem it ridiculous to root into. As for the vast body of laymen, who, after all, are the ones to be reached if any good is to be done, they will read the book not at all or in a state of mind made awry by curiosity that such a monstrosity of lewdness and hypocrisy can exist. It won't even make the intelligent proportion of them mad.

Where Lewis should have used a black snake whip he has substituted a slapstick, and into the slapstick he has driven twenty-penny nails.

I myself have been unfair in my enthusiastic disappointment. Sad as the book may be as a botched satirical panorama, it remains an immensely engrossing story—by far the most dramatic Lewis has written. The sequence with the lady revivalist seems a bit preposterous, but it is undeniably interesting. Elmer's wedding night with Cleo Benham is just about the finest implied tragedy Sinclair Lewis or anyone else has given us. And the end of Frank Shallard, (who should have been the central figure), I shall remember as the most thrilling and ghastly and overwhelmingly authentic bit of writing I know. If the rest of the book lived up to it, "Elmer Gantry" would be cause for shouting in the streets.

Whether or not Lewis can redeem himself is an open question. I fear that he will not. "Elmer Gantry" was borne on a rising wave of insane prejudice. It is one gigantic crescendo of wholloping filthiness, and I have the feeling that it carried Mr. Lewis before it, and left him stranded where not even himself can work his salvation.

(May 1927)

Part II
OTHER EARLY EXPERIMENTS

(1928-1932)

"Pygmalion"

"Pygmalion"; an unpublished poem (1928?)

Whether or not the following poem is the early "Pygmalion" Agee mentions in 1928 correspondence remains uncertain; the poem is significant, however, both as an example of early abilities and as an objectification of doubt about what all artists accomplish. More than likely this long poem was composed about 1928 while Agee was still a student at Phillips Exeter Academy. From letters and the autobiographical "1928 Story," written late in the nineteen-forties and also included in this collection, we know that he remembered his final year at Phillips Exeter as a time when he had high hopes as aspiring artist.[1] A "Pygmalion" poem about which Agee wrote to Father Flye in 1928 was read by Robert Frost who felt it was a satisfactory performance; however, no poem under that title was ever published. Also the typescript which has survived employs a later form of Agee's name, "James" rather than the usual Exeter "J. R." or "James Rufus."[2] Even if this poem is a somewhat later version of the 1928 "Pygmalion" it is important because it suggests what Agee was learning as artist, while it also is a correlative to his later artistic problem of developing proper forms.[3] This poem was first edited by Victor A. Kramer in 1966 and published in *The Mississippi Quarterly* in 1976.

Notes

[1] "1928 Story" is part of "Agee in the Forties, Unpublished Poetry and Fiction by James Agee," ed. Victor A. Kramer, *The Texas Quarterly*, 11 (1968), 9-55. (Reprinted in this volume. See pp. 239-258.)

[2] *The Letters of James Agee to Father Flye*, ed. James H. Flye (New York: Brazillier, 1962), 37.

[3] See Alfred Barson's discussion of this point in *A Way of Seeing* (Amherst: The University of Massachusetts Press, 1972), 24.

"Pygmalion"

World, my beloved world, scarce can I bear
The rending and transcendent joy that flows
High in my heart! Gone the dire loneliness
Of countless aeons past, when here I sat,
One Solitude pervading solitude,
Watching my ordered wilderness of space
Sweep past in still and solemn pageantry;
Watching the ordered swerving of the stars,
The rolling constellations, and the bright
Swoop of the screaming comets; when I heard
The swishing of the stars across the sky,
The smothered sighs of burring nebulae; [sic]
The hollow and reverberating crash
Of universes convolute . . . Until,
Sorrowful in my lifeless wilderness,
There surged into my brain a glorious dream
Of Thee, my World, as still thou art tonight.

Down through the sweeping, billowing veils of Space
I thrust my gentle and gigantic hands;
Heavy and damp in the warm, curving palms,
Lay thou, unborn, but flaming in my mind.
In a slow fever of delight I worked,
Worked ceaselessly as centuries ticked past.
Under the subtle smoothing of my hands,
The strong eternal soothing of my palms,
I moulded out a warm rotundity,
Plastic, and sheathed in one unbroken sea.

I pressed the sea with unrelenting palms
Until it sank deep in the followed earth;

And, with the roll of land that damply rose
From out of the girdling water, I began.
Here, with the pressure of my thumb, I scooped
A socket for one blue and bitter jewel—
That lake, which elevates its glaring plane
To flash the mirrored sunlight in my face;
From the moist earth I pinched thy little hills;
Down to the seas I dragged my fingertips,
And water sprang beneath them, and flows still;
Under the passage of my pressing palms,
Brown prairies hinged the rivers and the rocks—
And mountain-peaks I chiseled from the rocks,
And girdled them about with rolling mist . . .
Thou, multiplicit glory of my dream,
Lay in perfection, lifeless in my palms.

Stooping, I laid my fac[e] upon thy seas;
My wreathing breath swept round thy surface thrice—
Then burst from out the Life; I let it swarm
Into the warm and shallow seas. Thenceforth
Till now, and through eternity, I am,
Watching that Life unfolding and diffused;
Watching it scramble o'er thy splendid fram[e],
And try but vainly to remold my dream.

O world, what joy is mine thou canst not know!
To see thy beauty, formless, millionformed!
To hear the breathing of the sea at night,
The sagging of the wearied, sleeping hills,
The sensuous rasping of o'erlapping leaves—
To hear the breathless silence when the tide
Slinks through the darkness, outward from the shore—
To lose myself in that bell-haunted fog
Which stalks among the drenched and spiky pines
And broods above the terrified flat sea!
To see night spread her silent wings and flee
Swiftly the clarion assaults of dawn—
The swoop of glistening streams down to the sea,
The unperturbéd surge of misty plains—
Their verdure breaking high on mountain-sides . .

To see thy beauty parched and crackling,

Thirsty, and caked with summer dust—To hear
One raucous groan of color, dying out
As swirling leaf o'erlaps each fading leaf
And drains thy life-blood back into thy breast—
To see thy beauty sprawled and stark in death,
The staring of thy grey and glazed seas—
To gently shroud thee in my silent snows,
And brood above thee, holding in my heart
The calm sure solace of the spring to come—
Not in the memory of a million springs
Is there the joy of watching, through this night,
Spring, crouching noiselessly upon the hills!
I see thee shrink, thou tattered shroud of snow,
Discovering the body of my world,
Naked, and palpitant, with new-found life.
I press my face into the hot, sweet earth,
And hear the steady singing of the sap,
Trees! Thy red buds unfolding stickily—
Tumbling joyous hills and shouting brooks—
Full throated rivers—Pounding, shattering seas—
Seaweed, strangling the rusty rocks,
Mist-hidden mountains, cold and haggard crags—
Upward ye fling your arms, Upward ye hurl
Your voices in gigantic jubilance!

O world, too beautiful thou are today!
Be not afraid—I cannot but caress
The rondure of that hill—cannot but clasp
Thy teeming plains against my breast. Fear not,
Beloved earth—If I must strain thee close
'Tis to alleviate the agony
Of such a passion as I never knew
Could—Closer I must press thee, though I feel
The crumbling of thy framework, though thy seas,
Forced from their sockets, shiver into space . . .
In opalescent globes they slowly sink,
Weaving their trails of light among the stars . .
The stars, that swing in grand processional,
Ever and ever on.

                    Here in my hand,
I hold the bruised and broken form of earth.

Selections from *The Harvard Advocate*

Selections from *The Harvard Advocate*

Agee's writing for *The Harvard Advocate* included considerable poetry, fiction, and reviews produced over a four year period, 1928-1932. During his senior year he was editor of *The Advocate*, and during that year he also engineered a parody of *Time* magazine.

The twenty-six poems Agee published in *The Advocate* illustrate the manner in which he assimilated traditional writers; the *carpe diem* theme, perhaps the most important, predominates in these poems. Almost all of Agee's Harvard poetry has been included in *The Collected Poetry*, while only eight of the Harvard poems were used in *Permit Me Voyage*, seven as revisions for a sonnet sequence. As a writer, Agee seemed to lose interest in such conventional forms. The classical translation included here reflects, however, his precision in verse.

Much more important for any illustration of Agee's development as a writer is his early prose; and it is for that reason that more undergraduate fiction than verse has been chosen for this collection. Fitzgerald states that the Harvard poetry never seemed to possess the rhythm and power of the prose; all of the pieces of fiction chosen for inclusion here exhibit that power. These stories represent stages in Agee's development toward the more mature productions of fiction such as his story "They That Sow. . . ."

One can separate the Harvard fiction into two groups: stories which seem to rely heavily on imagination; and others which appear to grow out of personal experience, or at least which are limited to experiences which someone as young as Agee could have adequately presented. "You, Andrew Volstead" seems to be, at least in part, a self-portrait. "Boys Will Be Brutes," about the slaughter of tiny birds after they had been taken from their nest, is exceptionally well-focused because its basis is also so clearly in an actual, or believably portrayed, experience. All the prose selections included here are attempts by Agee to evoke the mental state of his imagined heroes as they are caught in the flow of events. His method is never as complex as in the slightly later story, "Death in the Desert," but he often suggests the fleeting consciousness of his characters. In these undergraduate pieces therefore we see him already moving toward the realization that a fiction writer's "actuality" is that series of moments which flow together to provide a unique texture.

Each of these stories provides additional insight into Agee's subsequent movement toward a focus upon the texture of particular moments. The stories "Near the Tracks," and "A Walk Before Mass," are perhaps rather predictable; these, and "You, Andrew Volstead," with its witty monologues, do however demonstrate that Agee could write entertaining conventional fiction. These stories seldom have the strength of the best prose of this early period which derives from an autobiographical impulse. Focus on the particulars of experience, however, is what gave impetus to Agee's best work—and this is clearly exemplified in "Boys will Be Brutes," and in many parts of "You, Andrew Volstead," "Near the Tracks," and "A Walk Before Mass."

"Near the Tracks"

Cold bit down on the hills like a vise. Light of the town thistled above it, frozen into the solid sky. The town, banked solidly against the sea, died out to the north in a straggle of shacks, arching their spines against the cold.

Jake, at work on his math, sat at the table, near the kitchen stove. The lamplight spread his shadow in a fan across the bed where his mother was sitting and his sister was sleeping. His mother took in washing and her stove was built to hold irons about its sides. Jake kept looking up foggily and thinking that the stove looked like a dirty diamond.

The door opened, and Ed Feeney walked in. "Hello, folks," he said.

"Jesus," Jake said.

"Shut up," said Mrs. LaRue. "How did you get out?"

"Let myself out. How about something to eat?"

"Got some boiled potatoes and I guess there's coffee left."

"Christ. Ought to have stayed in jail. Fry them up for me."

"How'd you work it, getting out?" Jake said.

"Oh, buy a paper." He walked toward the bed. "What's wrong with Mad?"

"What you mean, what's wrong?"

"Sleeping, this time of night."

"Can't she sleep when she wants to?"

"Sure. O.k. by me."

Mrs. LaRue and Jake looked at each other. Jake put wood on the fire.

"Say, fry up them potatoes, will you?"

"O.k. by me," Jake said. He took the dirty skillet out of the sink.

"Don't set that grease spitting yet," his mother said.

"Why not . . . oh."

"What you going to do, Ed?" said Mrs. LaRue.

"Well I ain't Santa Claus, and if I was a brass monkey I'd still be in a hell of a fix tonight. I figured you could put me up a while."

"What you think we are . . . Sailors' Snug Harbor?"

"Don't get too bright now, Jakie." He turned again to Mrs. LaRue.

"You needn't be scared. This cold snap can't last out the week, anyhow, and I mean to move out, first night the freight ain't iced to the rails. Anyhow, I'm here, and I'm staying here."

"Maybe we ain't so sore about it as you think."

"No, maybe we're *glad* you're staying here," Jake said.

"O.k. I guess Ed right you wouldn't bitch a friend."

"Oh no, not a good friend like you, Ed."

"We feel like you damn near belonged to the family." Jake turned away and sat at the table.

Mrs. LaRue turned to Ed. Her face was in shadow. "There's plenty wrong with Mad," she said.

"What you mean, wrong?"

"Oh, there's plenty wrong with her, all right."

"What you mean, wrong, huh?"

"Uh-huh. Damn poor guesser, ain't you?"

"Well, how the hell should *I* know what's wrong with her . . . in jail all this time?"

Jake turned around. "Who ought to know if you don't? The Mayor?"

"Listen here, what's all this funny business around here? What's wrong with her? I reckon I got a right to know, ain't I?"

Mrs. LaRue laughed. "Oh, I reckon you have, all right."

"If you still want to know, Mad's knocked up."

"The hell she is!"

"All right then, I reckon she's the Virgin Mary," Jake said.

"Jake! Shut your filthy mouth! Father Connly'd like *that*, wouldn't he?"

"Ugly little bitch . . . she *would*."

"Put on the potatoes now, Jake." Jake set the skillet on the stove. The grease relaxed and began to spit. Mad woke up and saw Ed standing by the stove.

"Hello Mad," he said, spreading his hands at the stove.

Mad kept looking at him; Jake scraped at the potatoes. After a little, Mad's mouth began to shiver. She turned her face to the wall and cried.

"Let me have them potatoes," Ed said. He'd eaten supper a little after dark. He sat down and ate methodically. The express went past. Ed looked up from his eating; Jake, at the window, saw the lights draw together like a closing accordion.

Ed drew a hand across his mouth and sat down on the bed. "Come on Mad, snap to," he said, bending a hand around her shoulder. Snap to."

In a minute Mad looked up at him.

"How'd you get away?"

"Oh, it was slick. Damned slick. Don't know why I never thought about it before. Never saw a guy get sucked like that."

"How'd you work it?" Jake said.

"Well, we had a lousy supper, and then along about seven thirty old Joe Torrey dropped around for a game of checkers. He'd beat me a game, and all of a sudden I got a hell of a gutache. He acted kind of sorry, so I thought I might as well make the most of it. So, along about the middle of the next game I jumps up and it begun to rain checkers. Old Joe was pretty sore about the checkers at first, but when he seen me on the floor, hanging on to my gut, he unlocked and come in, and bent down over me, real interested. I took aim, and landed a good solid kick, right in the old spot, and by Jesus if there wasn't old Joe rolling around on the floor! Nothing to do but trot out, after that."

Mad laughed a little. She seemed a good deal cheered up.

"You going to stay with us," she said.

"Oh hell no . . . just dropped in for tea."

Mad laughed some more.

"Old Joe's a good old guy," Jake said. "You didn't need to do him that way."

"Yeah? I suppose you want me to go out chasing monkey glands for him, huh?"

"No," Jake said. "All the same you didn't need to do him that way."

"Oh, what difference does it make how he done him. He's here, ain't he?"

"Yeah, and it looks like I'm here to do some time. Anyhow till there's a thaw."

Mrs. LaRue settled down on the bed again.

"Well, I got to get to work on this Math," Jake said.

"Aw let the Math go. Ed's tired," Mad said.

"Well, he can go to bed, can't he?"

"Oh, come on. You and Ma get on to bed."

"Who, me? What you think I am, to get in bed with my own son?"

"What the hell's he . . . Valentino?"

"I ain't going to sleep with my own son. Besides, it ain't right Ed should sleep with you."

"Don't see it makes a hell a lot of difference now," Ed said, looking at the stove.

"Well you can give me one of them blankets," Mrs. LaRue said.

Mad undressed while Ed banked the fire. He dropped his shoes beside the bed and rolled under the covers. She lay close to him; he didn't move.

After a minute Mad whispered, "What's wrong, Ed?"

"What you mean, what's wrong?"

"You ain't got any ambition."

"Who am I, Napoleon? Lot of good ambition would do me. I know you're knocked up."

"The hell I am. Who told you that?"

"Old Lady."

"God damn her soul, why can't she mind her own business?"

There was silence. Then Ed said: "Guess you think you got me where you want me now. Got to marry you now, huh?"

Mad did not speak for awhile. Then she said:

"God, Ed, do you think I'd bitch you like that? If you'd not broke jail you couldn't have married me could you? Then why do you think I'd make you now, just because I could run you in?"

Ed turned a little toward her. "By Jesus," he said, "By Jesus, Mad, that's awful white of you, no kidding."

"Oh, hell. Just be a bitch if I done anything else, that's all."

"All the same, that's damned white of you. No kidding."

Mad lay looking at the swollen red stove.

"I'm due to . . . have the kid, damn soon."

"Yeah?"

She waited a moment, but he didn't go on.

"I guess it must be pretty tough," she said.

"Yeah? . . . Oh—yeah, reckon it is, all right."

They lay looking at the stove. Coals stirred and slipped

inside it, and a few fell out into the tray.

Someone knocked at the door.

"What the hell," Ed whispered.

"Slide down under me." She snatched his shoes and clothes under the covers and bunched the blankets over him, lying partly on top of him.

"What you want?"

"We want in." It was the Sheriff, Fred Snow.

"Just a sec. I can't get up. Jake. Jake!"

Jake hurried to the door and let in Snow and two other men. The flashlight swept a cone around the room.

"What's wrong?"

"Plenty, maybe. Light up that lamp."

"What the hell? What have we done?"

"You heard me. Light up that lamp. Got a search warrant."

"What the—"

"Don't be a damn fool—light it," Mad said.

"Stay in here, Tom." Jake followed Snow and the other man into the front room.

Tom took the lamp from the table and looked under the bed, and punched and kicked at the clothes hung in the corner.

"What's it all about?" Mad said.

"That's up to Fred."

In a minute the Sheriff came back. Mrs. LaRue followed him, a blanket grabbed around her thin shoulders.

"Hope you're satisfied, rousting out decent people, this hour of the night."

Snow took a turn round the room.

"Looks sort of fishy to me," he said.

"Do you always sleep with your boy?"

"Who, me?"

Jake said: "Mind your own business, you filthy-minded bastards. Mad's sick, that's how come she's sleeping with me."

"Watch your talk you fresh little bum."

"Yeah—think I'm going to sleep with a girl that's sick?"

"She don't look too God damned sick to me. What's all this faking sick, anyhow?"

"Yeah, we ain't looked everywhere yet."

They didn't say anything, Mrs. LaRue looked scared.

"Well—," Mad began.

"Mad! Shut your mouth!"

"Well, if you don't believe me,—ask Father Connly am I sick."

"Mad!"

"I ain't going to get out of bed, to show you."

Snow and Tom looked at each other. "Jesus," Tom said. "God, we didn't mean no harm Mrs. LaRue. I'm awful sorry we rousted you out." "Well, you damn well ought to be sorry," Jake said. "Well . . ." "Guess we'll be getting along."

"Matter of fact, you see—Ed Feeney broke jail tonight," Snow said.

"Is that a fact?"

"Yeah, and we knew he knew—all of you, pretty well. So you see we didn't want to take no chances."

"Sure, I can see how you thought you better come on down. Say, I hope you won't talk this all over town it'll leak out too damn quick, anyhow."

"No. Oh Jeez no, we won't talk."

"Well . . . Let's get out of here Tom."

"Good night."

"So long."

Jake waited a minute, then locked the door.

Ed stuck his head out from under the blankets. "Judas! that was a close call all right. You sure worked that slick, Mad, I got to hand it to you."

Mrs. LaRue laughed. "Yeah, you sure worked that slick . . . God damn you. Ain't you got no decency at all?"

"What you mean, decency?"

"Disgrace your family, just to save that lousy bum."

"Oh, get on to bed," Ed said. "She couldn't have kept it dark much longer, when the kid come."

"No? Maybe the kid could have got lost in the woods," Jake said.

"You damn little fool! Fine Catholic *you* are! Sometimes I think you got no morals at all. Get on to bed . . . I got a little dose of hell to give you."

"Yeah, get on to bed and leave us be," Ed said.

"Huh! You're a sweet one to tell us when to go to bed."

"Oh, get on out, Ma."

"Put out the lamp, will you?"

"You can go to hell." She slammed the door.

Ed put out the lamp, and got back into bed. He dropped

his shoes out and rolled over toward the middle.

"Hello, Baby," he whispered.

None of them talked very much during the next three days. There seemed to be nothing to talk about. Jake was away at school or basketball or pool most of the time. Evenings, he came home sometimes and studied. Mrs. LaRue had to work overtime at the washtub; Mad's condition made things hard for her. Mad lay on the bed; Ed sat on the edge, reading a copy of Top-Notch to tatters. They didn't have much to say to each other. Every hour or so one of them would say something and the others would follow suit. It was:

"Oh, Christ, my back's just about ready to bust."

"Oh, Christ Almighty."

"Oh, Jesus."

Or:

"Move on down to the end, Ed I got awful pains in my gut."

"Judas, I'd think you'd be used to it by now."

"Try a backache for a change, you lazy slut."

If Jake was around, he'd wind it up: "Oh for Christ's sake" or "Oh, pipe down."

Then they would all be quiet for a long time.

Every once in a while one of them would dodge through the clothes that hung all over the kitchen and go into the bathroom, out of earshot. Then the talk was swift and intense. They got a lot said during those few moments.

It was:

"You little slut, he's going to marry you or know the reason why."

"But God, ma, it'll just mean they'll run him in again."

"Well, what if it does? What the hell do you care?"

"You going to bitch a guy like that, his only chance to get away?"

"You going to bitch *yourself* . . . only piece of luck you'll ever have, and didn't deserve that?"

"Damn right I will, if I have to."

"Not while I'm awake. What the hell, ain't I got something to say about this?"

"Not a hell of a lot, seems to me."

"Ain't I your mother? Ain't *I* the one that gets it in the neck, if you go wrong? How about . . ."

"Oh, shut up. He ain't knocked *you* up has he? If I could

do it without getting him run in I'd marry him, and he'd marry me, too."

"Yes, like hell he would."

"God damn it, he would, I tell you. He's a good straight fella. But they ain't a fella on earth would bitch himself on a break like he's got. Do you blame him."

"Course to hell I blame him. What's wrong with him is, he ain't got no morals at all."

"Huh! You're a hot one to talk about morals. How much did *I* miss being a bastard?"

"You little bitch, I'll smack your face in. I got married, didn't I? Didn't I get married, safe enough?"

"Yeah, and a whole month to spare."

"Well! Ain't that enough for any decent woman?"

There wasn't much Mad could say to that.

After that, Mrs. LaRue would usually begin in a different way:

"Listen Mad, you think I'm hard and everything. I ain't. I'm just trying to save your reputation. Just trying to do right by you, like a mother ought. I don't want no girl of mine to go wrong. If you ain't got sense enough to look . . ."

"I wish to God you'd let me ruin my own reputation."

"All right, if you won't talk sense, I can damn well make you act it . . . look out, here he comes."

They would say nothing until the next withdrawal.

"Well, what's the Old lady blowing off about now?"

"Oh, Ed, I'm scared as hell she's going to give you up to the cops."

"The hell she is."

"She'd just as soon as not, to get me married."

"Judas Priest, of all the snide . . ."

"It ain't my fault Ed. I swear it ain't my fault. You believe me don't you?"

"Oh, I reckon."

"Honest to God, Ed, I swear it ain't my fault. I ain't said a thing to her about it. I don't give a damn if you marry me or not . . . I swear to God."

"You don't, huh? What kind of girl are you?"

"Oh, don't talk so hard, Ed. You know I'd give anything if we could get married and . . . everything. But I'd a sight rather see you get away."

"Well, I reckon you know I'd marry you, if they was any chance."

"Listen, Ed . . . I got an idea."

"Yeah?"

"I got an idea if we told Father Connly . . ."

"Hey, don't go talking this around to anybody."

"Oh, give me a chance to tell you. I got an idea he'd marry us and never say a word about giving you up. I mean, it . . ."

"God, you're full of bright ideas, ain't you?"

"No, honest, Ed. I don't think he'd bitch you."

"Why the hell shouldn't he?"

"To get me married. Don't you see that means more to him than running you in?"

"Yeah, and why couldn't he marry us and then run me in?"

"Oh, we could get him around that, Ed. We could make him see what a hell of a trick it would be."

"Yeah, we could like hell. You can't reason with people like that. They got their duty. They ain't got no sense of decency."

"No kidding, Ed . . . oh, Jesus, Ed—I know he wouldn't give you up."

"Thought you didn't give a damn about getting married."

"Ed, I swear I won't do it if you think it's going to bitch you. I don't give a damn about my reputation, and all that crap. It ain't that. I just wish I could—I'd just feel so good, to be married to you. Even if you had to run off right away.

Ed looked at her. "It may be so, for all I know, but it sounds like hell to me," he chanted. "What difference does it make to you—if it ain't for your rep, and all that?"

"Ain't I just told you?"

"Didn't I say it sounds like hell?"

"Oh . . . I can't tell you if you don't see what I mean. I reckon . . . Oh, I reckon it's because I love you, Ed. I know that sounds like hell, but . . . I hate to talk teary like that, but I reckon that's what it is."

Ed didn't speak. She looked at him intently.

"Ain't you going to say anything?"

"What is they to say?"

"You ain't sore, are you Ed?"

"No, I ain't sore."

"Well what's wrong with you then?"

"Nothing wrong with *me*, is they?"

"Oh, Ed, I—Look out, here she comes."

It went on that way for three days.

Late Thursday afternoon the sky, which had been like dark clear ice, began to curdle and swirl down above the water. Great chunks of it tore loose and settled on the hilltops.

Ed and Mad and Mrs. LaRue sat watching the change. They didn't say a word. Mad kept looking very hard at Ed. Every once in a while he would get up and walk across to the window, and walk around a little, and sit down again.

Just before dark it began to drizzle. They didn't say anything, but they were thinking pretty fast. At about six, Jake came in. "Hello, folks," he said. "Its starting to rain outside."

He washed traces of white and green chalk from his fingers. "Better hurry up supper," he said. "Got a game tonight."

Mrs. LaRue looked at him and started to speak. She said nothing, and went across to the stove.

"Jeez, it's a lot warmer," Jake said. "It's warming up fast."

Mrs. LaRue turned on him. "We ain't all halfwits," she said. "I reckon it generally warms up when it rains."

"Yeah? Well, you don't have to act so sore about it. I'm damn glad it's warming up some, Christ's sake—"

Mrs. LaRue looked at him and he looked towards Ed. "Christ's sake," he said again, and decided not to talk anymore about the weather.

They sat down to supper. Only Ed ate much.

Jake said: "God, you'd think you two was playing, yourselves, tonight."

Mrs. LaRue set down her knife. "Don't be too damn sure you're playing," she said.

"What the hell, what the hell you mean, I'm not playing?"

Ed looked up at Mrs. LaRue. She became confused, and said:

"Oh . . . don't be so thick . . . You might slip up and hurt yourself."

"Har, har, har," from Ed. "God you're funny."

Nobody spoke during the rest of the meal. Jake pushed back his chair.

"Well, I got to be going."

"Come in here a minute," his mother said.

"What's wrong?"

"Come on in here a minute." She walked him into the front room and shut the door.

"God damn her, she's up to some dirty work," Ed whispered.

Mad nodded.

He grabbed Jake's hat and overcoat. "Well, I reckon my call's about over. So long." He started for the door.

"Wait, Ed."

"Look here, damn you—"

"Wait! You can't hop no freight before nine-thirty. If you go now Jake'll spread the alarm. They'll get you sure before then—"

"You trying to bitch me? God damn you, if you're—"

"No! No, I ain't. Use your head. Don't you see they'll get you?"

"I guess you're right at that." He tore off the coat and hung it up again.

"Don't you worry, I got it—."

"Shut up!"

Jake and his mother came back in. "Well," Jake said, very casually, "Guess I better be going along."

"Oh, yeah?" Ed said. "And where might you be going, Jakie?"

"Game, for Christ's sake."

"Oh, of course. Damn stupid of me to forget that."

Jake started to put on his coat.

"Just a sec, baby-boy."

Jake turned around, putting on his coat.

"Hang that coat right up there on the hook."

"What the hell?"

"The hell is, you're going to sit right here, tight on your little ass."

"Oh, yeah?"

"You heard me."

"Jake's going to that game," his mother said.

"Jake's got me to tell that first."

"You and who else?"

"I know damn well you mean to give me up. Christ, you can't put nothing over on me, you old bitch. Jake sits right here on his tail, and you sit on what's left of yours, till I say get up."

"Get your hat, Jake."

Ed grabbed Jake by the neck. "Look here now, I don't want to get tough, but—"

"Jesus Christ! You son . . . Turn loose of me!"

"You God-damned bum turn loose of him!"

"Ed—cut it out—turn loose of him! Turn *loose* of him a sec, can't you?"

Ed let him go, and stood in front of the door. "Well, now what?"

"Listen Ma—Ed—Get Father Connly—honest to God Ed, he won't bitch you. Get *him*, he'll marry us, and—"

"Yes, the hell he will, I just as soon a Sheriff gets me as a priest."

"He won't bitch you Ed—no kidding."

"I ain't taking no chances."

"Oh—Go on, Ma—go on up and get him. No use Jake's missing the game."

"No—that's a fact, Ma. Jeez, might's well—"

Ed said: "Look here, you trying to bitch me? You little—"

"God no!" She turned her back on them and looked very hard at Ed. "I ain't. You'll get away, this way, that's all . . . Don't you see? Ma, go on up. Don't tell him nothing, just say I want to see him. You ain't got nothing against Ed if he marries me have you Ma? You wouldn't give him up if he done that?"

"Not if he married you. I wouldn't."

"Well—I don't think Father Connly'd say anything, as long as he was going to marry us, do you?"

"I reckon he'd have to."

"Oh Jesus, I don't think so, Ma," Jake said, looking at the clock. "Anyhow he'd marry 'em."

"Yeah—he'd marry us, sure, Ma."

"Well—would you marry her, if you was sure to get away?"

"Hell, yes."

"Come on, Ma. Don't bitch him."

"Come on Ma, that sounds o.k." Jake said.

"Well—I reckon it's all right. Go on ahead, then, Jake, and get him."

"Aw, Jesus, Ma . . . I got to catch the bus, and he's way the hell out of the way."

"Oh, hell. I'll go—wait a minute. Mad, you ain't trying to pull nothing?"

"Hell no—we want to get married. It was just bitching Ed I didn't like."

"All right. Go on and catch your damn bus."

Jake got on his hat and coat and hurried out. "So long."

"Good luck," Mad called.

"Where's my rubbers?" Mrs. LaRue said.

"Don't know."

"You know, Ed?"

"How the hell should I know?"

"Don't get fresh, you crooked bum. And after I do you a favor like this."

"Oh, don't get on your ear, Ma. He didn't mean nothing, did you Ed?"

"She's touchy, that's all."

"Where the hell's my God-damned *rubbers*?" She looked under the bed.

"Oh," she said, and got them out.

"Here's your coat," Ed said.

"O.k." She went to the door. "God it's raining like hell," she said. She turned back in and shut the door. "We *got* to get a umbrella. Just sec." She went into the front room, and came out levelling a shotgun at Ed. "You better hang on to this," she said to Mad. "I don't mistrust you Ed, but I ain't taking no chances. Here." She gave the gun to Mad, who held it aimed at Ed.

"Well, I ought to be back before long." She went out.

"Don't hurry yourself," Ed said after her.

Mad waited for a safe interval, then lowered the gun.

Ed said: "Boy, I got to hand it to you. You sure used the old head."

Mad laughed. "I reckon you think quick, time like that." She got up and walked heavily to the cupboard. "I'll fix you up something to take with you."

"O.k."

He sat watching her move about. "Damn sorry, it turned out like this."

"How you mean?"

"Wish to God I *could* marry you, honey."

"Oh." Mad put her hands down on the table and looked at him. "Can't you stay, Ed? They won't be no trouble. I know they won't."

"Jesus, Mad. I can't take no such chances. Don't you see I can't? You know I'd marry you if I could, don't you honey?"

Mad began packing food into a shoebox. "It's all right," she said. "It's all right. I don't care, Ed." She worked faster. Ed didn't say anything. He sat looking at the stove.

She brought the box over. "There. That ought to see you through."

"Yeah. That ought to be fine."

"I wish they was a coat around here I could give you."

"Oh don't bother about that."

"Course you can have my coat, if you—" She laughed a little. "God you'd be a sweet-looking jailbird in that."

"I'll be O.k. Don't worry about me."

"I'll give you this blanket. That'll help—Get up, you lazy bum." She slapped him on the side of the head and he stood up. Mad pulled a blanket from her bed and rolled the lunch box up inside it.

"O.k. Mad. Thanks. Thanks lot."

Mad went to one corner and pulled up a loose plank, and took out an old stocking there. The foot was full of money. "Hell of a trick, but you need money worse than she does."

"Yeah, I reckon that's so." He took five dollars, and she put the stocking back.

She laid the shotgun on the floor, and they sat on the bed. For quite a while each waited for the other to say something. Outside, the express went by, the rails hammering rhythmically after it had gone.

"Well," Ed said. "Well, I better get going. It's couple of miles out to the grade."

Mad nodded. Ed got up and took an old cap from its hook in the corner.

"Well," he said.

"Oh, Ed! Mad ran to him and put her arms around him. "Ed—can't you take me with you?"

"Huh?"

"Can't you Ed? Take me with you!"

"Jesus Mad, I can't do that. Why—why you're due to pop a kid now, anyday. Oh for Christ's sake Mad—snap to. Don't get to crying—"

"Oh, Ed—please take me with you."

"Honey, don't you *see* I can't do it? Why, it'd kill you, sure as anything."

"I don't give a damn. Take me with you."

"Mad, how the hell would you hop a freight, in your shape? I tell you, you'd just get me caught, that's all."

"Listen here Ed: I've done all this for you. It does look to me like you could let me try, anyhow. I swear I won't make you no trouble . . . honest to God I won't, Ed. Listen. I'll walk out to the grade with you, and if I slow you up too much, I'll come on back. You'll let me do that, won't you?"

"Oh, for Christ's sake! Come on."

They crossed a great black field that sloped up into the rain. Ed spoke to her occasionally, but she saved her breath for walking. He decided to walk fast, to discourage her. She kept with him all the way, hanging on to his hand. "God damn it," he thought. "I wish she'd let go my hand."

They climbed the hill, and cut back through the woods to the left, overlooking the tracks. Back to the south they could see a haze of light shining through the rain. They sat down on a log.

For several minutes Mad could not speak. She leaned against him, almost crying through her hand, whistling breathing.

"There," she finally said. "There Ed. There, I told you I could do it."

"Mad, you sure have got the old guts."

"Oh, I got guts, all right." She threw her arms about him. "Oh, Ed—we're going to be all right now. It's awful white of you Ed, letting me come."

"You sure have got guts, Mad." Ed said again. He kept looking off down the tracks.

After a while he turned to her. "Look here Mad. You better go on back. You ain't got a chance in the world to hop that freight, honey. You'd kill yourself, sure."

"Oh, Ed . . . No kidding Ed, I can't stand it if you go and leave me."

"Listen honey, how about it? I'll come back for you, later on."

"Don't be a fool. You know you can't never see this town again."

"Well then I'll write you. Yeah, that's what we'll do. I'll write you, few months from now. Then you can break away and come to me. How's that, Mad?"

She thought it over. "Well . . . Well, I reckon that's O.k.," she said. "Yeah, that'll be O.k."

"Well, that's how we'll work it then. I'll get—Ho-oh—there's the train."

The freight was just pulling out across the field.

"Ed, I'd do anything for you."

"Good, I reckon you've showed me that. You been the nuts about it, honey."

They were silent for awhile.

The train was halfway across the field.

"Ed, I wish you could have stayed, I wish you could have been with me, while I was having the kid."

"I'd have to hide."

"Oh sure. But in the next room, I mean."

"Oh well . . . what the hell."

"Look, Ed—what you want me to call him?"

"Call who?"

"Oh, who the hell you think, the Mail Man?"

"Oh. Jesus, how do I know? May be a girl, anyhow."

"Yeah but I mean if he's a boy. You want me to name him after you?"

"O.k. by me."

"Don't you care what I call him?"

"Jesus, I don't care. Call him anything you're a-mind to . . . Ed's good as anything. What the hell you crying about?"

"I ain't crying . . . I'll call him, Ed, I reckon."

The train was getting onto the grade, now.

Mad spoke suddenly—"Ed!"

"Huh?"

"You swear you'll write me? You swear it, won't you?"

"What's eating you? Course I'll write you."

"For a minute I just felt scared as hell, that's all. Like I wasn't never going to see you or hear from you again."

"Oh, Jesus."

They could hear the train quite distinctly now. The rails began to click.

"I got to get down by the tracks now." Mad followed him down the embankment.

"Well, so long, honey," he said. "You sure have been the nuts about it."

"Oh, God Ed—Ed, you know I love you, don't you? Do you love me Ed?"

"Damn right I love you." He put his arms about her.

"Ed, I wouldn't care if you didn't give a damn about me.

I'd love you just as much. But you do, don't you Ed? You'll send for me won't you?"

The train leaned out along the curve, a little way down the track.

"So long honey." He kissed her quickly. She clung to him, trying to find his mouth once more. "Better stand back." He pulled her arms away.

"Ed—Ed—"

The engine went past.

"Ed—"

He kissed her hurriedly, on the cheek, so it happened, and pushed her out of the way with one arm. The cars ground past through the rain. He hitched the blanket and food up under his left arm, then threw them down. The blanket unrolled, the box burst with a sprawl of food into the wet cinders. Ed swung onto a car, and leaned out to yell back. "So long."

He hadn't kissed her, hadn't really loved her. "You'll send for me, won't you?" He hadn't answered that, he hadn't answered her. When the box fell she began to cry suddenly, unrestrainedly. For the flash of a second she stood staring at the light tatter of food on the cinders. Then, looking up, she saw Ed clinging against the side of the car like a cat to a tree.

There were three cars more. Ed saw her get ready for the first. "Mad!" he bawled. "You damn little fool, get back!"

She lost her nerve on the first. She thought she heard Ed calling . . . not that that made a hell of a lot of difference.

Now—

She grabbed out with both hands. They caught hold of the dripping rungs. She tried to draw her feet up to the bottom rung; no use—couldn't make it. Like a bale of hay, tied to her belly. "Oh, Christ Jesus . . ." So there she was, hanging on, her feet swung under the car . . . swung on like one of those little wooden parrots that balanced by their tails.

Ed could see her, swinging and hanging on. The train rounded a curve and started down grade. The cars leaned out in an arc between them. When they straightened she was gone.

He climbed in between the cars. "Christ!" He whispered. "Christ Almighty!"

After dark the next afternoon, he left the freight and picked his way out of the yards. He walked down the street running parallel to the tracks.

There were several lunch cars, scattered down the street.

It was early, yet, for many customers. He chose one that was empty and went in.

"What's yours," the girl at the counter said.

"Cook me up two steaks and French, rare."

"Two rare and," she called back.

"Judas fella, you must be plenty hungry," she said.

"I'm hungry all right. Hell of a night, ain't it?"

"I reckon it is. Damn sight better than this cold snap we been having, though."

"You said a big mouthful that time. Say, how about some coffee, just to get started on?"

"O.k. fella." She walked over to the tank and drew him a cup. When she turned around she saw him watching the lift of her skirt. The corners of her mouth dropped, and she hitched her hips a little as she walked back.

Ed smiled at her.

"Well, how they goin', kid?" he said.

"Oh, could be worse." She leaned on the corner, tapping her nails. Her dress fell away from her throat, and they smiled at each other again.

The shutter into the kitchen opened. "Two rare and," the old man said.

"Make the third medium," said the girl.

(June 1930)

"A Walk Before Mass"

He awoke at a little after four, and knew it was upon him again. It was scarcely daylight, and rain was dropping out of a bare sky. He watched blades of water delicately overlap and riffle down the pane. Mary was sleeping with her head thrown back, her mouth gently flared. For quite a while he lay staring at her, glancing up occasionally at the rain, trying to think it out.

Once more it had become unbearable, quite unbearable. He had gone through all this once before, so thoroughly, so pitilessly, that he had thought, "Nothing can ever hurt me again."

"From the many-venomed earth . .

. . . .

"Mithridates, he died old."

He'd always trusted Housman, and yet—here he was again, caught in the same inexorable cogs of pain. The first inoculation, then, had failed to "take." Yes, that was it: he had to be roused from the years of tundra-like discontent; his soul had to go on the table once more.

For over a week now, he had known. That was the really queer part of it; for a week he'd known, and gone ahead just as before. It had made no apparent difference. Indeed, he had been so foolish as to smile, silently quoting those silly verses of Housman's. Even the night before, the same unperturbed level of unhappiness had closed above him. Something profounder than a dream had moved toward this awakening.

He looked at his watch. Nearly five. He'd better try to get another hour of sleep, before they got up for Mass. "They?" He turned his head and looked at her for a long while as she slept. Could he ever again kneel at her side and take God into his body? How had he ever been able to, since first he had known it? How could he lie there beside her a moment longer?

And yet he did lie there, thumbs gnawing into palms; lay

staring down upon the sleeping head. In the brief months of happiness after their marriage he had often looked thus upon her and had thought, "It is like looking into a mirror." He remembered that now, and as he gazed more intently he saw dark floodgates spread like wings in his soul.

He pressed his knuckles into his eye-sockets, and tried desperately to pray. He couldn't make up his mind what he was to pray for. There was so much. It was so utterly beyond remedy.

He must pray for Mary. . . .

God . . . O God, deliver my wife out of her iniquity . . . God keep her, make her pure. . . .

Blessed is the fruit of thy womb, Jesus . . . .

Blessed is the fruit of thy womb . . .

Impossible . . . Blessed . . . Jerome . . . .

He must go to Jerome.

He got up, and tiptoed into the next room. Kneeling beside his son, he raised his palms and tried to pray. He looked at the window; water panelled it like a bird's wing, and beyond was black sky.

God . . . God. God!

Only when the child awoke did he realize he had spoken aloud. Jerome looked up at him, smiling, and he said. "Get up son. We must go for a walk."

The boy said nothing, but got up sleepily and began to dress. If Mary had made such a demand . . . or anyone except him. He sat on the edge of the bed, exulting in the quiet, the comprehending obedience.

Jerome stood puzzled, over a complication of buttons. He drew him between his knees, and finished dressing him. He held him for a moment, looking at him, then pushed the hair back from his forehead warm with sleep, and whispered, "Wait for me downstairs."

Quickly and silently he dressed, stopped at the door to look once more at his wife. Mary was sleeping with her head thrown back, her mouth gently flared. Vaguely he glanced at the mirror. It held only the rain-washed window. He shut the door quietly and stole down into the hall. They put on their coats and walked into the rain.

The street stretched downward like a hard cone. He took Jerome by the hand and they walked down the hill.

He walked heavily at first, dragging his feet through the filmy water. It seemed impossible to straighten his back and to hold his head where it belonged. In a despairing way he was still trying to think it out and to pray. As they came to the end of the pavement the country wind sowed rain into his eyes, and immediately he knew what had moved down his sleep in depths beneath dreaming.

Such a rain as this had fallen through that other dawn—just such a streaming silent mesh, drawn like a tent over all the sky and all his soul.

His shoulders straightened, and his head fell back upon them.

Before them stretched an expanse of spongy grass, belted by the river. On that other morning, he remembered, he had walked down here, alone, that time:

He had walked across the meadow and down to the river's edge; had stood beneath an elm; that elm at the bend. Alone. Jerome: He'd scarcely realized Jerome's existence then; Jerome was a baby. Only a few months old. Naturally, he hadn't given him a thought. Too little, almost, to be considered human . . . anything above, say, a helpless—

What was he dodging? What was his mind scurrying from on so many soft feet? What was there, hidden, that he could not—that he refused to remember?

Face it, admit it; confess it. Yet was it a thing to confess? He had scarcely thought it, certainly . . .

> I came down to the river, trying to puzzle
> it out, I couldn't bear to live with her any
> longer. And yet I knew I couldn't leave her.
> Jerome held us together, I thought, as if we
> were tied in a sack, I thought . . . I thought: If
> only *he* had never been born . . . or were out
> of the way . . .

Well . . . He'd admitted it now had confessed it to himself. He must confess it, now, to God, must—

But, was it a thing worth confessing? There had been no definite thought; the words had merely trailed across his soul, scarcely leaving a trace. It wasn't as if he had planned to kill his son. As if he hated him.

Hate Jerome! The child was all his heart and all his life. It was he who had made the whole thing bearable; no empty inoculation of pain. See how he had turned to him this morning, when God Himself gave him no help!

He looked down to the boy at his side as they kicked their way through the drenched grass. And he had thought, once, to . . . had wished his death. As dreadful, that, as murder. As wholly a mortal sin.

The elm was near at hand. He said to himself: "I will take him to the place where I thought it, and there I'll tell him about it and beg his forgiveness. Then we shall go to Confession and to Mass."

He took long steps, heedless of the sodden mounds and hollows in the earth. Jerome trotted after him, dragging at his hand. Breathless, they stopped beneath the elm.

After his haste his mind was broken and clattering. He put an arm around his son, and they leaned back against the tree. Above and below the bend the river stretched like a bolt of silk. Just at their feet the water roughened, but the rain quickly molded it into the smooth-skinned current. Rainpocks slid quietly down the surface.

He looked down at Jerome, and tried to begin.

"My dear, my beloved son . . ." he said . . . then caught him up and bruised the thin body against his own and with all his strength hurled him into the water.

The circles broke like bells against the bank, and smoothed away into the rain. For a few seconds he stood motionless, arms above his head, flayed eyes fixed on the water.

Suddenly he clenched his fist and so struck himself upon the temple that he had to lean against the elm.

(Christmas 1929)

"You, Andrew Volstead"

There were two people came in about the middle of the evening. One was a young man, and the other was a young woman.

"Let's take a table," the young man said, after he had ordered drinks. "We can't have any serious conversation at the bar."

"How thoughtful you are," said the young woman.

So they took a table in a fairly private corner, and both of them looked around.

"I like this place," the young man said. "It seems like old times, don't it?"

"If you mean it seems like last night, yes. If you mean it seems like last summer, no."

"I meant last summer. Here, you wanted the gin rickey, didn't you?"

"You ordered it."

"No, I ordered a whiskey sour."

"I mean, you ordered it for me."

"Oh, well. Here it is. Don't try to mix me up that way. You know I'm just a big wondering child."

"Yes, and that's all you have been, ever since you came down."

"Say, what's the matter with you? Here I try to be companionable and what do I get. You got something snotty for everything I say. What's matter with you, anyway?"

"Oh, darling, let's don't fuss about it. Hurry up and finish your drink and let's get out of here."

"Gee, Jake must have started putting alcohol in his liquor, since I was here last. What did you say?"

"You said that last night. Don't call him over here again and tell him."

"What did you say, about let's get out of here?"

"My God you don't mean to stay here all night, do you?"

"All night? What you trying to do, make me miss my train? You know darn well I got train to catch eleven thirty, eleven thirty-two."

The girl looked like Hope Williams two seasons late. "He asks me, don't I know he's got a train to catch," she said. She emptied her glass. "Oh, darling, *please* don't keep dodging me like this. Let's go where we can have a little privacy, darling. I want to talk to you, I want to see you. Dear, I haven't seen you five minutes the whole time you've been down I hav—"

The young man interrupted, quietly, and with measured justified grievance. "Now, that's not fair of you, honey. That's not even true of you. You know darn well I've been with you, every minute of two days, practically every minute. That's not even true of you."

"If you call dragging me around with your nifty friends being with me. And talking to them most all of the time being with me. If you call making me act pleasant to those damned souses—"

"Hey. Hey! Quit yelling that way. Quit that. Look at the way people are looking at you." He patted her arm. "You don't want people to be looking at you like that now do you honey?"

"I don't care who looks at me. I'm not so hard to look at. And for the God's sakes, please quit calling me honey!"

"Hon—dear—*please* don't talk so loud. Come on now, have another drink. Have one more little drink and you'll feel better."

"I don't want another drink. I hate this place. You've had too much."

"Come on now. Just another little drink and you'll feel lots better. You know you will. Hey, Jake!"

"I don't want it. I feel like a walking still now. Harry, come on. Come on up to the apartment."

"The girls'll bother us."

"No they wont. Dal's home for the weekend, and—"

"Mabel'll—"

"No, she won't. Mabel's a good sport. Come on, Harry!"

"Oh, but I like it here. It seems more like old times. Just a sec, Jake. What you want to drink, honey?"

"Give me a lime coke."

"Hahaha. That's a good one. Good one, hah, Jake? Come on now, honey?"

"Oh . . . *I* don't care."

"How about a whiskey sour? Make it two whiskey sours, Jake. Whiskey for me and sour for the young lady. Hahaha."

"Lime coke," he said. "Hahaha. That's a good one. That's more like old times." He patted her arm.

She did not say anything. He looked at her with some interest; she was intently watching the end of her cigarette.

He finally said: "Dear, I'm sorry about, I'm awful-ly sorry about, the way things panned out. Honest I am.

"I didn't know they'd take up so much time. You know I didn't know that, don't you?"

"Honest-ly, I thought you'd like to meet them, specially Randy. Didn't you like Randy?"

"I think they're a lot of heels. Every last one of them."

"That hurts," he said. "I can tell you, that hurts. But honey, let's not fight about them. We haven't got much time, honey. Only I just want you to know, I'm sorry they took up so much time when after all I came down to see you, and I didn't intend the least in the world to drink, much as I did."

"And, honey, I'm *awfully* sorry I passed out, last night. When I came to I was *awfully* sorry. You don't know how lousy I felt. Gee, I felt just *lousy*, darling."

"Yes. People usually do, when they've come to."

"Well, I didn't mean that way. Course I did feel pretty bum that way, but—"

"Of course you needed a few dozen drinks to set you back on your feet."

"Sure— I mean no. No. Honest, I didn't drink much. I had to drink some, to pick me up."

"And it's still carrying you pretty well, I notice."

"No, that's some I had later, at Tom's."

"Oh, I see. That must have been while I was waiting for you to call."

"My gosh Marian, you just *try* to mix me up. My gosh I thought I wouldn't call you till late because, well, we were all up awfully late and I didn't want to wake you up. I mean, I thought you'd be asleep."

"Thanks. That was very considerate of you, especially seeing that I didn't sleep a single wink, till nine a.m."

"What, why? Why? What was the matter?"

"He asks me: what was the matter! Listen here, if you'd been looking forward for God knows how many weeks to seeing someone you loved and then everything fell through and went wrong and then he had to go and pass out cold on you and turn into a first class mummy on the one night you'd just been living for God knows how many weeks and so you just went home to bed and lay there and cried and cried about it and you'd been dying to see him and talk to him and see him, I guess it would take half a dozen Simmons' mattresses and maybe a little encouragement with a hammer or laudanum or something to put you to sleep!"

The young man put down his cigarette and blew his nose. He said: "Say: Say, I didn't follow you. I couldn't follow you. Say that again."

"Oh: I don't want to talk about it. What's the earthly use of talking about it?"

"Well," he said. "Well, that's entirely up to you. Say, I'm awful sorry. I went ahead and drank my drink and yours too."

"Oh, don't worry about that."

"Look here, I'll get you another one, right away."

"No, don't."

The young man seemed rather puzzled. He lighted another cigarette and watched his discarded stub die a natural death. When fire had crawled down the stub and changed it into a rank haze and a cylinder of ashes, and, its work done, had itself handsomely become ashes, he put his fingers into the tray, flattened the cylinder, and fashioned ashes and stubs into an uncertain scroll-like design. He began, then, anxiously to turn and gently to shake his head, as if he were testing a universal joint at the base of his skull. He bit his lips and quietly molded them with the fingertips of both hands, and he rubbed his cheeks with the fingertips of both hands; and for a moment dropped his head into his two hands.

The young woman spoke: "Oh, my darling. My darling, you're so drunk. You're so tired, dear." She placed one hand on his shoulder, and set her knee against his knee. "Oh my dearest, it's been so awful. Dear, I've missed you so. You don't know how I've missed you. It didn't do a bit of good to write you, dear, it just wasn't a bit of help. And that's why I didn't mind your not writing me, much. Only darling, please write me once in a while, when you get back. I don't care if it's just a card. I know

you're awfully busy. But do write me, just once in a while, darling.

"Have you missed me much, dear? I've missed you,
dreadfully. Not all the time. It's funny. Some of the time I
don't even think of you, I hardly think of you, for days on end.
And then all of a sudden I'll think of you, and it just seems as if I
couldn't bear it if I didn't see you. I've missed you most at
nights, darling. Sometimes I've missed you so I just had to bawl.
I called you up twice, dear, but you weren't in, either time. But
it's all right. It's all right. I was so happy when I knew you were
coming down. I just couldn't think of anything else."

"Did you feel that way about it, darling?"

"And then ever since you came I've felt so damned futile,
dearest. You just can't know how I felt. It isn't I didn't like your
friends, sweetheart. I didn't mean a word I said about them. But
we had such a short time, lover, and it did seem so damned futile to spend it all just running around drunk with them. I kept
hoping you'd say, 'Well, I guess Marian and I will quit the party,
now.' Dear, they wouldn't have cared. I mean, they knew I was
your girl, and naturally you'd want to see me some alone,
wouldn't they?"

"I know that's what you did tonight, darling, and it was
sweet of you too. But it was last night, dear. That's when I
wanted you so. And the party just went on and on and on and
on, and I was *praying* you'd leave, sooner or later, and then you
never left except when you passed out and they took you to
Randy's in a taxi."

"I told them then that I could take care of you, dear.
Darling, I'd have loved to take care of you. I'd have been so
happy to have put you to bed and helped you if maybe you'd
been sick. But they must have thought I was too drunk myself.
They were nice about it, dear, but they said they'd better take care
of you."

"Oh—let's not talk about it, dear. We've got such a little
while left and I've got so much to tell you and ask you. That's
the reason I didn't write you much, dear. I thought, it's so much
lovelier to *talk* than just to write. And here we've sat and quar-
relled at each other, all the evening."

"Sweetheart, you look so unhappy. Don't be unhappy,
darling lover, when we've only got such a *little* while. Don't
think about it, dear. I don't mind. I don't care a bit, now. Let's
just forget all about it."

"Dear, try and be happy. Try and be gay, for my sake. No, hell I don't mean that but let's just try and be happy, the little time we've got left, darling."

The young man looked at her as if she were a broken mirror. He said: "Sure. Sure. That's right. Let's be gay." After a minute he said: "Sure. You got right idea." He straightened up and lighted another cigarette. "Don't you worry about me," he said. "I feel gray. Great."

"Darling, why don't you get another drink. It may pick you up. You better get another drink. Something real snappy."

"That's idea. Prick me up. I need pricking up. Jake!"

"You're sweet, dear."

"No I'm not. I'm all right. You wait a minute. I'm all right I tell you. I'm just sort of tired, that's all. But I'll snap to, all right. Don't want make you blue. I'll snap to."

"What do you want, dear?"

"Straight rye. Give me big straight rye."

"You're not blue, are you? Honey?"

"No darling I feel grand. How are you?" She smiled very brightly.

"I'm gray. Great. I wish he'd hurry up with that rye."

"He'll hurry. He's one of the best little hurriers I ever saw. Don't you love people that hurry, Harry?"

"Sure, sure, they're the sort make headway. Place in sun. Look at Lincoln. Look at Napoleon. Look Jimmy Walker. Not yet, you Peeping Tom. Now look. Ain't he a beauty? And he got it all by hurrying. What we need is more hurrying. Hurry for Harvard! Hurray! Boom!"

"That's the way to talk. Harvard's a great place."

"Harvard's gray place. Makes men. Men make women. Women make babies. Babies make—what do babies make?"

"Let's not talk about that."

"Let's not talk about Harvard."

"Here's your drink."

"That's stuff, Jake. You keep right on hurrying. Hurry get me big straight rye."

"No, hold it, Jake," she said. "Give me a little sip."

"Sure."

"Mmmmm. That's grand stuff. Just try that, Harry."

"Mmmmm. Grand. Gray. Great."

"Just like old times, hmm?"

"It's swell here."

"This swell place. Want a card?"

"Got one."

"You've got a card? Why you're wonderful. Wonderful girl. So bright and scarcely six. Gee this swell stuff. Better than electric belt. Fight shy of these electric belts, Marian. Don't wear a trusss. You can be strong and plum full vigor. If you were walking down street with your wife or sweetheart and a rough came and 'costed you for match, what would you do? You'd run, you pansy. No way to treat a Lady. Keep your muscles in trim."

"Keep your mind out of the gutter."

"Keep your muscles in trim and your mind out the gutter, what is the good of white bread and butter?"

"That's wonderful."

"I may be wonderful but I think you're wrong."

"Just the fifth Marx Brother."

"Let's form party of four to go through revolving door."

"Let's not. Let's sit here and talk. Drink your rye."

"You trying to get me drunk?"

"Darling, I wouldn't get you drunk. I couldn't bear it."

"Neither could I. It would break my mother's heart and after all, owe something to mother, don't we?"

"How much?"

"You mix me up. Honest mister, I paid my income tax. Honest Indian."

"An honest Indian is a dead Indian."

"Getting morbid on me. Oh mother Indian, you are my angel dear, you big louse."

"Mark but this louse, and mark in this, how—"

"Gad it's good to be alive. Or have you ever thought about it? I love to sit and think great thoughts."

"Do you ever play with Ideas?"

"What, those nasty little Ideas? I'm sorry they ever moved into our block, and if I ever see you playing with them I'll give you a spanking you'll remember. Just put that in your pipe and smoke it. Granger Rough Cut, the He-Man's tobacco. Grows hair on your chest. Grows moss in your lungs. Try it out on your faithful pointer. Throw it in the lake. Fish cry for it. It's better than blasting. Then, in the silence, a trout leaped. Quick, Watson, the bedpan, cried Holmes. And there we were, lost in the depths of the primeval jungle. That wonderful smell that is the East stole upon us, gnawed at our vitals. I tell you, boys, it was terrific. And I thought of England's peaceful mews and love stews, and I said: boy, have you ever played Rugger for Rugby? A boot flew through the air, and Tom Brown cried Stop! I'll carbonado your shanks, but leave that little lad to his confab with Jesus! And little Erminia looked up and said, Mama. What, cunning one, said Mama. Mama, a while ago I met three men. Two of them were terrible bums. And who was the one in the middle, said Mama. I don't know, he didn't give his name, but He was very, very kind. Mr. Gilchrist, can that be the star of Bethlehem? I wonder. The chimes swell out as the curtain falls. No thanks, we've just had tea. I want another rye."

"Jake! Another like it."

"Where was I?"

"Darling, I want to talk to you. Let's talk seriously for a while."

"Sure. I'm all for serious talk. No don't look like that. Honest I am sweetheart. You go right ahead and talk, I'll listen. Nothing like a good listener."

"Oh, please don't fool, Harry."

"Wasn't fooling. You think everything I say, I'm fooling."

The young woman thought for a moment, and said: "Did you miss me, dear?"

"Sure, Sure I missed you. Not all, not all the time you understand. But I missed you awful-ly, specially at first of the fall. Oh, Lord, why do you look that way? Darling? Are you sore?"

"No, I'm not sore."

"You miss me?"

"Not so very—oh but I did, Henry. There's no sense lying about it. I missed you terribly. Sometimes I didn't see how I could live, if I didn't see you."

"Gee, I'm sorry to hear that. O.k. Get me another one, Jake."

"I'm sorry you missed me that way."

She thought very hard for a minute. She said: "Dear, we've got to make a new start on things. Don't you see we have to? We can't just go on this way, with things just kind of in mid-air. Never writing each other, or seeing each other."

"Oh, darling, last summer was so lovely. We were so happy last summer. And now everything seems so different. I don't know what's the matter with us. Only I know we've got to *do* something about it, or the whole thing is going to hell. Don't you see we've got to?"

"Sure.   You're right.   Got to do something.   Things haven't been going a bit right." He stopped and looked at her curiously, and rather sadly. While he was looking he got rid of the rye in two gulps.

He said: "You know, friendship's a funny thing. You go along and you have a grand time with someone, and then all of a sudden things seem to be sort of going queer about it. Don't know what it is. Can't tell what it is."

"That's the time you've got to do something about it."

"You never do quite know what it is. It's funny, but you never do. People just kind of drift apart, and you never do quite know what's wrong. It's tough, that way."

"But we can get a new start on things."

"It's one of the toughest things a human being ever runs in to. It's awful. It causes all kinds of unhappiness—you know, agony even. Friendship is agonizing."

"Will you have your job back next summer darling?"

"And there don't seem to be anything to do about it. That's the hell of it. You know, the more I think of such things—"

"Oh, lover, you must *listen* to me. You've got to listen! I've got to tell you this. I don't want to make trouble or anything and if you say so, why of course I can get it fixed all right and we'll be just the way we were before, or dear we could be married secretly, but I've got to tell you, dear. I couldn't write it but I've got to tell you that I think I'm going to have a—a baby."

"I'll have a gin rickey, Jake! Where was I? Oh, yes, Friendship. Well I might as well come to the point. No use beating round the bushes. Point is that, darling, God Marian, oh Judas, I hate to make you feel bad, and if there was any way out of it, God knows I wouldn't for the world make you feel bad, but point is, I think we'd better break off our friendship. O.k., Jake. Lime Rickey and, what did you say you were going to have?"

"I'm not going to have anything."

"Oh, I thought you were going to have something."

She did not speak.

"Listen, dear. Let's drink to it. I want to drink to your good luck and you drink to mine. What do you say?"

"Do anything you want."

"Two gin rickeys. No. Got any wine? Got any port?"

"We got port."

"Two glasses port. That's stuff to drink hells with healths with. Well I was saying, Marian, dear, that's the only honest way to do the thing. I mean, as you said, we can't just drag it along this way. Can we? So we'll just finish it off the way a lady and gentleman ought, ought to. After all, when the thing's died, there's no use keeping it sort of dragging around your neck, like a like an albatross or something.

"Don't think it doesn't hurt me, darling. I've been thinking it over a long time, only I didn't write, because I decided the honorable thing to do was, come and see you. And honest to God, dear, I did mean to see you more, alone. I wanted to be with you all the time, and see if maybe we couldn't be happy again. I ran into Tom by accident. Entirely by accident. Maybe if we could have just been alone and taken things sort of easy, maybe we could have been happy only now I know there just isn't any use. It would just be painful for both of us. There isn't any sense in that, you know.

"Do you know that sonnet, since there's no help, come, let us kiss and part? Nay I have done, you get no more of me? And I am glad,? with all my heart,? yea I am glad. I can't remember it but, but darling I want you to read that. It's one of Shakespeare's, no I guess it isn't Shakespeare's but it's the way I want you to feel about this because it's the way I feel, and I want you to feel like that. O.k., Jake.

"Now darling, I drink to your good luck, and your happiness. Because darling you will be happy. You know you will. I want to drink to your luck and happiness and you drink to mine. Please darling. Don't feel bad. Say it, for my sake."

"I drink to your luck and happiness."

"That's great."

They drank. He said: "Darling don't look that way. I didn't mean to hurt you darling. You're not going to cry, are you?"

"No, I won't cry."

"That's great darling. Because I wouldn't for the world make you unhappy. I knew you'd be brave about it. You know, that's the only way to be."

He put his hand on her arm and they sat for a few minutes looking at each other. She said, finally: "What time is it?"

He took out his watch. "Say; my God! Eleven fifteen! Say, I've got to hurry! Just a sec, I want to settle up with Jake."

He left the table, and came back very soon.

"Well, dear, we got to be moving. Wish I could take you. Take you to your room. Will you ride on down to Grand Central? Taxi?"

She said: "I guess I'll stay here."

"Oh, Gee. You can't do that. You can't—"

"Don't worry about me."

"Well; listen: will you kiss me before I go?"

"Yes."

He leaned over and kissed her. He stood up and said: "No hard feelings?"

"No."

"Well I got to go. Don't worry about my things. Randy'll send them up.

"Well, the best of luck and happiness, Marian. You were swell about it."

"Let me rub those cigarette ashes off your face. Your mouth is all ashes."

"I'll clean up on the train. No time. Well, good-bye, darling."

He walked out, quite unsteadily.

(March 1931)

"Boys will be Brutes"

Highland Avenue projects various and diminishing qualities of paving through the suburbs of West Knoxville. It lies straight across a chaos of clay ravines, brambles, and tin cans. A few bungalows and signboards hang close on either side. The road lies straight across the field, and buries its head in a steep gravelly hill.

Half an hour before sunset, two boys emerged from a ditch in the field, and walked slowly toward the road. The larger boy, about eleven, was short and stocky. He carried a BB gun. The other, although nearly as tall, could not have been more than eight. Cupped against his shirt he carried a dead sparrow. When they reached the road he stopped, carefully laid the sparrow down, dabbed his fingers with spit, and tried to wipe traces of blood from his shirt. The older boy walked on a few paces, then stopped and watched him.

"Golly," Richard said. "I can't get this blood off."

"Well, what of it," said Joe.

"Well, Mama made me promise we wouldn't kill anything if I went."

"Well, I told you not to carry it like that."

"You did not."

"I did so."

"You did not."

"Did so. Well, what if I didn't? You ought to have known better, you darn nut. What did you carry it for?"

"My golly you told me to."

Joe picked up the sparrow and handed it to Richard. "Here. Hold it by the feet. No, down at your side, you nut. My golly."

A sparrow was sitting above the nearest signboard. Joe grabbed his gun into position, took quick aim, and fired. The bullet cracked against tin a few feet below the bird, which did not budge.

"Heck," Joe said. "That was the wind, did that."

He took very careful aim, and missed the sparrow again. Before he could shoot a third time, it flew away.

Watching for more birds Joe fired several shots at the coffee-cup that dominated the sign. He hit it twice.

Richard marshalled his courage and said, "Let me shoot, Joe."

"Aw, you can't shoot."

"I can so."

"How do you know? You never shot."

"Well, you never, till today."

Joe thought for a minute, "Well," he said. "I guess you better not. You got to know just how to handle these good old BB guns. No, I guess—Look."

High overhead, a flock of martens flew westward. Their song trailed across the field like thin rain following a cloud's edge. They flew toward the brightest sky, and flowed down behind the hill.

Joe shouldered his gun, and walked toward the end of Highland Avenue. Richard stood in the sudden silence, thinking of nothing in particular. When Joe reached the bank, he turned around and called. Richard trotted up to him.

"Where you going?" he asked.

"Up on the hill." He started climbing the bare bank. "Come on. There must be lots of birds up there."

Richard followed, taking great care not to harm the sparrow. The gravel slipped beneath his feet, and he heard it rattling faintly. He was tired, and the climbing was hard work.

"Hurry up," Joe called, ten feet above him.

"I'm hurrying." The sparrow's claws were moist and cold in his fingers. He looked down at it. One wing splayed out at an angle, from a bloody joint. The head bobbed and flopped as if hung from a rubber band.

"What you stopping for?"

"This sparrow."

"Throw it away."

"Golly, you said you wanted it."

"Heck no, I don't want it. Throw it away."

Richard tossed the sparrow behind him, and scrambled up to Joe's side, where he stopped breathless.

"You can carry the gun, if you want."

"Oh gee. Thanks Joe."

With the gun smooth and cool in his hand, it was much easier climbing. He reached the top only a little behind Joe. They kicked gravel over the edge, for the sake of the sound, and, tiring of this, turned toward the wood on the hilltop.

"Look," Richard said. "There's a bird." He caught the gun to his shoulder.

"Quit that," Joe yelled. "That's a robin. You can't kill robins."

"Golly. Honest, Joe, I didn't see it was a robin."

"You got to be mighty careful about that. My pop say's its mean to kill robins."

"Oh."

They walked on. "You better give me that gun. I don't want you to kill any robins."

Richard gave him the gun.

A sparrow flew over. "Watch me get him flying." Joe missed.

"Here." He gave Richard his cap. "When I say go, you throw this up, high as you can. You got to practise to shoot sparrows flying."

He failed to hit the cap a single time.

A sparrow alighted on a limb, very near them. He took careful aim, and pulled the trigger. The gun clicked emptily. He worked the pump, and set the muzzle close to the ground. The dust rayed out from the pellet of air.

"Gosh all mighty! Of all the times to run out of ammunition!"

"Got any in your box?"

"No."

"Gosh all mighty."

They walked aimlessly on.

They had not gone far when Richard said, "Look. There's a bird's nest."

"Where?"

"Up in that tree. Ducks on climbing."

"No, I'm going to climb."

"I saw it first."

"Oh, go ahead and climb if you want to be a baby about it."

Richard was already among the lower branches. Joe stood

beneath, watching him. "I don't care," he said. "It's an easy tree to climb."

Richard peered into the nest, and there was faint squeaking. For quite a while he said nothing; then he swung downward and called, "Four. Little teensy ones."

"Bring them down."

"Can't, too many."

"Aw, put them in our cap."

Richard straddled the limb and took the birds out gently. Then, very slowly and carefully, he climbed down. They held the cap between them, and looked at the birds."

"Gee, ain't they funny," Joe said.

"They're ugly."

"Gee, they're funny. Their mouths are so big."

"Maybe they're ugly ducklings."

"You darn nut, ducks can't climb trees. Ducks are born in the water."

"They wouldn't like it there."

"You darn nut they're ducks ain't they?"

A bird flew toward the tree, a worm in her beak. She dipped toward them and dropped the worm, chirping loudly as she wheeled about their heads.

"That's the mother bird," Joe said.

"It's a robin."

"I guess they're robins."

"Sure."

The birds stirred and opened their beaks very wide. Shrilly the mother answered their small gagged squeaks. She hooked close past Richard's head.

"We better put them back," he said.

"You can't put them back. They'll die."

"Why?"

"When you handle them, they die."

"Why?"

"They just do, that's all."

The mother flung herself straight between them.

"We *got* to do *something*."

After a minute Joe said, "What we got to do is, put them out of their misery."

"Out of what?"

"Out of their misery."

"What's that?"

"We got to kill them, you darn fool."

"Oh, why?"

"Cause. They'll die if we leave them here. They'll be cold."

"Gee. Why didn't you tell me?"

"Tell you what?"

"When you handle them, they die."

"My golly I thought any fool would know that."

Joe looked around. Nearby was a large flat of sandstone. "You take care of them," he said. He hunted about, and carried several stones, one by one, to the edge of the flat.

"Bring them here."

Ducking and dodging, and shielding the birds from their mother, he carried the birds over to Joe.

"Give them here." Joe took them out, one by one, and laid them carefully in the middle of the flat.

Together they stood and watched them. The birds were very young. A mildew fuzz covered their heads and backs, and along their wings lay little white spikes, like hair-fine fishbones. Through the membrane globing their monstrous bellies the children could see a mass of oystery colours, throbbing faintly. The birds kicked, and gaped, and clenched their wings, twitching helplessly in the middle of the stone.

The mother swept along an ellipse above them, and her distress streamed shrill behind her.

Richard said, "Joe. They're robins."

"Well, don't I know it."

"We're going to kill them."

Joe said nothing.

"Good golly Joe, we're going to kill robins."

After a minute Joe said, "They're only baby robins."

He set one of the robins apart from the rest.

"You kill two, and I'll kill two."

"I can't. It'll hurt them."

"It won't. They won't feel a thing. Look."

He picked up a flat stone larger than his head, held it above him, and dashed it down upon the bird. It was completely covered.

"There. You think he felt that?" He turned the stone over with his foot. "I guess that put him out of his misery, quick enough."

"No," Richard said, looking at it. "He couldn't have felt that."

"No I should smile he couldn't. Go on, it's your turn."

Richard set another robin aside, and selected the largest stone. He gripped it with both hands, strained upward, and threw it down with all his strength. Flesh splashed out as it struck.

"My golly," Joe said. "That was a good one! My golly, I guess you knocked *that* old bird into the middle of next week."

"Middle of next *week*? Middle of next *month*, you mean. Middle of next *year*."

"Golly, you sure fixed that old bird."

"Aw, that's nothing. I could do that any time. Gosh, that was easy. Watch this."

"Hey, who you think you are? My turn."

His face hot with excitement, he watched Joe dispose of the third robin. It was a less messy job.

"Yah! Didn't splash a darn bit."

"Heck, that was a little skinny one. He wouldn't splash."

"I bet I could make him."

"Bet you couldn't mess him up like that."

"Well, you messed him up all right, I guess. But any fool could do that. Just wait till I get to work on *this* old robin, though." He wrenched a large stone out of the loam and stood above the bird. "You better stand back. This one's going to splash all over the place. This one's going to splash all over West Knoxville."

"Do it, and then talk about it."

The rock was heavy and lopsided. With difficulty he raised it above him, and smashed it downward.

It barely caught the bird on one side, crushing a wing and opening its belly. The bird let out long-drawn reedy cries.

Richard stood watching its vitals pulse out of the wound. Joe's yell of derision scarcely pierced his fascination.

The mother's wing flashed across his face, and suddenly he ran to the edge of the flat, took a stone, rushed back, and threw it. He missed completely. The mother screamed about his ears. He threw another stone. It nicked the bird on the other side. The robin's belly burst and released its bowels. The mother wove wildly about him. He began to cry. He threw another stone, and another, and another. Half blind with tears, he ran into the woods, and pulled stones from the soft earth, scarring his hands, stripping his nails. Long after its squeaking had ceased, he piled rock on rock above the robin. Finally, exhausted, he sat down upon the little stack of rocks, and caught his head in his arms. Sobs tore through his chest. He was all but throttled with his crying. Suddenly he spread his knees; his head sank between them, and he vomited.

After that, his crying was less abandoned. Little by little he got it under control. He stroked his swollen nose, squeezed the mucus from it, and looked up. Joe was standing there, staring at him, helpless.

He said: "You all right now?"

Richard smothered a sob. "Yes. I'm all right."

Joe turned his foot on one side, and looked at the sole of his shoe. Then he looked up again, and said, "Let's go home."

"All right."

Without speaking they walked to the edge of the embankment.

Night was rising. Already it was above the city, and the dusk to the east was printed with lights. All the clouds had gathered beyond the hill; pure and crisp, they stood above open country. Wind blew steadily across the city, and brought with it a faint acrid odor of smoke.

They descended the hill, and walked more briskly toward home.

"Going to Sunday School tomorrow?" Joe said.

"Sure, you?"

"Sure. Catch me trying to skip again."

"Me too."

"Well, I guess I'll go on in to supper."

"Guess I better hurry up, too. I bet we're late."

"Shucks. My Ma don't care."

"Mine does."

"Be out after supper?"

"Sure, you?"

"Sure."

"Well, I be seeing you."

"So long. . . . Hey Joe!"

"Huh?"

"Will your Pop let you shoot on Sundays?"

"Don't know. I'll ask him."

"Well, see you after supper."

"Yeah, so long."

(April 1930)

"To Lydia"
Horace, Bk. I, Ode xxv

With violence diminished they rattle thy windows
Fast-joined—all the youths in their wantonness eager;
No more do they rob you of rest, and the door
  That often and silently

Swung on its hinges with ready complaisance,
Now lovingly lies in the sill's close embrace.
Now, seldom and seldom again do you hear:
  "O Lydia, Lydia,

"Now are you sleeping the long night through
While I perish, who love you?" Nay, now comes the time
When, forsaken and aged, down dimness of alleys,
  Of alleys deserted—

You wander and wail of the insults of rakes
Who beset you—While moon-maddened winds leaping down
From the Thracian highlands hold revel and riot;
  Then that furious lust,

That desire which with frenzy is prone to beflood
The dams of strong horses, shall rage in your vitals,
Shall foam round your ulcerous liver. Ah, Lydia,
  Not tearless ye mark it,

That Youth in its sprightliness sooner rejoices
In sap-singing myrtle and dusky-leaved ivy:
But dry leaves a-clatter in cold winds of Death,
  Youth offers to Winter.

(April 1929)

Part III
REVIEWS AND DOCUMENTATION

(1939-1945)

Time Reviews

Time Reviews

The over one hundred reviews Agee wrote from 1939 to 1942 for *Time* magazine cover a wide range of material. It should be remembered, however, that each writer was able to choose which books he would review. This selection is valuable because it indicates the kinds of books to which Agee was attracted. Also, it is apparent that his method is akin to that which he later refined for his movie criticism—he is always examining carefully the particular work under consideration and finding ways to relate that book to wider movements within the culture.

"Time and Craving"
After Many a Summer Dies the Swan
—Aldous Huxley—Harper ($2.50).

The Aldous Huxley whose early books so skillfully anat-
omized human viciousness and human hopelessness is no
more. With *Eyeless in Gaza* he turned to painful self-searchings.
With *Ends and Means* he grew stonily didactic. One of the gifted
moral satirists of modern times, he had become, by logical development, a definitely religious man. He still is, but in his new
book he turns to his earlier technique: uses once more the light
realistic fantasy and the sharp surgical analysis which first made
him famous, but uses them to say the most serious things he has
ever had to say.

The "Swan" of Huxley's sour fable is Jo Stoyte: old, half-
mad with wealth and power ("they are the same"), desperately
hanging on to his sexual potency, desperately afraid of its loss, of
age, of death. In his gigantic ferroconcrete chateau in Southern
California he lives with his young mistress, Virgina Maunciple,
a born courtesan with a short upper lip who frequently repairs,
for penitence, to the "Lourdes Grotto," which "Uncle Jo" has
built for her. Jo's other mainstay is sleek, Lavantine Dr. Sig-
mund Obispo who keeps the old man hopped up with hormone
injections, and searches, meanwhile, for the substance by which,
in Marxist John Strachey's optimistic phrase, "death might be
indefinitely postponed." The doctor enjoys Jo Stoyte's mistress,
old Jo himself does a bit of murder, and finally they all go to England, where Obispo uncovers the Fifth Earl of Gonister, who
nominally died a century ago. The secret of living indefinitely
has already been solved: the Earl, at 201, has matured into a raging fetal ape.

In the proper hands, it could be pulp fiction. In Aldous
Huxley's it is quite as plausible as highly intelligent satire need
be. In his hands, too, it is the excuse and occasion for the things
he particularly wants to talk about. Scattered in short (but stiff)

doses throughout the narrative, they are spoken by a Mr. Propter, the straightest and maturest straight man Mr. Huxley has ever permitted himself. As he speaks them, they are some of the firmest, most beautifully articulate essays Huxley has ever written.

Simple in essence, but by no means so simple as they sound, Mr. Propter's ideas boil down to this: "Time and craving, craving and time—two aspects of the same thing; and that thing is the raw material evil." Good, impossible within time, exists only on the animal level and on the level of eternity, of "pure, disinterested consciousness." That level is attained in the loss of wilfulness, of desire, of personality.

With that leverage on good and evil, talking with a rational clarity most mystics have lacked, Mr. Propter makes moral mincemeat of everything in sight, "good" or "bad," within the purely human sphere of endeavor. Some of his enemies—war and fascism—are popular pushovers. Others will leave Propter few takers. A partial list of targets for his dialectic: politics, capitalistic society, organized religion, romantic love, science, socialism, humanitarianism, language, virtue, selfless devotion, sex, art—in brief, all activities on the purely human plane, however disinterested, are productive only of evil.

"I believe," remarks Propter, "that, if you want the golden fleece, it's more sensible to go to the place where it exists than to rush round performing prodigies of valour in a country where all the fleeces happen to be coal-black."

.   .   .   .   .   .

Aldous Huxley went to Southern California about 18 months ago, not to write film plays but because of his eyes. In 1911 he contracted keratitis, which he says "left one eye slightly, and the other almost completely covered with scar tissue, besides inducing large errors of refraction." He went to Los Angeles for instruction in the Bates method of training his eyes to "relax." Although he moves about like a partially blind man, and his right eye looks blind (a blue film), he now reads without glasses, can do things "I couldn't have any more done than a fly a year ago."

In 1938 he wrote a film version of Eve Curie's life story of her mother. Garbo was to have played it, but the story was shelved. Just completed, in collaboration with Jane Murfin, is an adaptation of *Pride and Prejudice*, for Metro-Goldwyn Mayer.

For the past six months his home has been a secluded

wooden cottage in Pacific Palisades, overlooking Santa Monica. With his wife and niece he lives very quietly, takes long walks— sometimes 20 miles—in the Santa Monica hills. The only movie people he sees much of are Ronald Colman, Anita Loos, Directors Cukor and Mamoulian, and Charlie Chaplin, "an old and good friend." Another friend he sees fairly often is Bertrand Russell, now a professor at U. C. L. A. Recently he gave a picnic; the guests were Russell and Garbo.

As for rumors that he is developing a "new religion" he says: "There is no question of concocting a new religion. Certain people have been preoccupied with similar psychological exper- iments and with speculations concerning them for the past three thousand years. . . ."

(January 29, 1940)

Portrait of an Artist
James Joyce—Herbert Gorman—
Farrar and Rinehart ($3.50).

The utmost type of heroism, which alone is worthy of the name, must be described, merely as complete self-faithfulness; as integrity. On this level the life of James Joyce has its place, along with Blake's and Beethoven's, among the supreme examples. It is almost a Bible of what a great artist, an ultimately honest man, is, and is up against.

Of what that is Joyce himself has given such intense and definitive statement—directly in *A Portrait of the Artist as a Young Man*, by implication in every word he has written—that no biographer can hope to add to it. None should try. But any biographer may add much in the way of purely factual material.

Herbert Gorman cannot resist trying to comment as well as to present, and his comments usually fall short of their subject. But because he has a good deal to present that has not been presented before, including several excellent photographs, his book is by no means without value.

The general outlines of Joyce's life and many of the particulars are already well and widely known: the years of his youth in Dublin, the years of his exile in Paris, in Zurich, in Trieste, in Rome, again in Paris; his agonizing poverty during year after early year; the years of almost inconceivable misuse at the hands of publishers and, in his case, of printers; the horrifying succession of attacks on his eyes; his relief at length, thanks to Miss Harriet Weaver, from financial worry; the 34 years of unprecedented work he has done in the teeth of all deterrents: work which in the opinion of many mature critics gives him a place beside Shakespeare and Dante.

What Gorman valuably does is to add by the hundreds facts and anecdotes which intensify the significance of this quiet life and the image of the man himself. What he does still more valuably is to quote with some abundance from Joyce's own letters, unpublished verses and notebooks. Sample facts: His middle names are Augustine Aloysius; he used to sign himself Jas. A. Joyce. During his first visit to Paris, when he was 20, he often had no food for 40 hours at a stretch, was speechless with toothache when he did eat. At around 19, under the influence of Ibsen, he wrote a five-act play—lost—which he dedicated to his own soul. (His father, reading that in bed one night, bawled "Holy Paul!") Passing the Arc de Triomphe, Valery Larbaud asked him how long he thought the Eternal Flame would burn. "Until the Unknown Soldier gets up in disgust and blows it out."

Of Joyce's own writing the book contains, among other things: several of his letters to English publisher Grant Richards over *Dubliners*—as shriveling a statement of the artist-publisher situation as has ever seen print; an extraordinarily beautiful letter he wrote to Ibsen when he was 19; two invective poems which suggest Swift's and are quite as good. One of them, addressed to the Dublin Litterateurs he held in such contempt, ends with these proud lines:

So distantly I turn to view
The shamblings of that motley crew,
Those souls that hate the strength that
      mine has
Steeled in the school of old Aquinas.
Where they have crouched and crawled
      and prayed
I stand, the self-doomed, unafraid,
Unfellowed, friendless and alone,
Indifferent as the herring-bone,
Firm as the mountain ridges where
I flash my antlers on the air.
Let them continue as is meet
To adequate the balance-sheet.
Though they may labour to the grave
My spirit shall they never have
Nor make my soul with theirs as one
Till the Mahamanvantara be done,
And though they spur me from their
      door
My soul shall spurn them evermore.

(February 19, 1940)

Lynching Comedy
Trouble in July—Erskine Caldwell—
Duell, Sloan and Pearce ($2.50).

Briefly, *Trouble in July* is the story of how a colored boy named Sonny Clark is hunted down and lynched for a rape he did not commit. More elaborately it is an account of the behavior of Southern whites during such a man hunt. In particular, it is a tragicomic study of the plight of 300-pound Jeff McCurtain, sheriff of Julie County, Georgia.

The political situation is such that Jeff runs a fair chance of losing his job whether he lies low or takes action. Worse still, a Negro named Sam Brinson, of whom Jeff is very fond, has been grabbed out of jail to be a scapegoat if Sonny is not found. Jeff is reasonably sure Sonny is innocent; he knows Sam is. That he will sacrifice Sonny's life to his own political safety is, of course, a mere regretful reflex; at the same time he tries to find Sam at the risk of his job.

The manhunters gawp in her yard while the "raped" girl, dizzy with nympholepsy, shows off her breasts. Most of them know she is a slut, some of them doubt she was ever raped; but this is a nigger hunt. Later they break into Negro cabins, strip a Negro couple, whip the husband, turpentine his wife's belly, rape a mulatto girl. Before they get Sonny they drag Sam behind a car. After they have killed Sonny the girl confesses his innocence. They stone her to death.

Standpat Southerners deny such stories with heat and hatred; non-Southerners know too little to have any right to an opinion. Author Caldwell's taste for close crowding of extremes of cruelty, pity, irony, inconsistency and comedy; his occasional tendency to stack his cards, still further obscure these important facts: that the South is a country of incredible extremes; that for all his faults Caldwell is one of the best and fairest recorders of them.

(March 11, 1940)

Genius-à-la-King
The Hamlet—William Faulkner—
Random House ($2.50).

The locale of *The Hamlet* is Frenchman's Bend, a little clump of houses sunk 20 miles deep in the country from Jefferson (presumably Oxford), Miss. The time is the late 19th Century. What the story's essential subject is, God—and just possibly William Faulkner—knows. Apparently it is a study of the village itself, chiefly in terms of an evil clan of intruders named Snopes. The volume is built in four books, like the four movements of a symphony.

Book One is a sort of muted epic on those tricks of sharp rural trading which become the legendary material of country store gossips. It tells how cold Flem Snopes, a tenant farmer's son, gains complete power over Will Varner, who virtually owns the town. Other Snopeses turn up on the horizon.

Book Two is a piece of natural history in human terms; the story of a queen bee. Eula Varner is a semi-superhuman embodiment of unmitigated sex, already embarrassingly female at the age of eight. As she ripens, the male community establishes itself in quavering, fighting concentrics of courtship: first raw boys, the slick sports in shiny buggies. But it is Flem who finally gets her. He takes her to Texas.

In Book Three the idiot Ike Snopes falls in love with a cow. Mink Snopes murders a widower named Houston. The villagers, to cure the idiot of "stock-diddling," slaughter the cow and require him to eat of her. In a gruesome scene Houston's hound attacks Mink. Mink is caught and jailed.

In Book Four Flem returns from Texas with a string of insanely wild piebald ponies and sells them to his neighbors. They break loose in horrendous slapstick and pervade the countryside. Mink gets a life sentence; Cousin Flem doesn't lift a finger to help him. Two bourgeois and a desperate peasant invest all they have in a plot of land where Civil War treasure is known to be buried. They find Flem has hoodwinked them as he has every-one else. When last seen, Flem is on his way to larger opera-tions in Jefferson.

If that were all there was to the book it would be plenty, though no man could quite judge of what. But for Dionysian William Faulkner the story is, as usual, a mere set of spring-boards and parallel bars for the display of one of the most daz-zling and inchoate talents in contemporary letters. The reader who takes in the show exposes himself to so furious a narcotic cyclone of Poe, Melville, Mark Twain and original Faulkner that the best he can do is to hang on to his hat and wits. As the storm screams past he may discern a number of things, mainly favor-able to the author and to his own pleasure:

Through his people, both normal and daemonic, through his animals, through his fascination in the mysteries of gesture, tones of speech, stature of objects, phases of weather, and through his magical ability to isolate them in words, William Faulkner records the much-investigated South more subtly and truly than any dozen more simple reporters on it.

If an anthology were made of it, this novel would contain perhaps 100 each of almost incredibly beautiful poems, lyric paintings, scenes from motion pictures. Faulkner has learned more from films, and could give them more, than any other writer.

Whatever their disparities, William Faulkner and William Shakespeare share these characteristics: 1) Their abun-dance of invention and their courage for rhetoric are bottomless. 2) Enough goes on in their heads to furnish a whole shoal of more temperate writers. 3) By fair means or foul, both manage to play not for a specialized but for a broad audience.

In passages incandescent with undeniable genius, there is nevertheless not one sentence without its share of amateurish-ness, its stain of inexcusable cheapness.

(April 1, 1940)

Messiahs
The Heart is a Lonely Hunter
—Carson McCullers—Houghton Mifflin ($2.50).
Joy of Man's Desiring
—Jean Giono—Viking ($2.50).
Wartime Letters of Rainer Maria Rilke
—Translated by M. D. Herton Norton—Norton ($2.50).

Published last week were three books which, utterly divergent in most respects, all operated in a common, powerful magnetic field. Each centred in a Messiah.

First Novel. Slightest of the three was *The Heart is a Lonely Hunter*, the talented first novel of 22-year-old Carson McCullers, Georgia girl.

In a deep-southern mill town a half-mad anarchist, a Negro doctor desperate to free his race, a girl who loves music, and a quiet, watchful café owner all come to share a mystical admiration for deaf-mute John Singer. Out of Singer's stunned face and his silence, each of the four constructs an image of absolute understanding, a godlike sounding board for prayerlike confessions. The fact that Singer himself is coolly puzzled by them, is himself even more piteously dependent than they, escapes them. The fact that no one of them can understand the other they scarcely realize. But when they lose John Singer, three of them lose the mainspring of their precarious spirits. Only the restaurant owner remains relatively intact.

The book is such a study in the relationship of human Christs and semi-Christs to a suffering world as Dostoevski made into the most annihilating literature of his century. As a candidate for high honors, however, Mrs. McCullers flunks out flat on a crucial matter. As a writer of words, she is never distinguished, never in one glint verbally original.

Prose Poem. Jean Giono was arrested last September (*Time*, Oct. 23), to prevent his leading a band of his French peasant neighbors in a flat refusal to go to war. (He was released in November.) Last fall the innocent movie version of his innocent novel *Harvest* was shown at a few U. S. theatres. *Joy of Man's Desiring*, published in France in 1935, though in form a novel, is about as intense and unabashed a poem as any prose could be.

A serene wandering acrobat named Bobi settles for a couple of years among the farm people of a lonely plateau in Southern France. All he cares about is joy—in useless beauty, in the
purity of animals. Carried away by his precept and example, the
farmers reduce their planting to what they can eat, turn their animals loose, crowd their fallow land with narcissi, make friends
with a stag and his doe. Having set up his earthly paradise,
Giono regretfully proceeds in his closing chapters to knock it to
pieces. He does so none too logically.

Jean Giono has a genius for observing, and recording, the
splendors of the natural world, the beauty of natural tasks and
pleasures. The book has been given an excellent translation.

Thumbprints. The third Messiah is no fable; he struggles
with fact. Rainer Maria Rilke was one of the most devoted, most
profoundly endowed religious artists whom this century has
produced. As such he was, for his generation, one of the focuses
of human consciousness. Of what happens to a bearer of such
consciousness in time of actual war, this volume of letters is a
direct record.

The effect of war upon the sources of Rilke's poetry was
simple enough; they were so atrophied that they did not recover
full life until 1922. But he kept a virtually blind knowledge that
a past had existed in which that high form of consciousness was
possible; that a future must ultimately emerge in which it might
live again; that during war "one's deepest obligation seemed to
be to give up nothing of what mankind had previously gained
and acknowledged after honest search. . . ."

Sometimes Rilke's letters seem like the handwritings and
idle thoughts of a safe, sickly gentleman, sometimes like definitive statements of truth:

"Why is there not *one* who cannot endure it any more,
will not endure it any more; did he but cry out for one night in
the midst of the untrue, flag-hung city, cry out and not let himself be pacified, who might therefore call him liar?"

"The whole of distress is always in use among men . . .
only the distribution varies."

"Fearful as the war is in itself, it seems to me still more
dreadful that the pressure of it has nowhere contributed to bringing man out more distinctly, to forcing him . . . face to face with
God, as great tribulations in earlier times had the power to do.
On the plane meanwhile cultivated, on which the newspapers
are able to give a conscienceless verbal cross section of all that

happens . . . an incessant equalizing of all tensions is created and humanity becomes accustomed continually to accept a world of news in place of realities which no one has time or is minded any more to let grow large and heavy within them. I never was and *cannot* any longer become a newspaper reader. . . ."

"The intellectual would of course have to be . . . an opponent and disavower of revolutions; he of all people knows how slowly all changes of lasting significance are accomplished, . . . how inconspicuous they are and through their very slowness, almost imperceptible, and how Nature, in her constructive zeal, hardly anywhere lets intellectual forces come to the fore."

The letters of the three years following the war are a record of slow convalescence. In them it becomes clear that the years of silence, and daily absorption in horror, despair and death, contributed incalculably to those continuously illuminated days in 1922 during which Rilke completed the *Duino Elegies*, those poems through which he felt his existence had been justified.

(June 10, 1940)

With Columbus
To the Indies
—C. S. Forester—Little, Brown ($2.50).

Cecil Scott Forester's narrative is so excellent that it cries out loud for the one thing it lacks: a touch of the terse hypnosis that Hemingway manages with words. Aside from this lack, there is nothing to regret about *To the Indies*.

Don Narciso Rich, like Forester's Horatio Hornblower (*Time*, May 1, 1939), is capable of intelligent reflection; but he is not by nature a man of action. He is, rather, a sort of Leopold Bloom light-ballasted for a more adventurous sailing pace: plump, humane, timorous, uneasily involved in thoughts which set him, in the late Middle Ages, on the borderlands of heresy and of the Renaissance. Without quite understanding why, he has committed himself, in the middle of a tabby life, to sail with Columbus on his third voyage, as guardian of the Spanish King's interests in the New World. On the voyage his mind fumbles toward the invention of the sextant, the use of Indian hammocks at sea, of pumps for bilge, copper sheathing against marine borers. He is fascinated—and so is the reader—by every detail of medieval navigation, by Columbus (half inspired zany fur-collared "thespian"), by the cloudy jumble of zombie myth and fetal science which throng Columbus' mind.

On fresh-found Trinidad he sees his first Indians—as touching a set of noble savages as any romantic could wish; and poking along the Orinoco Delta he suspects, by the size of the river, the vast land that bears it. But Columbus is too sure he has found the Earthly Paradise to waste conjecture on a mere South America.

When they get to Española (Haiti) Don Narciso sees what just six years of white rule can do: Christianized Indians who die rather than work and who, through mere imprisonment, die in a few days "like fish in a bucket." Hardly has Don Narciso got his shore legs when he witnesses the burning alive of sixteen heretics; he sees next what happens to 20,000 Indians in spontaneous desperate rebellion. Stark naked, all of them, men, women, and children, they advance in a brown wave, using stones and sharpened sticks, to dissolve into panic before the first volley from the crossbows. Narciso is enough a man of his time to get bloody excitement out of his first kills: when, with four hours' daylight left, his companions begin to slaughter merely for sport, he "followed fascinated." It was easy enough to see what had been incredible: how, in six years, half of these Indians—a million—had been obliterated.

Columbus' brothers, in charge of Española, are by no means trustworthy, his ex-valet Roldan is in open revolt. Columbus himself is arrogantly, piteously aware that there is not a man on earth he can trust. It is Don Narciso's business to report to his King that "the Admiral was not fit to govern a farmyard, let alone an empire." He dislikes his task, but takes comfort in the thought of sailing, on the morrow, for Spain and the quiet life. Kidnapping, hurricane, shipwreck, a Crusoe sequence delay his return. When he finally sails, a more distinguished passenger is Columbus, in chains, with a ham actor's pride in his martyrdom; still hopeful, hot-eyed, still straining after the Golden City of Cambaluc.

C. S. Forester so skillfully constructs the silences of unbruised continents, the dreadfulness of events, that he inevitably challenges the memory of Archibald MacLeish's *Conquistador*. His story has the pity of that poem, some of its beauty and power.

(July 29, 1940)

Liebestod
Love in the Western World
—Denis de Rougemont—Harcourt, Brace ($3).

Swiss Philosopher de Rougemont's ambitious thesis is that Europe and the Western Hemisphere owe their desperate plight to their over-susceptibility to passionate love. Ancient Greeks and Romans, says he, regarded love as a mental aberration, an unqualified misfortune; Orientals so regard it today. Only in the Western world has it taken a hold in the mores, been accorded respect. Taking Tristan and Iseult as the archetypes of passion, he hangs on their necks more weight than Freud ever hung on Oedipus.

Immediate ancestors of the Tristan myth were the troubadours of Provence. They were Albigensians, heretics, and their songs, their protocols of courtly love, were simply the elaborate double-talk of a theology driven underground. With them, in the 12th Century, passion took root in Europe. Thence sprang the whole of European literture, the whole shape and vocabulary of European mysticism, the whole ferocious timbre of European warfare, the whole possibility of such megalomaniacs as Hitler, the whole suffering wreckage of European love and marriage. De Rougemont believes there is an almost universal schizophrenia, a tide rip created in millions of individuals between two hopelessly incompatible systems: the socially responsible, Christian type of love ingrained by Family, Church and State; and the anarchic, unappeasable passion which is literature's (and the cinema's) degraded heritage from the troubadours. An unattainable "happiness" has replaced an unattainable divinity. Under such circumstances it is inconceivable that any human marriage can survive.

Thus having spoken, De Rougemont flogs the daylights out of contemporary conceptions of marriage, of happiness, of romantic love. In a last chapter whose eloquence becomes all but desperate, he expounds his personal solution: a marriage in which fidelity is observed neither for love, money nor hope of inner reward but "by virtue of the absurd," that is, by virtue alone of having taken oath to it. Right or raving, De Rougemont's reasoning is often ingenious, always arresting, fascinating in detail.

Edible Slice-of-Life
In the Money
—William Carlos Williams—New Directions ($2.50).

Ever since Zola, writers have tried to commit to paper the daily living of average families. "Naturalism" had a notion that an account of how such a family struggles through its oatmeal, breeds another generation to do likewise, could present all human life fearlessly and whole. The result of this literary theory has been some good amateur anthropology, a titanic amount of dullness, little art.

Part of that little is the work of William Carlos Williams. A Rutherford, N. J. baby specialist and poet, Williams in his best verse gives the simple objects of existence the glistening integrity of pebbles in a quick stream. In *White Mule*, three years ago, he trained his poet-doctor's eye on the ordinary living of a U. S. middle-class family, set down their record in noiseless, antiseptic prose. *In the Money* is a continuation of *White Mule*. It is also a broad advance on the naturalist front.

The materials of *In the Money* are so simple that, judged even by the flattest traditions of Naturalism, they scarcely exist. Joe Stecher is a German-American, his wife Gurlie is Norwegian, his daughters are Lottie, 5, and Flossie, 2. They live in Manhattan, on 104th Street, and the year is 1901. Joe has quit his job (he is a printer) and is trying against stiff, not to say dirty, opposition to set up in business for himself. He lacks the proper piratical zest; Gurlie is hell-bent to get him—and herself—In the Money. In the long run he succeeds, they get a house in the suburbs. Meanwhile Gurlie has snubbed her neighbors and fought bitterly with her mother; Joe has had a personal interview with President Theodore Roosevelt and has not been impressed; Flossie, her parents blandly unaware of it, has acquired the neurosis which will give her whole life shape; the children have been vaccinated and have visited aunts in Vermont; and Gurlie, at the end, is beginning to show a sourness toward Joe which suggests unhappy events for a few volumes to come.

It could be, as such things always have been, as dull as dipsomania. But *In the Money* is as fully fleshed, as complex, and as curiously beautiful as daily life. So Williams lifts his material clear of the stodgy fog banks of Naturalism. To this central ability he brings an impressive set of spare tools. Joyce himself has scarcely greater precision with dialogue, and only Richard Hughes has written so well of the behavior of children. Without one line of comment, Williams makes clear "social significances" which the authors of *Middle-town* can only bumble over. With scarcely a skid into deliberate lyricism, whole chapters become lyric. Dickens without gush, Dreiser without fat, Lardner without cynicism, might combine to approximate it. On his subtle, flexible, non-literary monotone, Dr. Williams seems to carry, without gasp or gesture, the whole load of daily living in the U. S.

Abstract Prose
Ida
—Gertrude Stein—Random House ($2).

Most readers require of prose that it make concrete sense as they think sense should be made. So Gertrude Stein, who uses prose to build a series of abstractions, either infuriates most readers or elicits defensive jeers. But readers who are willing to read words as they are willing to listen to notes in music—as things without an explicit message—can get from her work a rare pleasure. The three stories in her earliest (1909) book, *Three Lives*, being anchored to sense, are good ones to start on. Her latest book, *Ida*, much more abstract, is a good one to go on with.

The heroine of *Ida* is purportedly modeled on the Duchess of Windsor. That fact need trouble no one, short of a tenth reading or so. Ida is a woman who likes to rest, to talk to herself, to move around. In the course of her lifetime she has several dogs, marries several men (mostly Army Officers), lives in several of the 48 States. She seems at times to be some sort of dim, potent symbol or half-goddess, sometimes a plain case of schizophrenia, sometimes a stooge for Miss Stein. In the long run, after several icily beautiful pages of suspense, she appears to settle down with a man named Andrew.

How much or how little sense *Ida* makes as a story is not important. The words in which it is told are stripped of normal logic, and totally cleansed of emotion. The result is something as intricately clean as a fugue or a quadratic equation.

For those who wish to make the effort, the following suggestions:

> Read it with care, but require no sense of it that it does not yield.
> Read it aloud.
> Read it as poetry must be read or music listened to: several times.
> Read it for pleasure only. If it displeases you, quit.

Gertrude Stein says of Ida: "Ida decided that she was just going to talk to herself. Anybody could stand around and listen but as for her she was just going to talk to herself."

(February 17, 1941)

A Mirror for England
Between the Acts
—Virginia Woolf—Harcourt, Brace ($2.50).

The late great Virginia Woolf's last book is not one of her major works; it is almost a "light" novel. But it compares with the run of light novels as a Mozart opera compares with one by Sig Romberg. It is also the most nearly public of her exquisitely private books. Its subject is no individual, but the whole of England.

On the lawn of a country house, on a summer afternnoon in 1939, a group of upper-class English people watch a village pageant and retire with its ambiguous messages fading on "the sky of the mind." By this time the afternoon is over. Mrs. Woolf has conjured up a heroic image of the whole splendor of English literature and history, from the age when rhododendrons crowded Piccadily to the moment when, puzzled, uneasy, a little offended, the audience beholds itself torn to pieces among the flashing mirrors of the village players in their finale, called *England: Ourselves.*

These spectators are a sultry, mercifully drawn set: a restive wife, her sullen husband; his aged, beak-nosed, naive father, dreaming of youth in India; his delicate old Aunt, cherishing a crucifix between her bony hands; an assortment of eligible neighbors. The pageant they have come to see is a half-talented, half-parodied hodge-podge which in actual performance would have been sad, silly, and typically British, but which, in Mrs. Woolf's hair-line contexts, is moving too.

While Queen Bess and other principals hold the forestage, for instance, village supers clad in sackcloth creep among the trees, unable to make themselves heard through the wind as they chant: "*Digging and delving, hedging and ditching, we pass . . . Summer and winter, autumn and spring return . . . All passes but we, all changes . . . but we remain forever the same. . . .*" They remind you of Evelyn Waugh; yet in Mrs. Woolf's many-planned perspective they are also in truth the nameless human swarm.

Nature and machines are other characters in the larger drama. A wedge of planes blasts to bits the Rector's fuddling interpretation of the show; and butterflies are deluded by bright costumes on the grass: "Red Admirals gluttonously absorbed richness from dish cloths, cabbage whites drank icy coolness from silver paper."

After the show, the two elders of the household, dreaming of the glories of a vanished England move up to bed, to death. The younger couple, a sorrowful, sadly mismated Adam and Eve, are left alone to their marriage and to silence, sailing like disconsolate swans on the exhausted calm of a summer evening, and on the edge of one of the steepest chasms in history.

"Alone enmity was bared; also love. Before they slept, they must fight; after they had fought, they would embrace. From that embrace another life might be born. But first they must fight, as the dog fox fights with the vixen, in the heart of darkness in the fields of night."

Virginia Woolf was the unlikeliest artist on earth to stoop to propaganda, or to any form of public ingratiation. She did not do so here. Yet England and its people, its present, past, innocence and disease, are here summarized in much the way a night wind can summarize a continent.

(October 13, 1941)

Guidebook for a Labyrinth
James Joyce—Harry Levin—New Directions ($1.50).

The review of *Finnegans Wake* by Harvard's Harry Levin was one of the few that gave James Joyce the sense that his book had a reader. Mr. Levin's volume on Joyce is designed to be read along with Joyce's works. On Joyce's powers of characterization, on his Swiftian moral grandeur, and on that almost Shakespearean humaneness which alone could delight the plainest of readers, he is obtuse as only a hyper-intellectual can be. But on those intricate obscurities which put off most plain readers, and on Joyce as a technician and theorist, he has written the best guidebook and the most brilliant criticism to date.

Of all modern artists, Joyce was the most bitterly uncompromising, the most tortuously responsible to his vocation; as a result, he was "the most self-centered of universal minds." His obsessive subjects, the city and the artist, bracketed the whole conflicted matter and spirit of modern civilization. *A Portrait of the Artist* is self-centered, naturalistic; and Levin tells a tantalizing little of its earlier 1,000-page version, which was far more so. The multitudinous date of *Ulysses* vibrated like cold made-lightening between the cathodes of the most fluoroscopic symbolism and the most granitic naturalism. In *Finnegans Wake* naturalism and the artist himself all but disappear; the book is a shimmering death-dance of chameleon-like symbols; an attempt at nothing less than a complete serio-comic history of human consciousness—in Levin's neat phrase, a "doomsday book," culminating in a Phoenician paradox of dissolution and resurrection.

Though history was, to Joyce, "a nightmare from which I am trying to awake," he made some frightening images of the history of his time. *Finnegans Wake* derives much from the philosopher Giambattista Vico's cyclic theory of history, which is highly apposite to the present. According to Vico, and Joyce, the first of a civilization's four phrases begins, and the last, collapses, in fear of thunder, and a rush for underground shelter; and in that sheltering cave, religion and family life begin again. Today the ambiguous thunder talks above every great city of the earth and the shelters are crowded, and a civilization, if it is ending, is no less surely germinal. In one great warning work of literature after another, meanwhile, a similar mental cavern is retreated to and explored (Joyce's was a Dedalean Labyrinth). Levin quotes St. John's "Except a grain of wheat fall into the earth and die, it abideth by itself alone, but if it die, it beareth much fruit." That, says he, is "the burden of the manifold texts of *Finnegans Wake*," and of Dostoevski, Tolstoy, Ibsen, Zola, Gide, Eliot, Mann.

(January 19, 1942)

Dark-Ride Through Dawn
Go Down, Moses
—William Faulkner—Random House ($2.50).

Reading the new Faulkner is like taking what carnival people call a "dark-ride": one of those slow Tunnels of Love which alternate blank darkness with suddenly illuminated views of dancing skeletons or Swiss lakes. *Go Down, Moses* is a dark-ride well worth taking. Stretches of it are blank enough; but some of the views beat those of any other U. S. writer.

The book is made up of seven stories. They are about the same set of people: Mississippi planters and Negroes and their descendants; and have a common theme: the land. A linked theme is that of blood and its heritage. Negro-white miscegenation pads through the pages like a housecat, and the presence of Indians makes a sort of bottomless pit into the past. Sub-themes, which have more interest for Faulkner than for his readers, are money (one 100-page story centers on his old theme of buried treasure) and what he calls the "curse" which is laid on the South.

Poetically rather than rationally, Faulkner manages to bulldoze the reader into believing that the South is indeed accursed, but he is never very clear why or how. On mixups of money and genealogy he constructs passages as intricate but not as rewarding as a five-voiced fugue. On the pre-cotton Southern wilderness he is superb. Nearest thing to a central character is old Ike McCaslin, who has retained, throughout his life, the born huntsman's anarchic feeling for the wilderness.

In *The Old People*, Ike, at twelve, kills his first buck and is initiated into manhood: the "son of a Negro slave and a Chickasaw chief" steeps his hands in the deathblood and marks his face.

In *The Bear*, the wilderness is epitomized in Old Ben, an almost immortal bear; Ike, now 16, is in at his death, at the death of the dog who was fierce enough to hold him, at the death and primeval funeral of Ike's Indian mentor. Not many years later Ike sees the beginning of the wilderness' end. The forest is sold to a Memphis lumber company, and Faulkner's description of the sinister little locomotive prodding in the wilderness is one of the best passages he has written.

In *Delta Autumn*, Ike, in his late 70s. comes again, perhaps for the last time, 200 miles from Jefferson down through the slowly peeling palimpsest of civilization and of his memory to what little is left of true wilderness, cramped in the deep inverted apex of the Delta.

Faulkner knows his own country as few men do. His details of farming, hunting and folkways are as tangible as rusty nails and as tough as legal writ. There are magnificent flashes of a dirt lane which runs "pale and dim beneath the moonless sky of corn-planting time"; of a godforsaken Arkansas farmhouse in which an ex-slave sits in a frock coat, reading through lensless spectacles; of a blow across the "hard hollow-sounding face" of a mule; of a rattlesnake's "thin sick smell of rotting cucumbers"; of some moving, semi-literate pages from an old plantation ledger:

"Percavil Brawnly 26 yr. Old. cleark @ Bookepper. bought from N. B. Forest at Cold Water 3 Mar 1856 $265. dolars

"and beneath that, in the same hand:

"5 mar 1856 No bookeeper any way Cant read. can write his Name but I already put that down My self Says he can Plough but dont look like it to Me. sent to Feild to day Mar 5 1856"

Faulkner is perhaps the most gifted of living U. S. writers. He can be as funny as Mark Twain, as exalted as Melville, as solid as Joyce and as dull as Dreiser; but he has never done a book which has the sure, sound permanence of any of these men. *Go Down, Moses*, like most of Faulkner, is brilliant and uneven. Its special value is its evocative (though local) exploration of the U. S. national source and dawn. In it is a sometimes merely yeasty, sometimes 100-proof sense of those powers and mysteries of land and the people on it which make a nation.

(May 11, 1942)

Inquest on Democracy
Walt Whitman. Poet of Democracy
—Hugh l'Anson Fausset—Yale ($3).

This compact, brilliant critical biography is 1) an excellent life of Walt Whitman, 2) a just, if merciless, evaluation of him as poet, mystic and prophet of democracy, 3) an arduous, provocative sermon on the nature and responsibility of democracy and of art. Unlike most Whitman critics, Author Fausset avoids the extremes of most books about Whitman. He neither damns nor admires Whitman for being a homosexual. He does not claim that Whitman's poetry is as great as Homer's or merely a free verse Sears, Roebuck catalogue. He simply tries to explain what Whitman achieved in poetry and mysticism, what he failed to achieve—and why.

Critic Fausset's thesis is simple: if Whitman was a great poet, it was his business to fulfill the responsibilities of one. If he was the evangelist of democracy, it was his business to write a true, not a heretical, gospel. In Fausset's opinion, Whitman never quite succeeded in being either poet or evangelist. He wrote some great poetry and some amazingly energetic verse. But on the whole, he shrank even from such responsibilities as he was equipped to recognize. He perceived a great number of democratic half-truths. He lacked the intellectual equipment or spiritual stamina to make the half-truth whole. Reason: Whitman, the man, was never really whole.

Bisexual. All human beings, Critic Fausset observes, are to some extent bisexual. But Whitman had a great deal more of the woman in him than men normally have. This schism in his nature, Fausset believes, was in part the source of such greatness as he had. It was also the chief source of his failures. Whitman's femininity gave him his tremendous powers for the passive absorption of experience, for sympathy, for the almost bottomless endurance (as in the Civil War hospitals) of massive suffering. But it also accounts for the sentimentality, effusive-

ness, extreme over-assertiveness, pseudo-masculinity and egoism of many of his poems.

Because he feared and never quite understood himself,
because, in all probability, he never felt normal sexual desire in
his life, his hunger for the easy comradeship of simple men developed. "More intent on excluding none than on wholly finding one," it was inevitable that he should remain innocent to
the end of his days of psychology, character, the true nature of
individualism, personality, tragedy, evil—all of which considerably complicate the problems of the poet and of the democratic
theorist.

Womblike. Due to the same schism, Whitman never really understood the essential duties of an artist. Real harmony
of form is "created from within." It demands "an act of unified
being in the artist himself"; the more he enters "into the depths
of his own soul, the deeper he [enters] into the meaning of
things." And "there [is] no other way of achieving creative insight in place of an external and generalized view." Whitman
achieved such insight and such harmony only rarely; notably,
Fausset points out, in a sense of death as womblike as his frame
of mysticism or the childlike attachment to his mother, which
he never broke. Much of the time he substituted, for truly dis-
tilled perception, declamations, loud affirmations, a catalogue of
beloved objects, and worked in a vocabulary too superficial and
meager, and in a formal pattern too loose, to produce anything
that can be called true poetry.

His bisexualism also involved Whitman in other difficulties. One can be as hopelessly tethered to flesh by Whitman's
sort of "false relish," Fausset observes, as by the Puritanism
which he was over-reacting against. The errors and half-truths
of Whitman's gospel in general are brought out most clearly,
Fausset believes, in the celebration of sex, *Children of Adam and
Calamus*. Whitman "affirmed far too easily the identity of body
and spirit . . . and this evasion resulted in an almost complete
sacrifice of the distinctively human values to biological forces."

In these poems, Fausset shrewdly remarks, "the faces of
men and women in love, the eyes of their intelligence, hardly
ever meet." He also finds symptoms of frustrated sexual impulse in Whitman's spurious "primitiveness": "A primitive
man may think *in* his bodily organs. But he would be the last to
think *about* them or to display or exploit them consciously." In
short, "to attempt [as Whitman did] to resolve the conflict of

self-consciousness and sex by merely sinking to the biological level . . . was to abandon the hope of human integrity without recovering an animal innocence."

War. By 1860 Whitman's work as the poet-propagandist of democracy (*Song of Myself, Song of the Open Road, Children of Adam*) was almost finished. Democracy's crisis, the Civil War, was to provide him with the source of his greatest poetry and the great central act of his life. Being a simple man, he liked the glamor of war, liked still more its courage and comradeship. He wrote half-Hitlerish lines on the glories of immolation en masse. He also wrote the maturest poems of his life, possibly the finest that have ever been written about war. And in the hospitals of Washington he lived his gospel of brotherhood more eloquently, truly and bravely than he had ever managed to write about it.

The rest of his life was decline. Like any old soldier, Whitman faced, and faced nobly, a different gambit of heroism: the slow endurance of anti-climax—failing poetic powers, the wrenching death of his mother (for which, at 54, he was as emotionally unprepared as a child), the paralysis which he endured for 20 years of his remaining 27.

Those years were not uniformly dreary. They were warmed by the half-filial, half-erotic friendship of many young men, notably the young Irish streetcar conductor, Peter Doyle. They were cheered by the startling letters of Mrs. Anne Gilchrist. She had read the *Leaves* and wrote their author: "Nothing in life or death can tear out of my heart the passionate belief that one day I shall hear that voice say to me, 'My mate. The one I so much want. Bride, wife, indissoluble, eternal' . . . O come, come, my darling, look into these eyes and see the long ardent aspiring soul in them."

Orbic. Whitman was still active. He went West, like the nation, and saw the Rockies. Their grandeur reminded him of his own poetry. But he was aging. He began to say he had never read Emerson before he wrote *Leaves of Grass* (he had), to be a little cagey about money, to blossom a little senilely at his few remaining birthday parties to welcome the less fantastic of his admirers. They were not the common workmen he had written for, but those poets and cultivated hangers-on who are the fate of poets in general. He kept adding to *Leaves of Grass*. It had become "a habit." He wrote *Democratic Vistas*, a book of prose more perceptive of the weak spots in U. S. democracy than anything Whitman had written before. He had outlived his pre-Civil War hopefulness, but he was still capable only of vague "orbic" statements about the leadership of "the divine literatus," and preached once again "his old back-to-nature illusion." He still professed his uncritical confidence in the deep instinctive virtues of "the People." Author Fausset believes that this confidence is part of Whitman's pathetic fallacy.

Like his masses, Whitman lacked the self-mastery, the intelligence and the creative idea whereby true democracy becomes possible. He glimpsed "the necessity of bringing the moral sense into a new relation with intelligence," but he could "only link them loosely and hopefully together." He vaguely foresaw "the basic problem of democracy, that of reintegrating the individual in a social whole and converting a semi-conscious mass into a community of responsible persons," but "he overlooked the cost of integration, as he had overlooked it in himself." And "his lack of insight into the nature of imagination and the spiritual cost of creating great literature was paralleled by his ignorance of the nature and cost of the 'soul-consciousness,' whose development he insisted, rightly enough, it should be the one purpose of all government in a democracy to encourage."

(June 15, 1942)

Baying at The Moon

John Steinbeck's *The Moon is Down* (*Time*, March 9) has stirred up (as book and play) the year's liveliest literary fight. By now the battle has become a general war, involving book reviewers, theater critics, editors, people who write letters to the newspapers, diplomats, college professors and Dorothy Thompson. Two great questions are at issue: 1) Does Steinbeck put too much faith in the moral superiority of democracy? 2) Is Steinbeck wrong in portraying German soldiers as human beings?

It has even been suggested that *The Moon* is veiled Nazi propaganda. In Manhattan the Belgian Commissioner of Information objected to Colonel Lanser, one of Steinbeck's Germans who recalls how, in World War I, an old Belgian woman killed twelve Germans with a long black hatpin. Said the Commissioner: "Mr. Steinbeck . . . does a disservice to the Belgian reputation for dignity and fair play."

Prominent among those who think that the Steinbeck moon is made of green cheese are:

New Yorker Critic Clifton Fadiman ("It seduces us to rest on the oars of our own moral superiority").

Humorist James Thurber ("This little book needs more guts and less moon. . . . If these are German officers . . . I will eat the manuscript of your next play . . .").

The pinko *New Republic* ("Don't think that Mr. Steinbeck's Nazis are the people who actually invaded Norway. If they were, the free nations wouldn't need planes tanks and gasoline rationing to defeat them. The job could be done effectively with dynamite and bonbons").

Warmest defenders of *The Moon* are Novelist Pearl Buck, Drama Critic Brooks Atkinson, Dorothy Thompson, Book Reviewer Louis Gannett. Gannett called the "totalitarian crusade" against the story "a depressing example of wartime hysteria."

Said Dorothy Thompson: "I know dozens of German officers who were thoroughly mature when last I enjoyed friendly
relations with them, and they were just like [Colonel Lanser], . . .
The enormous power in Mr. Steinbeck's drama is that it is *not*
an attack on *Nazis*. It is an attack on *Naziism*."

Meanwhile *The Moon is Down* is doing quite nicely. As a
novel, it has sold 450,000 copies. As a play, it has entertained
when it closed last fortnight, some 56,000 theatergoers. Producer
Darryl Zanuck, who paid $300,000 for the film rights, is rushing
production of the movie version.

(June 22, 1942)

"It is Written"
The Dream Department
—S. J. Perelman—Random House ($2).

S. J. Perelman picks up business where he left off with *Look Who's Talking* (*Time*, Aug. 12, 1940). One passage should suffice to give traffic signals to such readers as remain unfamiliar with Perelman's work. The passage was inspired by a notice to the effect that moving pictures would be used for department-store advertising. The title is *Kitchenware, Notions, Lights, Action, Camera!*

Scene: *The music room in the palatial villa of Mrs. Lafcadio Mifflin at Newport. Mrs. Mifflin, a majestic woman in a slimpin Bemberg corselet well boned over the diaphram (Stern Brothers, fourth floor), is seated at the console of her Wurlitzer, softly wurlitzing to herself. Mr. Mifflin, in a porous-knit union suit from Franklin Simon's street floor, is stretched out by the fire like a great, tawny cat. Inasmuch as there is a great, tawny cat stretched out alongside him, also wearing a porous-knit union suit, it is not immediately apparent which is Mifflin.*

There are many other pieces under such titles as *Beat Me, Post-Impressionist Daddy, Caution—Soft Prose Ahead, P-s-s-t, Partner, Your Perstalsis is Showing.* They handle, with the expertness required for delivering a two-headed baby, the aching half-lunacies which turn up as a normal part of U. S. life. They use one of the rangiest and most microscopically exact vocabularies in modern letters—a vocabulary drawn entirely from those ancient current and emergent clichés of which Flaubert and Joyce were both collectors and which are as diagnostic of a civilization as any ten themes on the *Zeitgeist*, and a thousand times as entertaining.

They are, as Perelman's pieces have been for some years, overformularized: yet even at their most manufactured they have a surface and a perfection of rhythm which little contemporary prose can touch. At their best, they stand with the best of

Ludwig Bemelmans and of James Thurber as a shocking commentary on most of the nominally more solid and earnest books being written in English.

The Author is less well known than his work. Said he last week:

"Button-cute, rapier-keen, wafer-thin, and pauper-poor is S. J. Perelman, whose tall, stooping figure is better known to the twilit half-world of five continents than to Publisher's Row. That he possess the power to become invisible to finance companies; that his laboratory is tooled up to manufacture Frankenstein-type monsters on an incredible scale; and that he owns one of the rare mouths in which butter has never melted are legends treasured by every schoolboy.

"Perelman's life reads like a picaresque novel. It began on a bleak shelf of rock in mid-Atlantic near Tristan da Cunha. Transplanted to Rhode Island by a passing Portuguese, he became a man of proverbial strength around the Providence wharves; he could drive a spike through an oak plank with his fist. As there was constant need for this type of skilled labor, he soon acquired enough tuition to enter Brown University. He is chiefly remembered there for translating the epigrams of Martial into colloquial Ambaric and designing Brooks Bros.' present trademark, a sheep suspended in a diaper.

"Perelman like many another fledgling writer headed posthaste for Montparnasse. A redoubtable tosspot and coxcomb, he was celebrated throughout the Quarter for drinking Modigliani under the table; his fondness for this potent Italian aperitif still remains unabated. In 1925, disguised as Ashton-Wolfe of the Surete, he took to frequenting the *milieu*, the sinister district centering about the rue de Lappe. As 'Papa' Thernardier, he organized the gang that stole a towel from the Hotel Claridge and defaced the blotters at the American Express Co. A *demarche* from the Quai d'Orsay shortly forced him to flee Paris.

"When, in 1928, the meteoric career of Joe Strong, the Boy Plunger, ended abruptly with the latter's disappearance from Wall Street, few knew that Perelman had ended another chapter. In bloody Cicero, Illinois, swart Sicilian mobsters fingered their roscoes uneasily, dismayed at lightning forays by a new rival. In a scant eight months, no shell of needled beer touched lip in Chicago County without previous tribute to 'Nails' Perelman. Implacable, deadly as a puff adder, the hand that triggered a steely automatic could caress a first Folio with equal relish. Able to snatch in fifteen minutes the rest most men required a night for, Perelman spent the balance dictating novels (*Jo Bracegirdle's Ordeal, the Splendid Sinners*), essays (*Winnowings, The Anatomy of Gluttony, Turns with a Stomach*), plays (*Are You There, Wimperis?, Musclebound, Philippa Steps Out*), and scenarios (*She married her Double, He Married Himself*).

"Retired today to peaceful Erwinna, Pa. Perelman raises turkeys which he occasionally displays on Broadway, stirs little from his alembics and retorts. Those who know hint that the light burning late in his laboratory may result in a breathtaking electric bill. Queried, he shrugs with the fatalism of your true Oriental. '*Mektoub*,' he observes curtly, 'It is written.'"

(February 1, 1943)

At the Still Point
Four Quartets
—T. S. Eliot—Harcourt Brace ($2).
(This review written in collaboration with Harvey Breit.)

In a little short of 900 lines, these subtle, magnificent religious poems contain more beauty and sense than any book
within recent memory. They are capable of charming, and teaching many thousands among the great general reading audience.

T. S. Eliot has never been an artist likely to please the bulk
of that great audience. Simply as a rather solemn American-
turned-Englishman, he is personally unsympathetic to many.
His work lacks commonness in the good sense of that word as
well as the bad. It requires a patience of ear and of intellect
which many readers lack; patience not merely in one reading but
in many. For a long time, too, it was easy to misjudge Eliot,
thanks to certain of his admirers, as the mere precious laureate
of a Harvardian coterie. But that time, fortunately, is well past.
So levelheaded a man as Somerset Maugham has recently (in
his *Introduction to Modern English and American Literature*—
anthology; *Time*, May 24) done both poetry and plain readers a
notable service by introducing Eliot to a large audience, without
talking down and without so much as mentioning his "obscu-
rity," as "the greatest poet of our time."

Eliot is, to be sure, not a poet in the grand antique sense of
spontaneous and unprecedented song. But as a devoted artificer
of words and as a distiller of experience, he has always been a
poet, and a particularly fine one. Unlike many greater and lesser
poets, moreover, he has constantly grown and changed. In his
youth he was most notably a satirist; then a mosaic artist of
exquisite sensibility, a man who used the perfect expression of
past artists as frankly as he used his own to arrange, fragment by
fragment, edge by edge, an image of the desolation of his time
(*The Waste Land*).

In 1928, with considerable hauteur, Eliot professed himself
an Anglo-Catholic, a royalist and a classicist, and the chaplet of

lyrics (*Ash Wednesday*) which celebrated his conversion remains the most richly beautiful of his poems. In the '30s, taking hints in diction from his brilliant junior W. H. Auden, he wrote the poetic dramas *Murder in the Cathedral* and *Family Reunion*. Now, at an age (54) when the talent of many good poets is dead and buried, he publishes the harvest of his last seven years, these four "quartets." Of all his poems they are the most stripped, the least obviously allusive,* the least ingratiating in image and in diction, the most direct. They are set in a matrix of subtly intensified, conversational style. To many readers they will look, and remain, flat and forbidding. But those who will give them the care they require will find here, the finest work of a distinguished lifetime.

Beethoven and Eliot. Readers familiar with the great "last quartets" of Beethoven will suspect that Eliot derived from them his title, much of his form, elements of his tone and content. They will almost certainly be right, for no other works in chamber music fit the parallel. Both Beethoven and Eliot are working with the most difficult and quintessential of all materials for art; the substance of mystical experience. Both in the effort to translate it into art, have strained traditional forms and created new ones. Both use motif, refrain, counterpoint, contrasts both violent and subtle, the normal coinage of both arts, for purposes more profound and more intense than their normal coinage, for purposes more profound and more intense than their normal transactions.

Beethoven was a man of colossal genius, originality and definitiveness; Eliot is not. That might make all the difference in the world; it makes a good deal less than might be supposed. For Eliot, if he lacks major genius, is nevertheless a man of fine intellect, of profound spiritual intelligence, and of poetic talents which, if "minor," are nevertheless unmatched in his generation. And his subject is of a dignity which, if approached with these abilities, makes excellent poetry unavoidable and great poetry possible.

---

*E.g. In one quartet, *East Coker*, there are disguised quotes from the 16th-Century Sir Thomas Elyot and from St. John of the Cross; but each is linked by appropriate transitions with what goes before and after, so that readers unacquainted with these not-widely-read authors will not be conscious of missing anything.

There is poetry of both kinds in *Four Quartets.*

"Time Past and Time Future." The heart of Eliot's meditations is Time. Not time as that hypnosis of clocks and of history which holds all human existence captive—though this sort of time gets his attention too—but time as the mystic apprehends it, "at the still point of the turning world." Time beats in these poems like the seabell which, in one of them,

> *Measures time not our time, rung by*
> > *the unhurried*
> *Ground swell, a time*
> *Older than the time of chronometers. . . .*

The first quartet opens with a quiet statement which could as easily have been J. W. Dunne's in his *An Experiment with Time,* as a religious poet's:

> *Time present and time past*
> *Are both perhaps present in time future,*
> *And time future contained in time past.*
> *If all time is eternally present*
> *All time is unredeemable.*
> *What might have been is an abstraction*
> *Remaining a perpetual possibility*
> *Only in the world of speculation.*

But the religious implications of that statement are clear:

> *Men's curiosity searches past and future*
> *And clings to that dimension. But to*
> > *apprehend*
> *The point of intersection of the timeless*
> *With time, is an occupation for the saint—*
> *No occupation either, but something*
> > *given*
> *And taken, in a lifetime's death in love.*
> *Ardor and Selflessness and self-surrender.*

For those of us who are not saints ("human kind cannot bear very much reality")

> *. . . there is only the unattended*
> *Moment, the moment in and out of time.*
> *The distraction fit, lost in a shaft of*
> > *sunlight*
> *The wild thyme unseen, or the winter*
> > *lightning*
> *Or the waterfall, or music heard so deeply*

That it is not heard at all, but you are
    the music
While the music lasts.   These are only
    hints and guesses,
Hints followed by guesses; and the rest
Is prayer, observance, discipline, thought
    and action.
The hint half guessed, half understood
    is Incarnation.
Here the impossible union
Of spheres of existence is actual . . .
And here all opposites are canceled, become one:
The dance along the artery
The circulation of the lymph
Are figured in the drift of stars
Ascend to summer in the tree
We move above the moving tree
In light upon the figured leaf
And hear upon the sodden floor
Below, the boarhound and the boar
Pursue their pattern as before
But reconciled among the stars.
For we are here
At the still point of the turning world.
    Neither flesh nor fleshless;
Neither from nor towards; at the still
    point, there the dance is,
But neither arrest or movement.   And
    do not call it fixity,
Where past and future are gathered.
    Neither movement from nor towards,
Neither ascent nor decline.   Except for
    the point, the still point!
There would be no dance, and there is
    only the dance.
I can only say, there we have been
    but I cannot say where.
And I cannot say, how long, for that is
    to place it in time.

Time Conquers Time.   There is an opposite pole to this stillness.   It may be discerned behind "the strained time-ridden faces, distracted from distraction by distraction," of any great city, any "place of disaffection":

> *Descend lower, descend only*
> *Into the world of perpetual solitude,*
> *World not world, but that which is not*
>   *world,*
> *Internal darkness, deprivation*
> *And destitution of all property,*
> *Desiccation of the world of sense,*
> *Evacuation of the world of fancy,*
> *Inoperancy of the world of spirit.*

a darkening of the soul whose opposite and whose one cure is "the darkness of God":

> *I said to my soul, be still, and wait*
>   *without hope*
> *For hope would be hope for the wrong*
>   *thing; wait without love*
> *For love would be love of the wrong*
>   *thing; there is yet faith*
> *But the faith and the love and the hope*
>   *are all in the waiting.*
> *Wait without thought, for you are not*
>   *ready for thought:*
> *So the darkness shall be the light, and*
>   *the stillness the dancing.*

Time, moreover, is our savior as well as our destroyer. It is the air we must breathe, the lens through which we perceive timelessness, through which we become conscious:

> *Time past and time future*
> *Allow but a little consciousness.*
> *To be conscious is not to be in time*
> *But only in time can the moment in the*
>   *rose-garden . . .*

[The moments of mystical illumination]

> *Be remembered, involved with past and*
>   *future.*
> *Only through time time is conquered.*

Theme and Variations. Upon this theme in poetry rich in paradox and reward in mystery, in symbol, in despair and ultimately, in hope, Eliot develops his great variations. The sere, cryptic titles of the four quartets are the names of places intimately associated with his experience. *Burnt Norton* was a Gloucestershire manor near which he lived for a while. *East*

Coker is a Somerset village which was the home of his ancestors. *The Dry Salvages* (accented like *assuages*) is a group of rocks off Cape Ann, Mass. *Little Gidding* was a 17th-Century religious community established by Nicholas Ferrar. Each of the poems has not only its earthly-mystical locals but its season of the year and its Aristotelian element as well—which is not in every case clear. Of the first, the season seems to be spring, and the element air. Of the second: summer and earth. Of the third: fall and winter. Of the fourth: "Winter spring" and fire.

Throughout the poems, in constant undertone and, more often than not, by indirection. Eliot writes of the time-bound society he lives in, and of the war:

> *The dove descending breaks the air*
> *With flame of incandescent terror*
> *Of which the tongues declare*
> *The one discharge from sin and error.*
> *The only hope, or else despair*
> *Lies in the choice of pyre or pyre—*
> *To be redeemed from fire by fire.*

The dove may be either Spitfire or Messerschmitt, or the Holy Ghost, or both. The redemption from fire by fire may be either the crucial moral dilemma of war—kill or be killed—or the redemption from hell-fire through heaven-sent fire, or both. That the fire is heaven-sent, literally as well as through the mere figurative agents, doves and bombers, Eliot has not doubt. For the lyric continues:

> *Who then devised the torment?   Love.*
> *Love is the unfamiliar Name*
> *Behind the hands that wove*
> *The intolerable shirt of flame*
> *Which human power cannot remove.*
> *We only live, only suspire*
> *Consumed by either fire or fire.*

(June 7, 1943)

Against Intolerance
History of Bigotry in the United States
—Gustavus Myers—Random House ($3.50).

When the late Gustavus Myers first conceived this book (in 1925), he may not have thought that his theme would become more topical than the perpetuity of human malevolence. But since World War II began, surges of intolerance have grown so commonplace that the 20th Century, long accustomed to regarding itself as the most civilized age in human history, has been able blandly to disregard the fact that it has become the most savage. Race wars, class wars, the mistreatment of Negroes in the U.S., the deliberate efforts to exterminate the Jews in Europe, the cold-blooded, scientific murder or enslavement of whole populations, the destruction of orderly life throughout the world and the preaching of hate as a doctrine—all these are present-day manifestations of bigotry, of fanatical intolerance of any but one's own race, class, church, ideas.

In this 495 page book, Historian Myers gives bigotry one of its most strenuous workouts. He puts at the disposal of those who would combat bigotry, and who would preserve merely credulous and ill-informed people from the infection of intolerance, a tremendous arsenal of fact and of reference. Not content with the merely local effects of bigotry, Gustavus Myers moves, with exhaustive industry, in the iceberg depths of precedent and origin—deep into England, deep into ancient Rome.

Under his calm scrutiny of fact, myths small and large explode like popcorn. Mr. Myers' explosion of three U.S. myths is particularly notable: the Myth of the Puritan, the Myth of the Catholic, the Myth of the Jew.

The Myth of the Puritan, dear to millions of U.S. hearts, is the belief that the Puritans were, and remain, responsible for U.S. bigotry in all its more characteristic forms. The facts, says Historian Myers, prove otherwise. In all the American colonies the general spirit was that prevalent in England. That spirit was one of rampant persecution. Quakers were hanged in Massachusetts, but they were persecuted in Virginia as well. Not only in Massachusetts but in Maryland, long famed for its religious tolerance, the penalty for inveterate blasphemy was death; and blasphemy was any doubt that the Bible was the Word or that Jesus was the Son of God. Blue laws began not with the Puritans but in England, in 1448, "when all England was Catholic." Every America colony, Puritan and non-Puritan Quakers included, had its quota of blue laws.

The Myth of the Catholic became the new focus of bigotry as Puritan theocracy faded. From the early 1830s up to the Civil War and again among sheeted Klansmen, and in the weird, oratorical soapsuds of Alabama's Senator Tom Heflin, and in a grand climax during Al Smith's Presidential campaign, Catholicism was a favorite target for bigots. At the root of much of this bigotry lay Samuel F. B. Morse's *Foreign Conspiracy Against the Liberties of the United States* (a kind of anti-Catholic *Protocols of the Elders of Zion*), which decades later was still misinforming those who wanted to be misinformed. *The Awful* [and disproved] *Disclosures of Maria Monk* (1836) are still exhaling sulfur fumes on many a small-town bookshelf.

But the true sources of this fantastic brouhaha are not literary. They lie deeper in human nature and history. Just as the Great Fire of London was blamed on the Roman Catholics of 17th Century England, the burning of Rome was blamed on the Roman Christians of Nero's time. The moth-eaten charge that monasteries and convents are sinks of iniquity got its immortal impetus when Henry VIII sent forth investigators under instructions to furnish him with an alibi for pillaging the church. A favorite yawp of those who like to insist that Catholics have never stood for liberty—Pope Innocent III's annulment of Magna Charta—disregards the fact that Magna Charta was drafted by Catholics, and is happily ignorant of the fact that Catholic priests and prelates fought for and preserved it in defiance of the Pope.

The myth of the Jew, ever evil and ever active, burgeoned in the U.S. when Hitler came to power in Germany, had been quietly prospering for years. Ritual murder, the most sensational charge against the Jews, was originally charged against the early Christians. The charge against the Jews was especially popular in medieval Germany; and there are plenty of people who believe it today.

Myers effectively disposes of the myth that Jews control trade and finance, are incurably deceitful and tricky. He points to "the many successive laws—a long line of them century after century—which Parliament found necessary to enact in the effort to suppress deceit and fraud"—during the long periods when no Jews were allowed in England (1290-1655). Myers also discusses the most colossal of all libels against the Jews, *The Protocols of the Elders of Zion*, once more gives the data which years ago proved it a rampant forgery.

It is not likely that Mr. Myers' history will change the heart or the mind of a single bigot. For bigotry, it is pretty clear is a disease as constant and incurable as it is appallingly dangerous.

(September 27, 1943)

"James Agee by Himself"

"James Agee by Himself"
(1942)

Assertive and caustic, this essay speaks for itself. Not published during Agee's life, it provides a record of an ambitious writer's frustrations, and is an example of his skill with language. While revealing Agee's anger with an apparent failure to write what he wished, it is also a clear example of how he was slowly coming to realize that his best subject was himself.

"James Agee by Himself"

Mr. Agee, James "Rufus" Agee, was born in Knoxville, Tennessee, in November, 1909, scarcely one hundred years after the birth of Abraham Lincoln, of parents verging on the bourgeois, but honest. At three he inquired of his mother: "Mama"—he called her Mama in those days—"who made God?" (P.S.: He got the job.) At four he was run over by a bicycle, but later learned to love the irresponsible fellows. After a brief sojourn in kindergarten, for which he showed no more than average aptitude, he entered the public schools, and at these, and others, he spent no few years in ardent study of the back of the nearest head and of the nearest exit. At ten he proposed to write a monograph on torture, but lacking the training in research necessary for such a task, soon put it by. At fifteen he visited the London of Ramsay MacDonald and the Paris of the *Hunchback of Nôtre Dame*, where he explored the "slums," watched out for American moving pictures, and climbed the cathedrals. He scarcely minded the bedbugs at all . . . an oversight which was to amaze him in maturer years.

At Phillips Exeter, whose motto is that there are no rules until they are broken, he fought Caesar's Gallic War for the third time, swam the backstroke, and was awarded ten volumes of Rudyard Kipling for excellence in English Composition. At Harvard he made many valuable contacts and spent what must always seem to him the four happiest years of his life.

Originally purposing to be an Eagle Scout, a naturalist, a Late Roman Emperor, a concert pianist, a master criminal or a movie director, Mr. Agee has interested himself in writing only during the past seventeen years. Prior to settling down to it really seriously, he occupied himself in turn as delivery boy, hitchhiker, harvest "stiff," road mender, unskilled laborer, *Fortune* writer, Guggenheim applicant, amateur psychiatrist, bush-league messiah, armchair anarchist, soil analyst, unpaid agitator, picketer, conversationalist, international spy, mule skinner, dishwasher, bone crusher, tennis-court marker, spring-toothed harrow, roving reporter, potato masher, and scout knife. He was with Time Incorporated during the death of Calvin Coolidge. He was with the Loyalists heart and soul when André Malraux spoke in the ballroom of the Hotel Roosevelt. He was with Borodin on a telescope when Shanghai fell on Rayna Prohme and Sheean got the wound that made him think. He was with Negley Farson on the follow-up. He was without funds at the time of the Nazi-Soviet pact. He found no peace. His suggestions as to the proper way first to avert the Second World War and, later, to end it, were universally rejected, but he bears no grudge toward any living creature. "Only wait," he likes to say. "Things will work themselves out in time." And thus far, none has dared to dispute it.

At present, Mr. Agee lives modestly in a little "flat" in Cornelia Street in the Italian, not the Anglo-Bohemian, quarter of "The Village." There he entertains rarely, save for a few really close friends. He has done little of his own "stuff" during the past two years, being far too fascinated by what he laughingly calls his "private" "life," and by his task of book-reviewing for one of the great weekly magazines. "Why write," he queries, "when one may read, and read, and read, the superb work which is done by others?" His creditors are at a loss for an answer.

Mr. Agee is tall, faintly rustic in appearance, with slightly walled eyes. He is gentle when not aroused, and always kind to animals. Thanks to an inexcusable bit of carelessness he has lost several teeth, but still retains a legal sufficiency to bite the God of War, should their paths cross. He is a great believer in democracy and fair play, and spends much of his time trying to draft adequate fan letters to Dorothy Thompson, whose gracious femininity he finds exquisite, and to Walter Winchell and Westbrook Pegler, whose sturdy use of the native idiom he so admires. On the work of such artists as Margaret Bourke-White, Andre Kostelanetz, Phil Spitalny, "Poldy" Stokowski, and Thomas Benton, he is all but inarticulate. "To think," he murmurs huskily, "that artistry such as this can live—and be rewarded—in our time." He is also an urgent rooter for the Museum of Modern Art. "Art has a home worthy of it at last," he points out. He is pronouncedly schizoid, and a manic-depressive as well, with an occasional twinkle of paranoia. He breakfasts on the better-publicized dry cereals, dusted with Benzedrine Sulphate. He is not a Party member. He has never voted, but is the most faithful of taxpayers. He is an insomniac, rises late, and is interested in the psychology of sex. He has published two volumes one of verse, one of prose, both literary bonanzas in their day. "Gee, isn't it great to be an American," he says, and according to well-wishers he means every word of it.

Mr. Agee is shy at parties, though not antisocial in the clinical sense. He loves to seek out quiet corners behind layettes or refrigerators and there, with someone who really speaks his language, to carry on truly worthwhile conversations. He does not like to be called Aggie, Uhgee, Egg-gee, Ag-you, Ank-*yow*, or Rufus. "Don't call me that," he says. Due to some domestic or Christian trauma sustained in early youth, he is kindly in proportion to his hatred.

**The Complete "Work" Chapter
for *Famous Men***

The Complete "Work" Chapter
for *Famous Men*

Throughout *Let Us Now Praise Famous Men* Agee constantly assures the reader that it is impossible to know a way of life or to evoke it with any verbal approximation. He also insists there is no "average white tenant family." But his love for the persons he came to know, and his concern for their degradation drove him to sketch the "dignity of [their] actuality." His text, what he once called a "dissonant prologue," provides an image of a way of life.

What is sometimes forgotten is that Agee wrote considerably more than could have been included in his 1941 book. The chapter "Work," as printed in the book, was only a shortened version of the complete chapter. The complete version is provided here. This chapter was first edited from a carbon copy manuscript by Victor A. Kramer for publication in *The Texas Quarterly* in 1972.

"WORK"

To come devotedly into the depths of a subject, your respect for it increasing in every step and your whole heart weakening apart with shame upon your self in your dealing with it: To know at length better and better and at length into the bottom of your soul your unworthiness of it: Let me hope in any case that it is something to have begun to learn. Let this all stand however it may: since I can not make it the image it should be, let it stand as the image it is: I am speaking of my verbal part of this book as a whole. By what kind of foreword I can make clear some essential coherence in it, which I know is there, balanced of its chaos, I do not yet know. But the time is come when it is necessary to me to say at least this much: and now, having said it, to go on, and to try to make an entrance into this chapter, which should be an image of the very essence of their lives: that is, of the work they do.

It is for the clothing, and for the food, and for the shelter, of which I have told you, by these to sustain their lives, that they work. Their work is without any hope or reward beyond this, and without any question, from the moment they are born, of escape. Into this work and need, their minds, their spirits, and their strength are so steadily and intensely drawn that during such time as they are not at work, life exists for them scarcely more clearly or in more variance and seizure and appetite than it does for the more simply organized among the animals, and for the plants. This arduous physical work, to which a consciousness beyond that of the simplest child would be only a useless and painful encumbrance, is undertaken without choice or the thought or chance of choice, taught forward from father to son and from mother to daughter; and of its essential and few returns you have seen most: the houses they live in; the food they eat; the clothes they wear: and have still to see what it has done to their bodies, and to the consciousness; and what it makes of their leisure, the pleasures which are made available to them. I say here only: work as a means to other ends might have some favor in it, even which was of itself dull and heartless work, in which one's strength was used for another man's benefit: but the ends of this work are absorbed all but entirely into the work itself, and in what little remains, nearly all is obliterated; nearly nothing is obtainable; nearly all is cruelly stained, in the tensions of physical need, and in the desperate tensions of the need of work which is not available.

I have said this now three times, in one paragraph. If I were capable as I wish I were, I could say it once, in such a way that it would be there in its complete awefulness. Yet knowing, too, how it is repeated upon each of them, in every day of their lives, so powerfully, so entirely, that it is simply the natural air they breathe, I wonder whether it could ever be said enough times.

The plainness and iterativeness of work must be one of the things which make it so extraordinarily difficult to write of. The plain details of a task once represented, a stern enough effort in itself, and one beyond me, how is it possible to be made clear enough that this same set of leverages has been undertaken by this woman in nearly every day of the eleven or the twenty-five years since her marriage, and will be persisted in in nearly every day to come in all the rest of her life; and that it is only one among the many processes of wearying effort which make the shape of each one of her living days; how is it to be calculated, the number of times she has done these things, the number of times she is still to do them; how conceivably in words is it to be given as it is in actuality the accumulated weight of these actions upon her; and what this cumulation has made of her body; and what it has made of her mind and of her heart and of her being. And how is this to be made so real to you who read of it, that it will stand and stay in you as the deepest and most iron anguish and guilt of your existence that you are what you are, and that she is what she is, and that you cannot for one moment exchange places with her, nor by any such hope make expiation for what she has suffered at your hands, and for what you have gained at hers: but only by consuming all that that is in you into the never relaxed determination that this shall be made different and shall be made right, and that of what is 'right' some, enough to die for, is clear already, and the vast darkness of the rest has still, and far more passionately and more skeptically than ever before, to be questioned into, defended, and learned toward. There is no way of taking the heart and the intelligence by the hair and of wresting it to its feet, and of making it look this terrific thing in the eyes: which are such gentle eyes: you may meet them, with all the summoning of heart you have, in the photograph in this volume of the young woman with black hair: and they are to be multiplied, not losing the knowledge that each is a single, unrepeatable, holy individual, by the two billion human creatures who are alive upon the planet today; of whom a few hundred thousands are drawn into complications of specialized anguish, but of whom the huge swarm and majority are made and acted upon as she is: and of all these individuals, contemplate, try to encompass, the one annihilating chord:

But I must make a new beginning:

WORK: 1

If I had been born a tenant farmer's son, there would have been no question about it: no question of 'education', none of learning a skilled trade, none of knowing except as the cloudiest kind of a dream the existence of a world different from that I was foundered in: even in my own world, all except those of my own class would be strangers to me; they would move and appear in the strangeness of people on a stage, or seen through a thick sheet of glass: there would be no question about it, what dialect I was to use, what clothes I was to wear, what was to go on in my mind, what I was going to eat all my life, what sort of house I was to live in, what people I was to be at ease with, what sort of girl I was to marry, what sort of life we were to have together, what sort of work I was going to do; what sort of work she was going to do: above all else no question, no question at all, but what I *would* work, hard, with my hands, with my body, with all my strength, learning my trade in my childhood and youth, and working hard in my childhood and in my adolescence, and from the day of my marriage on, working with all I had, that we might stay alive, and scarcely better than staying alive, for that work, and helpless in my leisure.

That I was not born a tenant farmer's son is no doing of mine: nor is it any doing of mine that I was born as I happened to be, among relative advantages. But every human advantage is a theft: and the worst of it is, that by this theft by which one gains, another is deprived; and that the one who is deprived is the one who has earned what he is deprived of by hard and hopeless work, or his children who must suffer for him. I feel intense guilt towards every such man and woman and child alive; and I suggest that you need to feel it too; and that that sense of guilt cannot possibly be intense enough, nor the wish to expiate sufficient.

It is in the terms of this intensely felt guilt that I wish I could write of a tenant's work: in such a way as to break your back with it and your heart if I could: this implies consciousness greater than they have. That consciousness has been described near here as more limited than this, but still more: in such a way that "innocent" of them though you are, you might go insane with shame and with guilt that you are who you are, and that you are not what some one of these persons is, who is living, while you are living. Good God, if I could only make even this *guilt* what it is: not just some piece of pathology or of metaphysics, but the literal thing it is, the literal thing. The literal fact that you and they are living in the same earth. That because you are as you are, they are as they are: living persons, each with as sacred a claim upon all existence as your own: and that of this existence, they get what they get of it, and are made what they are made, and you get and are made what you are.

There is never any question about this work. It is the heart and centre of living. That is one thing: another is, that it is done to hold life together. Not relative comfort or discomfort or one or another degree of social standing, but life: food, and clothing, and shelter, of what sort you now know little: for a man, and a woman, and their children: for just this life and nothing more: and with no possibility that the work will ever let up.

You might say, yes, but there is leisure. Yes, there is, a good deal of it; but, it is not by any means an enviable kind of leisure. There is no sort of equipment for the use of leisure, for one thing: for another, there is so little to live on that leisure is merely terror or despair. I am not speaking falsely but truly when I say that nearly all conscious existence here (of these people) is focused on and poured into work, very hard work, without hope, beyond the plainest expectations between staying scarcely and a little less than scarcely alive, and certainly without any choice or question of not working: so that work and need and continuousness and hopelessness and knowledge of infinitely meagre reward are all blended in every day in every grown brain and body in a sort of tension, relaxed only a little in leisure, or to an apathy known as 'shiftlessness', of which I will say more later; and this tension, a kind of central spring at the heart, involving every muscle and every faculty, this tension, and quiet, unquestioned, fatal is the knowledge of enslavement, is the whole tone or key of living at all.

This is what a tenant child is born into. Even at its birth it is many generations old and seasoned in hopelessness and changelessness, so that his whole substance is made of it; and he draws it in with every breath. It is his from the start, I suspect from long before the beginning of his working. For if as has been shown (by Freud, for instance), a child is sensitive to the relationship between his parents, and is shaped by it, it seems likely he is sensitive too, to the whole tone of existence surrounding him: and if this is as I have said, so lean and strained and weary, and so resigned, and with every mouthful of food and every inanimate object a corroborator of it and a harmony with it, then surely this has considerable effect.

There is no thought or reason for thought, on the part of his parents, that he shall be otherwise than as they are; and he relives their childhood. There is nothing else to do, and nothing else imaginable.

Of children's work, and 'child labor', I will try to write later. Here I am wanting only to sketch work in a life, its general shape and rhythm: and perhaps I had best say next, what it is in a family as a whole, what a family is in relation to work.

[The] family exists for work. It exists to keep itself alive. It is a cooperative economic unit. The father does one set of tasks, the mother another; the children still a third, with the sons and daughters serving apprenticeship to their father and mother respectively. A family is called a force, without irony; and children come into the world chiefly that they may help with the work and that through their help the family may increase itself. Their early years are leisurely; a child's life work begins as play. Among his first imitative gestures are gestures of work; and the whole imitative course of his maturing and biologic is a stepladder of the learning of physical tasks and skills.

This work solidifies, and becomes steadily more and more, in greater and greater quantity and variety, an integral part of his life.

Besides imitation, he works if he is a man under three

compulsions, in three stages. First for his parents. Next for himself, single and wandering in the independence of his early manhood: 'for himself', in the sense that he wants to stay alive, or better, and has no one dependent on him. Third, for himself and his wife and his family, under an employer. A woman works just for her parents; next without a transition phase, for her husband and family.

Work for your parents is one thing: I shall try to tell of it later. Work 'for yourself' is another. They are both hard enough, yet light, relative to what is to come. On the day you are married, at about sixteen if you are a girl, at about twenty if you are a man, a key is turned, with a sound not easily audible, and you are locked between the stale earth and the sky; the key turns in the lock behind you, and your full life's work begins, and there is nothing conceivable for which it can afford to stop short of your death, which is a long way off. It is perhaps at its best during the first two years or so, when you are young and perhaps are still enjoying one another or have not yet lost all hope, and when there are not yet so many children as to weigh on you. It is perhaps at its worst during the next ten to twelve years, when there are more and more children, but none of them old enough, yet, to be much help. One could hardly describe it as slackening off after that, for in proportion with the size of the family, it has been necessary to take on more land and more work, and, too, a son or daughter gets just old enough to be any full good to you, and marries or strikes out for himself: yet it is true, anyhow, that from then on there are a number of strong and fairly responsible people in the household besides the man and his wife. In really old age, with one of the two dead, and the children all married, and the widowed one making his home among them in the slow rotations of a floated twig, waiting to die, it does ease off some, depending more then on the individual: one may choose to try to work hard and seem still capable, out of [duty] and the wish to help, or out of 'egoism', or out of the dread of dropping out of life; or one may relax, and live unnoticed, never spoken to, dead already: or again, life may have acted on you in such a way that you have no choice in it: or still again, with a wife dead, and children gone, and a long hard lifetime behind you, you may choose to marry again and begin the whole cycle over, lifting on to your back the great weight a young man carries, as Woods has done:

That is the general pattern, its motions within itself lithe-

unfolded slow, gradual, grand, tremendously and quietly
weighted, as a heroic dance: and the bodies in this dance, and the
spirits, undergoing their slow, miraculous and dreadful changes:
such a thing indeed should be constructed, of just these persons:
the great sombre blooddroned beansprout helmed fetus unflow-
ering within Wood's wife: the infants of three families, stagger-
ing happily, their hats held full of freshly picked cotton: the
Ricketts children like delirious fawns and panthers: and secret
Pearl with her wicked skin: Louise, lifting herself to rest her
back, the heavy sack trailing, her eyes on you: Junior, jealous and
lazy, malingering, his finger sore: the Ricketts daughters, the
young stepping beautifully as a young mare, the elder at the
stove with her mouth twisted: Annie Mae at twenty-seven, in
her angular sweeping, every motion a wonder to watch: George
in his Sunday clothes with his cuffs short on his blocked wrists,
looking at you, his head slightly to one side, his earnest eyes a little squinted as if he were looking into a light: Mrs. Ricketts, in
that time of morning when from the corn she reels into the
green roaring glooms of her home, falls into a chair with gasp-
ings, which are almost groaning sobs, and dries in her lifted skirt
her delicate and reeking head: and Miss-Molly, chopping wood
as if in each blow of the axe she held captured in focus the
vengeance of all time, and Woods, slowed in his packing, forced
to stop and rest much too often, whose death is hastened against
a doctor's warnings in that he is picking at all: I see these among
others on the clay in the grave mutations of a dance whose
business is the genius of a moving camera, and which it is not
my hope ever to record: yet here, perhaps, if not of these archaic
circulations of the rude clay altar, yet of their shapes of work,
I can make a few crude sketches, remarking, too, how nearly
basic, how near to source, these motions and collaborations
are:

A man: George Gudger, Woods, Fred Ricketts: his work is
with the land, in the seasons of the year, in the sustainment and
ordering of his family, the training of his sons:
A woman: Annie Mae Gudger, Ivy Woods, Sadie Ricketts:
her work is in the keeping of the home, the preparation of food
against each day and against the dead season, the bearing and
care of her children, the training of her daughters:
Children: all these children: their work is as it is told to
them and taught to them until such time as they shall

strengthen and escape, and escaped of one imprisonment, are submitted into another:

There are times of year when all these three are over-lapped and collaborated, all in the field in the demand, chiefly, of cotton: but by and large, the woman is the servant of the day, and of immediate life, and the man is the servant of the year, and of the basis and boundaries of life, and is their ruler; and the children are the servants of their parents: and at the centre of all their existence, the central work, that by which they have their land, their shelter, their living, that which they must work for no reward more than this, because they do not own themselves, and without hope or interest, that which they cannot eat and get no money of but which is at the centre of their duty and greatest expence of strength and spirit, the cultivation and harvesting of cotton; and all this effort takes place between a sterile earth and an uncontrollable sky in whose propitiation is centred their chief reverence and fear, and the deepest earnestness of their prayers, who read in these [machinations] of their heaven all signs of a fate which the hardest work cannot much help, and, not other-wise than as the most ancient peoples of the earth, make their plantations in the unpitying pieties of the moon.

Words can do anything: perhaps: hurried and green, how-ever, I see no way of making in words what human work is: each of whose thousands of gestures should be transliterated into the bones of any one who reads, yet not even only that: for besides, each such gesture, must be set in the whole meaning, rhythm, tension and texture, of each individual life: so that I might write almost illimitably long, listing merely, not embody-ing, all those things which we who do not know this work, who are merely examining, must ask ourselves simultaneously to imagine, and to know the pressures of: and to know these pres-sures intimately in the exhaustions of individual lives; or to know, only for instance, to imagine, to try to compute, not lightly nor merely mentally but in our exact bodies, the sum and whole series, each by each and day upon day and year upon long solemnly draughted year, of each of these gestures and exten-sions of effort between pressures of need and deprivation in no hope and friendlessness, which just one such creature, Mrs. Gudger, has made, in the course of only twenty-seven years, that she now stands made as she is in the photograph in this book, the beautiful, and dreadful, and piteous, and irretrievable creation of what she has had to do: or merely, but again literally, to know the sum of these efforts as they are extended and reflexed upon the lives which comprise the living of one family, from the birth of each of two parents until they shall have sunk in death, leaving their children standing, saplings sprung fresh between thin roots, what energy, what incalculable expence and persistence of the hear[t]s has wrought up and spread and held and seeded this simple family flower: what energy, what straining and draining dry of all strength and love and hope, has composed even this one living generation of even this one shallow city of such flowers who in their grand and sterile field on this southern country are dedicated, making their landlords neither the happier nor the better nor more than a little the more rich, into the raising of the cotton plant, that they may by incidental hold the frayed string of existence together within each of them: and these unfolded backward upon all past generations into the sources, and spread in horizontals such that the planet and its cities are one glittering membrane of these unpaid agonies; and postulated upon the future into what hope of change: and driven against all minds that have ever searched or meditated and against all braveries which have acted the question which of its self is accusation, what is it you have done for this: and [done] into our hearts and brains who read or make record of this: by what ways and means and by what rights are you advantaged of this to differ from it in the least:

Such computations then all drawn and trained upon the literal work and living even of one: might begin to suggest the simple and scarcely conscious features of opening land with a plow, of sweeping a floor, in their true proportions, and might begin to make it possible that these gestures be told of as they should be: in language so simple, physical, and dispassionate that it is incapable of holding sense beyond or less than the literalness of that action which it is trying to embody.

I, though: I cannot hope or pretend to touch a one of these things as they deserve to be touched, but must sketch and guess and be grateful if I shall suggest mere fractions, and that the fractions are not wholes:

A woman's work: a man's: a family[s].

The Gudgers follow the classical family pattern which I have sketched, in which a man's and a woman's work are divided, and their children are apprentices; with full collaborations in the service of the cotton:

The Woods family is hovered between this and a still more antique pattern, and with the further illustrant of one in old age, a widow, who is making her home:

The Ricketts family: the man and the boys hold true to pattern; the rest is modified or disintegrated: of these last two, more to say:

Of the Woods:

In mountain and primitive families, with the tradition of the man as the hunter, it still persists, though not in full force, that the woman does the plowing and cultivating. Mrs. Woods, young and tirelessly strong, is a natural primitive, or parallels it in her anarchic lack of embarrassment before custom: she likes to plow, and likes all the work tenant men are supposed to do. Her husband forbids her doing it. It goes against his own tradition of what is right: still more, he dislikes it because he is older and weaker than he wants to appear to himself or to others, these others being critical of his having remarried at his age.

Mrs. Woods' mother is what happens when a family is broken: she lives among her married children. The old and widowed are thus taken care of, automatically. Quite as automatically, they are (usually) dropped out of existence, noticed as little or perhaps less than the youngest of the children. No one necessarily answers or even appears to have heard them, for instance, when they speak; and they make up their existence out of their own thoughts and out of companionship with the younger and more leisured of the children. This oblivion increases in proportion as the mind and the interest and strength to be of use are [diminished], so that at its far end, which is not uncommon, the aged are as the grandmother in Tobacco Road, an old, deathly silent, witless, bent-up animal, tied up in rags, whose occupation is gathering sticks, and whose loss or death is more casually noticed than that of a neighborhood dog: Mrs. Woods' mother is much luckier: strong, fierce and full of comedy; able to help powerfully with the work: she has, even, a loquacious and almost living companionship with her daughter and son-in-law: as if through a thin and perfectly transparent but unbreakable membrane of glass.

Of the Ricketts:

Fred Ricketts is as classically the 'provider', and his sons are being grown in his image, and the younger of the children are as is normal; the centre of disintegration is in his wife and in the strength and maturity of his daughters. The falling apart of her mind is hardly distinguishable from the falling apart, in living, of the whole family, and there the causes are not measurable beyond the guess that they are interactive. However the proportions and full causes may be it is so that whereas there is method, plan, constancy and clarity of action, consciousness, and purpose, in all that goes into the running and living of the Gudgers family, and all this only a certain amount loosened and apathetic in the Woods family, there is in the Ricketts family almost nothing of the sort, beyond the kind which might be the imitative and soon-abandoned impulses of children playing family, so that it is constantly uncertain and casual who is its cook the next meal, who is to do the milking, what vegetable will be planted, when a washing will be done, who is watching out for the safety of the children,—all the things which are the tasks of home: with this afterword necessary, that none of the three women is by any means 'lazy', or leaving it to the others: and with this rough and fairly constant change of the pattern from normal, and rebalancing: that Margaret, the oldest, has taken over the central work of her mother, the cooking, and the minding of the children: that the mother, who cannot bear the indoor heat and closed air of the stove, does the more outdoor work in a frenzy of effort equal to her dim knowledge of her weakness, her unbegrudged disenthronement, and her guilt and grief of her inadequacy, a frenzy which tears her down almost into nausea within two hours, and its renewed as soon as possible, whether or not there is need for it; and that Paralee is auxiliary between the two of them, with Margaret, next to her father the physical head and central magnet of the family, and the mother the spiritual head and the centre of love:

With these patterns and balancings briefly laid out, it is time to try more nearly to substantiate the individual tasks of a woman and of a man.

Which is 'the harder', a man's work, or woman's. How do they differ by rhythm and shape.

It can seem to me that the woman's work is the harder, both by its continuousness from day to day, as against the seasonal intensities and relaxations of the man's work, and by the fact that it is she who is, most essentially, the servant and secondary, the bearer and developer of the heavy weights and drainages of one child after another, the centre of all psychologic and physical vicissitudes among the children, and the inheritor of the greater multiplicity of tasks: and this may be so: but I see no real way of measuring or knowing. The man's work breathes in and out more slowly, as the year does itself, and during the months in which it is required of him is profoundly heavy and arduous, as her tasks in the main are less; and are not favored of those islands of leisure which during most months of the year relieve his wife a while each day in the middles of mornings and of afternoons, but are continuous from early morning into the late dusk, and are given their ventilations only by his economics and deliberations of effort and reasonably frequent short pauses, which are the practice of every accustomed manual worker. He has this entire bulk of the land work to lift upon his shoulders, with the assistance of his family in certain times of year; he has besides this, the entire bulk and responsibility of the empty times of the year, in midsummer and in winter, the terrible bulk of needing work which can scarcely be found; the weight of the work if it is found: and besides these the weight of all flanking tasks, the taking of cotton to gin and corn to grist, the killing of the hog, the harvesting in of all crops and the supervision of his family in this, all the physical repairs or efforts at improvement, the care of the stock: and besides this, the entire literal and symbolic weight of his situation as centre, king, and provider of his family, responsibility for it towards each member, and towards himself, and towards the world, all business negotiations of every kind: it would be foolish to say that either is the more difficult: one can only say of each, that it totally fills and absorbs and exhausts the whole substance of each life, of whatever sex:

And still I have so scarcely suggested: for I have as yet said nothing of each individual task: and even if that were done, there would be the even greater difficulty of making it clear, how each of these tasks is the weight not merely of itself, but of itself in the twenty thousandth repetitions, with twenty thousand more to come, and in relation to other tasks which have been finished that this one may be taken hold of, and in relation to still others which must be proceeded to when this one is finished, and each of these in its relation to the thousands of times it has been done before, and to the thousands of times it must be done again, in days, circular weeks and slowly drawn seasons which repeated themselves like blue carbons of one another, the

letters less and less legible, and the words finally so far beyond
meanings of words they have become meanings of music and
even these effaced, so that it is all done blindly in the infinitesimal focus of the immediate action and in the dim volumes of a
dream, rhythms, long waves, only faintly felt behind and
known, by memory rather than by anticipation, ahead, so that
the apathies of a cast of players who have performed the same
drama eight times a week for five years before a more and more
degraded and degrading type of audience is as nothing before
such requirements as theirs whose lives are a drama without
situation, relish, hope, or any interest, played over and over, day
upon day, its greatest cycle a year, before no audience whatever,
and with never more development than that the flower girl
becomes the bridesmaid and at length the mother-in-law, in
every hour, without intermission, approbation, or even the
[experience] of boredom, for ten and forty and seventy-five years,
as if from a low and stifled, featureless sky, softly, one musing
silver gray suffusion, rain stove and compounded itself upon
the world a full quiet smothered century:

And so if I were to try to detach each of the tasks of a
woman in one day: each of the tasks of a man in one year: each
of the tasks of a son: each of the tasks of a daughter: each of the
tasks and repetitions of tasks that is stored up into the wearying
body and eyes of just one of these parents from the first gay emu-
lations of childhood into this present day, and into all that is to
be required of him tomorrow, and like wise on the day after, and
like wise throughout every day of the succeeding week, and so
into that time in which he is withered and grown small into the
ground: the lifting up out of an iron farce of rest each early
morning; the making of the fire; the putting together of flour,
salt, soda and water into one mass and the heating of this in an
oven; the breaking of eggs and their seasoning while they fry; the
cutting and frying of salt fat meat; the openings of oven doors;
the servings of a family; the clearings of a table; the washing of
dishes; the milking of a cow; the churning of butter; the washing
of the churn; the hanging of the dasher on the wall; the taking
of the butter and milk and buttermilk and cream to the spring;
the getting of water; the sweeping of the rubbish and loose dirt of
the backyard nearest the house into the cotton at the side of the
house, the making of the beds, the folding up of the pallets, the
hanging up of each night garment, the mending of the broken
knee of a pair of overalls, the patching of the shoulders of a shirt,

the designing and cutting and stitching and trimming of a new
dress, the laundering of clothes, the gathering in of vegetables
for dinner, the making of the fire, the mixing of corn meal, salt,
lard and water and the putting of the mixture into a flat pan and
into the oven—

Or the breaking down of the stalks, the harnessing of the
mule, the running up of the terraces, the broadcasting, the first
bedding, the second bedding, the harrowing, the planting, the
putting down of [fertilizer?], the first sweeping, the weeding, the
putting down of the soda, the second sweeping, the weeding, the
chopping, the third sweeping, the spreading of poison, the weeding, the fourth sweeping, and picking, the weighing, the loading,
the ginning, the harvesting in and shucking of the corn, the
gristing, the making of sorgham, the killing of the hog, the cutting of him to pieces,—

And here I have only begun merely to name the more ordinary of the tasks—

I would have first, taking each one of these apart from all
the others, and getting as deeply as I could inside the body of one
of these persons so that if possible I lifted the whole and exact
weight of this body in its leverages upon this task, to give inch by
inch and in every conceivable exactitude each smallest detail of
the task in all five senses as it is, in its exact time of accomplishment and balance within the rhythm of other duties, of the day,
of the week, of the year, of the lifetime: and to do this same of
every one of these tasks, not omitting nor speaking more briefly
of any one, since no such omission is possible in work:

And I would have second, of each of them, and of all of
them in sum, to bear in mind and to establish those repetitions
of which I have spoken and their unthinkable cumulation and
weight:

And I would have third, to try to say, what this work has
done to the body and to the being of each one of these persons as
they stand at this day, arrested an instant in life, in the summer
of 1936, watching and recording in each person each blemish and
distortion and effacement, each insult which has been visited
upon each of them: and knowing a little in each child the past of
his parents, and in each young adult the youth of the old, and in
each parent the future of each child:

These things, these first minimum requirements of one
who would claim to write of the work of working people, and
which, done as they should be done, would compound such a

driving symphony of gesture, pain, fury, and effort as has never been made save continually in most living human creatures, and which I hope might nearly kill a hearer with personal exhaustion, anger, guilt, and purpose; I lack the ability to do these things, and the space, and the time, though I cannot so easily get rid of the obsession that they must be done: but the least I can do is to have suggested them, and I hope that in some measure I have: and to point out to you, in such a way that it will not be possible to avoid, that none of this is a matter of mere personal fancy, conjecture, or emotion, but is existing fact, far beyond my power to state or to suggest the weight of: and as a body of fact, is quite as open to your consideration as to mine, and quite as much your obligation to consider as mine to write of. And so I earnestly suggest of this whole subject that, if only with such materials as I manage to give, you make up your own mathematics and meditations on it, and your own problems of pity, understanding of cause, and conscience; trying to determine, for instance, whether you can ever get solidly enough into your body and into your consciousness the full sum of the work each one of these persons has done and must do, and the full sum of what it has done to them, and the full sum and complexion of the causes, and the full sum and complexion and confliction of the possibilities of rectification, and the full sum and depth of each person's responsibility not merely to write or read it, not merely to think of it now and then, but to be incapable of forgetting it, of not enlarging by your own intelligence my failures in telling you of it, and to be incapable merely of pitying or deploring, or of taking courses of action which may ease your conscience but which, more scrupulously examined, may be insufficient; and to be incapable of rest save in the rightful leisures and digressions and oblivions of those who work hard in the worship of existence and the knowledge of the deathliness of any too stonily centred allegiance, and of peace save in this dangerous rest and digression, and in the constant effort to determine, towards whom or what must be my present and future allegiances and actions; how are these things to be changed; how are they to be made right; what is 'right'.

Of all the work of the women, the heavy bearing and rearing of the children, the teaching of the daughters, the subjection to the men, there is no room to tell, and I do not know how I could tell it if there were: I can only beg you that you know it by their tasks, some of which have been named: that you know in

what terrible fulness it exists, and is done, in every day; and I
suggest of whichever sex you are, a way by which you can know,
if only a little about it, still, much more than I can tell you; unless as may be, you know it already. It is simple enough. For
every day of one month, prepare all of your own meals, for yourself, if you are alone, or for your family; clearing the table and
washing the dishes after each meal. If you want to make it a little more exact, prepare breakfast at about daybreak, at whatever
time of year, dinner at about noon, and super about six. As for
your leisure, do not allow yourself to read, play or hear music or
news, play a game, or entertain yourself in any way save by sitting still quietly and, if there is a companion, by quietly talking,
being careful to keep your talk, in words of one syllable, your vocabulary and conversation limited almost entirely to things
which can be seen and touched. This will not be nearly enough;
but it will be something. By what this little bit alone does to you,
and by adding to it in your imagination all other such responsibilities as I have named, and by multiplying the whole of this
upon your self by twelve, a year, and then by the years of a lifetime; and then by condemning yourself to another month of it;
and by trying to recognize that for those you are emulating there
has never been and never will be any escape except briefly in extreme sickness and finally in death: by these exercises, I believe
you can take more of the meaning of it than by anything I can
possibly say.

I would particularly recommend, small an image though
it is, the monotony of washing the same dishes three times in
each of these thirty days. That alone can begin very quickly to
have a stupefying effect on one who isn't used to it; and is a
small measure, anyhow, of the effect it has on those who are so
used to it that it has never occurred to them whether they are
stupefied or not. I had better add this suggestion. You may en-
large your understanding if you cook the same breakfast each
day, the same dinner, and the same supper, permitting yourself
no meat except fried or boiled salt pork, and the other foods as
they have been described.

Of the man's work, I know of no way you can get an idea
short of taking his place. But here again, for what little they are
worth, are a few suggestions. For one month: or you might use
for it your next vacation: do either the hardest manual work you
can find or contrive, or do sitting-up exercises and liftings of

weights. Do these, if possible, in the broad heat of the hottest sun available. Whether it is work or exercises you are doing, begin it at about six in the morning, and do not stop for more than an aggregate ten minutes of any hour between then and sunset, excepting a half hour out for food in the middle of the day. During all this same time, deprive yourself of any money more than eight cents at a time, do not borrow, have no conversation with anyone who is not an unskilled laborer or a member of his family; do no reading, nor writing, nor hearing nor playing of music or news, nor looking at paintings, use only tactile words and ten of the plainest generalizations you can think of, and wherever you go, go on foot unless you can obtain a mule. Kick your dog a few times each day. Fuck your wife each night on as uncomfortable a bed as you can find, in a room occupied also by children. Do not by any means despise her, but make yourself incapable of looking at her or speaking to her with any love. Have acquaintances, but no friends. Be rather careful how you speak to any man of property, no matter what he may say to you, and how you look at his women or daughters. If you can pay the poll tax, which you probably cannot, vote the straight democratic ticket. Make yourself feel shy in entering any small town; you haven't much right there. Dread the law; it is not for your kind. Wear the clothes which mark you for what you are.

Of the children, too, I cannot tell much; yet a little:

I would say a tenant child has two kinds of work; that which he does at home, and that which he does in school. In school, from about six on for a while, he is locked into a sort of factory in which he has little or no desire to work: and in the course of time this work is ended in favor of the other kind. It is ended for no one reason but for several: because beyond a minimum literacy it understandably enough seems to his parents, to himself, to the landowners, and usually to the teachers, thoroughly irrelevant to the way he is to spend the rest of his life; because he is bored with it and there is a strong odor of maturity in having quit school for work; because his parents need him; and finally, if having by chance escaped these reasons, he persists in school, because the landowner employing his father does not by any means approve of higher education, meaning that beyond the sixth grade or so, for those of the tenant class.

His other work, his work at home, could be divided into two kinds: chore-work and general assistance on the one hand, on the other, apprenticeship. They overlap, of course; every task, in the course of learning it, is an apprenticeship, or even a personal ambition, and to some extent the more complex tasks remain so until breaking away, independence, and parenthood (the ultimate competitive gesture of a child against his parents) sets on everything he is and does the new mark he will wear all his life. But every task, too, soon loses much of novelty and of ambition, and quickly absorbs more and more of the flat and finally demolished taste of drudgery; and these I am absorbing under the heading of chores and general assistance. There is nothing of slave driving about any of this; there doesn't have to be. A child begins because he is imitative and interested, before he is ever told or taught; then he is taught; the work becomes more regular; it is more and more regularly and casually expected of him: a number of set requirements, say, in each day; and a number more of less regular or expected and less pleasing interruptions. There is no slave driving, and no question or consciousness of it either in the child or the parent, but let the child object, if he is beyond a certain tender age of irresponsibility, and he will learn quickly and solidly enough to attend to his business, and that he has a hard boss.

I have seen the labor of tenant children written of as if it were a brutal responsibility of the landowners, or as if it were forced on the children (and their unwilling parents) by exigencies peculiar to the tenant system. I think there is a sort of truth in this: I think also, though, that on the whole it is mistaken. It is true in this way: during two parts of the year, in chopping and in picking, labor on a cotton farm is intensely concentrated on that one crop, which the tenant plants not by desire nor for any profit by contract, and for his landlord, and to live as a tenant at all; and these two operations require every bit of help which can be had, down to the youngest who are competent for anything but getting in the way. If a competent child were withheld from this work, and if his parents themselves approved or tried to defend this withdrawal, I am quite certain no landowner or overseer would let it pass lightly. It would run against every principle he had. But since it would first have run against every principle the parents have, and every principle also which the child had ever heard of, it would not be likely to happen. There is another way, too, already mentioned. By the time the child is old enough to begin learning something in school, he is also old enough to put almost as much strain on the lean resources of his family as would an extra adult, and in that same proportion he is able, and obligated, to relieve this strain by working. If he were held out of this work, it would be a rare and violent gesture against every thin-stretched economic law by which he and his family must so scarcely live, and against every principle, emotion, and belief which these economic facts have produced in himself, in his parents, in his class, in his teachers, and in those who use his class and for whose use it must remain in its present perfectly available solution of complete need and ignorance. Every year more learning, every year less involvement into the work of staying alive, is an enormous and brilliant badge of the meanings of money and of need: and to compensate and to hold captive all divisions in their places, whole religions of habituation and belief are formed which hold each individual securely from without, and which are seated also at the roots of his self-esteem, his loyalty, and his fear. The trap is strong enough, and searching and flexible enough, to hold all individual variants save the few most extraordinary among each ten thousand, and even of these, few can modify themselves far: few can get at large more loose realms whose keys (without the mysteries of unlocking) are given to others for nothing, save the price of the blood of those who carved them and shall never so much as see them flash in the sun.

This too, you could in a sense say, is a 'responsibility' of the landlords', but only by the chance that a landlord hires that family. It could be more properly said thus:

The work of tenant children is harder than that of other farm children, in as much as tenants must work harder; and is done for nothing and for the landowner, in as much as he works without pay for his parents and they in turn work for next to nothing for the landlord: and their youth is focused into a payless apprenticeship to the landlord, in as much as they will almost surely become tenant farmers when they are grown: this is true and is important but there is more to remember:

Simply: that these children would be worked, and worked hard, without pay or the thought of it, quite regardless of any landlord or future as tenants, out of the nature of a farm family merely as such: a nature which is intensified in proportion to poverty and the 'ignorance', 'simplicity', or 'primitiveness' of the family. It is so natural, simple and inevitable, that it needs little or no further explanation. Every family, of whatever class, is among other things, and as a part of its essence, an economic problem and an economic group, and if it is a family with lives cut of the immediate land, the plain skin of the teeth of the earth, and the plain skin of its own teeth, all disguises, softenings, and modifications are stuffed away and it is beyond this grim fact, only that little else which can by a miracle remain in those whose living is so skeletal of the capacity for thought and feeling (and by this miracle,[2] more remains, and commonly, of gentleness and nobility than is by a good deal so commonly discernable elsewhere). Each of these families is a small primitive nation, to which the children owe their lives: and the feeling for this patriarchy is sharpened and simplified in proportion with the depth of withdrawal from 'civilization'. I don't know of the present but as an instance I do know, as of not many years ago, how mountain families came into mill towns, once a crop of children was raised to the useful age, and how the parents sat in the porches of the shacks at their ease while their children, in the spinning mills, paid them back what little they could for having brought them into the world.

I am astonished to have written so much that has seemed necessary, even for this necessarily brief sketch of what the work [is], and to have said so little that is to the immediate physical point: that the tenants use their strength and learning in certain given tasks by which they stay alive; what these tasks are; some kind of representation of each of them at work at them, some kind of representation, too, of what their leisure is, and of what this life has made and is making them. I have been aware that like one in a snowstorm I have been going in circles; and that has pleased rather than dismayed me, for each of the circles, such as it is, has been turned in obedience of an intense need and wish to make clear, however blind, and if as each has rounded past remembered landmarks any sense of dead and heavy weight and of oppressiveness has added itself upon you, then I am grateful, for it was in that hope that I kept on with the circlings: in the hope that by the slowly wound inane and earnest brutality and boredom of their reincidence a little might be set upon you of the unspeakable weight, and monotonies and cumulations, of the work itself: and in the hope that no task or process named or described could seem as merely one but as one of thousands in each person and of billions in the millions of them: but now I have come to where I must go into these singled particulars, and I myself am so dizzied, and so disturbed over my lack of proper space, that I do not know quite where or how to anchor: or whether I had better not discard all I have written on this subject, and try to make some more clean and succinct start.

It was here and in this attempt that I wrote what I have used as if as a preface to this chapter, and I suggest that it be called to mind now.

Notes

[1] The manuscript of Agee's "Work" chapter has been printed here as it appears in the carbon copy typescript now in The Harry Ransom Humanities Research Center, The University of Texas at Austin. In a few places errors of spelling have been corrected, and omissions of words by Agee are indicated by the editorial addition of a word, always indicated by brackets. Names have been changed to correspond with the names used throughout the book. Except for punctuation, the opening pages of this version are substantially as they appear in the book. Therefore these passages are used with the permission of Houghton Mifflin, Inc.

[2] Not so very [much] a miracle; in a world where every advantage is starved and corrupted in the mortal sin of money wrung out of others, every excellence that accrues of it is more or less discolored; and a human being stands his chance of mere elementary purity only in proportion as he is sequestered of this syphillis: and how ever little he may become that was in him to, yet his hands are relatively clean of this particular blood and excrement: yet also: nearly as much horror, of a different order, is forced on him by its lack, as is forced on others by its having: and any beginning of morality, humble to be sure, must come of a use, not a starvation, of materials: but only of a use by which no other human being is in the least deprived. Meanwhile, "poverty" seems among the few possible personal approaches. [This note is Agee's.]

Unused *Time* Articles

Unused *Time* Articles

These unused articles are relevant because they examine the problems of acting as a responsible person in a world where unindividualistic ideas had become what Agee called "Popular Religion." Neither article was printed; yet because they supply information about how Agee was thinking immediately following the end of the World War they are valuable. Each article is indicative of his disappointment with man's inability to act as an individual. Both are edited from typescripts which were also accompanied by an autographed working draft.

The first of the two articles was to be prefaced by scripture: "Consider the lilies of the field. . . ." The article which followed is an explanation of the fact that, while most persons in the western world were nominal Christians, "The world's history, and the daily and future destiny of every individual, are given shape, meanwhile, by the thousands of great and trivial assumptions, taboos, fears, prejudices, which men in effective numbers believe so fully that they act accordingly." The malformed opinions Agee listed ranged from views about the "nobleness of war and democracy," to the conviction that groups and races can be guilty *as* groups or races, or that it is possible "to enjoy the benefits of materialism without being liable to its hazards." Such beliefs were really what caused people to act. Seldom did they act out of personal conviction or religious belief. More often than not, they simply adopted the incorrect thoughts of others.

The second of the two articles was written for the Christmas (1945) issue of *Time* and is a meditation about how all men bear the Christ child in their hearts. The typed manuscript of the story is heavily edited (whether by Agee is impossible to say); but it is relevant to note that the Christmas issue of *Time* that year contained only a watered-down version of Agee's draft, part of which was a long quotation from St. Matthew.

Popular Religion

Consider the lilies of the field, how they toil not, neither do they spin; yet Solomon in all his glory was not arrayed like one of these. Therefore take no thought for the morrow, whether ye eat, or whether ye sleep, or wherewithal ye shall be clothed; for verily I say unto you, all these things shall be added unto you. Sufficient unto the day is the evil thereof. (QUOTE CHAPTER AND VERSE: CK QUOTE)

If every man in the Christian world were asked whether he believed these lines, it is probable that a surprisingly large minority would say, and sincerely mean, that they did. If everyone who said and meant that he believed these lines were asked in what degree he put, or even tried to put, his belief into practise, the affirmative minority would, judging by contemporary evidence, be infinitesimal. Such beliefs can be put into practise only by those who so thoroughly believe them, that every demand, responsibility, pressure and need of daily existence seems trivial beside them. A good many Americans, to limit the field, honestly enough claim to believe in God; and a good number try, honestly enough, to act accordingly. But the world's history, and the daily and future destiny of every individual, are given their shape, meanwhile, by the thousands of great and trivial assumptions, taboos, fears, prejudices, which men in effective numbers believe so fully that they act accordingly. If the same poll mentioned above were applied on the questions, for instance, of spitting on one's flag, or of striking one's mother, the answers would be far more vigorous.

Some of these conditioned reflexes are as ancient as any known religion; some have developed as recently as this fall. Some are all but universally accepted; some are accepted only by one economic or social or mental class, or by one sex, or in one region, and are as vigorously contradicted by another. Some appear to have strong elements of good; others are not only patently or implicitly evil, but appear to guarantee disaster as thoroughly in this material life as in each personality or in any world to come. Aware that few if any such beliefs apply to everyone; that none apply only to some historically ineffective minority; that the correct boundary of application is often impossible to define; and that in most human beings, including the compilers, it is never wholly possible to correct the tendency to assign to one's neighbor, or to one's enemy, shortcomings which are most profitably examined in oneself, TIME here briefly lists a few examples. Insofar as seems roughly possible, and especially relevant, these will be followed by limiting classification and by comment. From time to time, in subsequent issues, the list will be added to.

The following beliefs have developed or have been notably intensified during or since the war:

#That in war, it is no longer shameful to confess fear; but is, indeed, all but obligatory. (This is perhaps more generally believed by civilians and by propagandists than by combatants. It arises perhaps in part from a more mature and more scientific understanding of courage; in part because it helps the safe and more or less guilty civilian, or propagandist, share the illusion of unity with the combatant.)

#That war is just "a dirty job that has to be done". (A reaction against overblown statements of war aims and meanings; something relatively new in self-justification; this too is more often articulated by non-combatants than by combatants.)

#That the U.S., and the U.S. alone, entered, fought in, and emerged from this war with its motives and ideals clean and uncompromised.

#That the war brought on a profound and widespread religious revival, which is still deepening and broadening. That it is deep and broad enough to save mankind. That religion is 1) essential to our daily life, private, public and international; 2) non-essential, and indeed unemployable, but a good thing all the same.

#That the American Way of Life is the best on earth, and the best in history, and the best conceivable.

#That no American wants war; that no Russian wants peace; that no European wants to do anything for himself which he can get Americans to do for him.

#That to follow a generous impulse disinterestedly is to be played for a sucker.

#That anyone who did not recognize the viciousness of fascism after 1941 is to be mistrusted; that anyone who recognized its viciousness before 1940 is even more to be mistrusted.

#That all men except Germans, Japanese and potentially Russians, are created fundamentally good; or in another phrasing, that the laws of heredity are absolute in the case of enemies or potential enemies, those of environment in the case of ourselves and our friends. An important variant: The Anglo-Saxon stock is the best on earth; the Teutonic, when Americanized, is almost as good. Latins, etc., are not at all necessarily "bad" people; but with a few notable exceptions (Jesus Christ, Joan of Arc, etc.) they cannot hope to live down their inferior stock.

#That though it may be impossible to keep the secret of the atomic bomb, American ingenuity will always guarantee us a comfortable lead.

#That man has only to learn to master the machines and the techniques he has developed, to live happily ever after.

#That it is possible to enjoy the benefits of materialism without being liable to its hazards.

#That those who talk of a world control commision [sic] for atomic energy probably have right on their side but their heads in the clouds; that those who believe that such control would prove useless unless the world were also politically and economically unified, are 1) harmless, 2) dangerous maniacs.

#That those who doubt that our best efforts towards peace will be sufficient—people variously called skeptics, pessimists, destructive critics, prophets of doom, calamity howlers, etc. etc.—are dangerous and irresponsible citizens, and should be shut up. (Older version "Don't knock—Boost.")

#That tolerance of other races and religions, since it marks the difference between democracy and fascism, must be encouraged; but that the Anglo-Saxon stock is still the best; and that outside of befriending one or two outsiders to prove your tolerance, it is best to stick to the superior races.

#That war is obligatory if you are attacked; that any means used to defeat the enemy is all right if you are fighting in self-defense, and if they started fighting dirty first. That you must do your share; that if you don't, you are Unamerican.

#That if there is another war, it will be because we let another Hitler rise to power. That wars are not caused by people, but by dictators and by fascism. Anything fascist is bad; anything communist is worse; anything democratic, liberal, progressive, or antifascist is above both suspicion and reproach.

#That a serviceman or veteran is right because he is a serviceman or veteran, and deserves all we can give him, especially when it makes good publicity (see NATIONAL AFFAIRS—"dream week" in Penn.Hotel). That a man with campaign ribbons and a Purple Heart is most right and most deserving of all. That because mothers "gave" their sons, and wives their husbands, they too must be treated right.

#That democracy can be taught.

#That democracy can be forced on others.

(1945?)

Christmas 1945

Lully, lullay
Thou little tiny child,
By by, Lully lullay.
O Sisters too,
How may we do
For to preserve this day
This poor youngling,
For whom we sing
By by, lully lullay?

Herod the King
In his raging
Charged he hath this day
His men of might,
In his own sight,
All young children to slay.

That woe is me,
Poor child, for thee!
And ever morn and day,
For thy parting
Neither say nor sing
By by, lully lullay!
—The Coventry Carol; ??th Century.

It is not likely that Christmas has ever held more grateful meanings than it does this year; or meaning more pitiful. Nearly everywhere, though most of the world is still drowned in anguish, the war, at least, is over. All over the world, people who have long been heartsick for home, or in their empty or ruined homes, are together again; home to stay for Christmas. In most homes, even those which call themselves Christian,

Christmas has long ago ceased to be regarded as much of a religious feast; it is chiefly domestic. This year, even in the U.S., which has managed cheerfully to ignore the suffering of the rest of the world, and the responsibility which that suffering imposes, the delight in family shines like childhoods' best dreams of a Christmas tree.

Yet few people, this year, can hear the words "peace on earth" without unbearable sadness or bitterness. Even during the war, when Christmas came, there was the ravenous and often noble hope for peace itself, and for what peace would bring. But peace brought the world about as near the dead end of hope as life can sustain; brought terror as pervasive and as valid as man has ever contrived for his destruction; brought such a great disordering decline and suicidal nervelessness in beliefs, values, allegiances, as the world can ever have known. To this country, in particular, it brought a depth of moral anesthesia from which we shall with great difficulty, if ever, awake. Pressures ever increasingly severe for more than a century now, with the new peace, became so grim, that it is now something of a miracle for any man even to remain moderately human—to say nothing of undertaking responsibility toward all that is best in him.

In this year of Our Lord 1945, Christmas has ceased to be regarded as much of a religious feast; it is chiefly domestic. Yet in unimaginable millions of men and women, this Christmas, Christ is born again: a Child Whom may stand for all that is most brave, most innocent, most loving, most kin to the divine in all men, whether Christian or not. All that may be called the soul, all that awakes or fructifies the soul, is touched once more to life. It is all that is excellent that all men in all the world most earnestly love and desire; that unbelievably massive yet individual vitality of goodness which blooms in such tragic paradox in ways and which, far more tragically still, appears unable to save us now.

For even if the Child could save us, it is hard to imagine how in most men, even in those who most dearly value and desire His Life, He can survive so much as the day of His Birth. For to say nothing of the outward and, it would seem, mortally deranged and incurable world, each personality is at war within itself, since Each of us must recognize in himself not only the Child, but also the Mother and the Foster-Father, the Shepherds and the Magi, the Angels and the Beasts, and Herod, as well. And in the world as it is today, only the accidents of moral genius or imbecility can prevent any of us being, most of all, Herod. Moreover, it is clearer than perhaps ever before, that there is no outward way to flee from Herod; no Egypt in this world. There is possible only, in each man, a dangerous and difficult withdrawal into the depths of his own conscience and his own forgotten nature, into his own land, in fact, of ancient bondage, if he desires that this Child survive the Herod in him.

But it is more difficult than that. For the Parents did not flee with the Child into exile, or conceal Him, or protect and raise Him, in order that he might live[,] far less return to seize power from Herod or Herod's successor. All this was done purely in order that He might increase in wisdom and stature, desert even his Mother and his Foster-Father, act in entire faithfulness to His own nature, and, in the fulness of time, desiring it no more than any man, choose to accept death.

. . .

This guardianship, ripening and acceptance is the only end available to all that is best in anyone. Nothing else, by comparison, is of the least importance. Most other considerations, including many that for excellent reasons mean a great deal (or, as we say, "the world") to most men serve chiefly and, it appears, inescapably, as obstruction and defeat.

Not many people have the reckless honesty to admit, or even rationally isolate this fact—a fact especially obscure in a nation whose chief sense of all life, as of Christmas, is an invincible belief in Santa Claus; yet in their hearts, an infinite number of people know it. If enough people were to believe it, and practise it, in the reckless honesty, without which it lose its existence, the world's one hope of survival might quite incidentally reside in just that action—with such an extravagant dissolving of all that we know as civilization, as can scarcely be imagined. It appears pretty clearly, on the other hand, that the world's survival rests in no other kind of hope or effort. Least of all would it reside in any of the efforts, at present pretending to some vigor, to exploit or compromise religion for any purposes of security, such as a "Christian society," or indeed for any purposes other than its own. For in any such doubtful eventuality, soul and world would be destroyed as one.

For man is a rational animal—a significant fact which has never successfully been resolved with his spirituality and, unlike contemporary pressures, is hardly likely to be. He is also the most intricately selfish animal—a terrifying fact, the ends and implications of whose terror move, through vast and often very tireless fertile areas of self-justification capable of cryptic infinitudes of self-deceit. Judging by past and still more by present performance most men, kindly and well-meaning and tragically trapped as they are, will find destruction, rather, through the most earnest and piteous efforts to protect much more, and other, than their own souls. In these efforts they will use their best intelligence, guided by self-interest, described, at its most ruinous, as "enlightened".

For these reasons nearly every man, even as he first looks at the newborn Child within him, knows that He must not be allowed to survive His infancy.

That is the basic reason, however faintly realized, why Christmas this year is remarkably dear to so many, who are trying to compensate their central despair insofar as they can, in prodigally loving and giving, with all their resource, in those few living creatures they can trust.

For men who have shown themselves careless of woe even of their Allies, to say nothing of forgiving, far less loving, their enemies, it is why this year, at its root, is an inexpressibly sad season—a season in which much of the human race gazes with longing at all it most loves and, helplessly, betrays it. Whereas for some men, whom the rich tyranies [sic] of Herod can no longer bully into civility but at last, in their insupportable arrogance, send underground. But it is also a day of such untouchable beauty, such irreducible hope and gratitude, as the Christian world can hardly before have known, save in the First.

Part IV
CULTURAL AND
AUTOBIOGRAPHICAL
EXPERIMENTS

(1945-1948)

Three 1940's Sonnets

1940's Sonnets

These poems demonstrate the intensity of Agee's unhappiness during the years after the Second World War. The first of these sonnets is written about those who gave their lives in the war. In that poem the speaker pleads that impossible patriotic excuses should not be given to account for the inexplicable deaths caused by war. Two other sonnets are entitled "November 1945" and are more personal. Together they indicate Agee's doubt that he could continue as an artist in a period which seemed so bleak.

Three Sonnets

We soldiers of all nations who lie killed
Ask little: That you never, in our name,
Dare say we died that man might be fulfilled.
The earth should vomit us, against that shame.
We died; that is enough. Many died well,
Of both sides; most of us died senselessly;
Ask soldiers who outlived us; they may tell
How many died to make men slaves, or free.
We died. None knew, few tried to guess, just why.
No one knows now, on either side the grave.
If you insist you know, by all means try,
That being your trade, to make the knowledge save.
But never use, not as you honor sorrow,
Our yesterdays to garnish your tomorrow.

"November 1945"

I

Now on the world and on my life as well,
Ancient in beauty, infant in such fear
As no time else had dreamed, nor shall dispel,
Loosen the ashes of another year.
Whether by nature's will, man's or my own,
I who by chance walked softly past a war
Shall not by any chance the world has known
Be here, and breathing, many autumns more.
Only, with all who in past worlds have died,
I had, till lately, faced my death secure,
Knowing my hunger only was denied;

All I most loved and honored would endure.
But this year, dying, struck wild as it fell,
Ending itself, me, and the world as well.

II

This being so, and thirty and five years
So nearly vanished, and so little used;
All delights turned as trivial as all tears,
All meanings altered and all hopes refused;
By what means shall I, in what little while
Abides my being, on such narrowed span
As will and world allow, find out that trial
Of strength wherethrough, well fought, I die a man?
O long, long, idle in tribulation,
Grown fat in all I did because I must,
I dreamed at least I knew my own salvation:
Now I begin to wake, and it is dust.
Where is the Angel in whose rage alone
Wrestling, I live? The night is nearly gone.

"1928 Story" (1948)

"1928 Story" (1948?)

This short story is the first sustained piece of autobiographical writing which Agee completed in the nineteen-forties. It is a lamentation about the contemporary spiritual climate and therefore can be associated with other analytical and autobiographical pieces included in this collection, but it is also an example of Agee's ability to take memories from his earlier life and use them for fiction. This method clearly foreshadows the autobiographical fiction of *The Morning Watch* and *A Death in the Family*. This story has been transcribed from a pencil manuscript. It was edited by Victor A. Kramer in 1965 and first published in my dissertation and then in *The Texas Quarterly* in 1968.

"1928 Story"

He had not been home long when he found that one of the things he cared most for was playing the old records. His wife liked some of them too, very much, and when he put on the oldest of them she remembered, he could see, how pleased he had been that she recognized how much better they were than most of the later ones. But now that he was playing them again, and she showed how warmly she enjoyed them, he had to realize that her associations were very different from his own, referring entirely to their times together just before the war; and that she was using these already different and inadequate associations a little too eagerly, to get close to him. He knew, sadly enough, that it was still not easy for either of them to get close to each other, and he felt gentle towards her for taking whatever means she could. But he knew too that it was worthless to try to exploit this music, and its so very different associations, for any such purpose. She was badly mistaken to try. And he had to realize that he was badly mistaken himself, to use the records in his own way: that whatever was done about this music, estranged them still further, rather than bringing them together. It seemed quite possible, for that matter, that he was using them as a way of retreating from her, and from everything else. He felt that he had no business doing it, to her, or for that matter to himself. He had to get used to living in the world again, after all. And when he thought of it at all he realized that the world he had once lived in, and could never live in again, and that could never again exist, was no great loss, to him or anyone else. He had better recognize this fact; he knew that very well. Even the nineteen thirties had been increasingly distasteful, one year worse than the next before it; then the war, which in one curious sense hardly counted as a part of living—or how much did it count? He still did not know. He wondered whether he was ever likely to. And now, the middle, the last half, of the nineteen forties. Only the meanness, and fatness, and insanity, seemed to survive, as it had also survived the Depression; and in whatever ways these had changed, they seemed to have changed for the worse. There had been a kind of innocence in everything about the old years, that gave some sort of charm even to the worst of it. In a way, of course, the innocence had survived everything too. But it seemed a kind of innocence, now, that has no business being so innocent. And the sophistication, such as it was, was the most blinding thing of all. (What do I mean, he thought; but lacked the energy to specify.) Very likely, he realized, all this was purely subjective—a matter simply of his having been young during certain years, older during certain other years, and, God knew, older still right now. That, and beginning to learn about himself that he was infantile, to use a word out of a vocabulary which sickened him; that he had never really grown up, whatever that might mean, or even wanted. Good Lord, he thought, if I'm not careful I'm going to find out I'm a Conservative, after all.

Or was he. Was it even true that he had not grown up, or hadn't wanted to? He had certainly been filled with a lot of easy hope, back during the Depression, when he and practically everyone else he knew had gone Left. And even when he found he was far less sanguine than most of his friends he had for a long time remained hopeful, and active. For several years his reflexes and ideas had been as thoroughly Marxian as they were Freudian, in the purely smattering way, that is, that he knew anything about either. Then his Freudian ideas had frayed out among the renegades and the schools, and his Marxian ideas had frayed out to something, he supposed, that was most easily defensable as political agnosticism, and for some years now, though he still used the same vocabulary and reacted to a great extent, he was afraid, according to the same reflexes—with a few additions which he supposed and hoped were his own—he had found it almost never possible to trust either his own judgements or those of anybody else. Certainly, by now, he felt no trust or hope in anything, that anyone might do or even say. It was a stupefied country, and evidently a stupefied world, and as stupefied as anything else was his sense of universal mistrust and of hopeless regret, his dependence on mere taste, his pleasure in the sensuous, his miserable reluctance to live in the world as it was, and to discard the pleasures of recall.

If I could write about this, he thought, maybe it would amount to something, or maybe at least it would help clear my mind. But he knew that he was quite unqualified to write it, and that he had no heart even to try, or even to think about it in terms of writing. It was so long since he had really felt any heart for that. During the war it had seemed, for a while, as if something had returned—yes, actually, for a while, he knew it had returned. First industriously, then more and more irregularly, finally petering out, all but entirely. He had kept a journal— which as it petered out turned more and more into guide notes—and he realized that there had been some pretty good things in the journal, here and there anyhow. Yet he was not sorry that he had destroyed it. And he was rather more sorry than glad that of the five poems he had written he had sent one, the Christmas one, to his wife, and that she had sent it along, without asking him, to *Partisan Review*, which had printed it. He remembered rather bitterly the letter a quite good poet (but not after all so *God* damned good himself) had sent him: the poem was not thoroughly finished—understandingly enough under the circumstances, and was indeed in many respects a remarkably fine job—in some respects, in the poet's opinion, "far and away ahead of anything else you've done." He was delighted to see new work after so long a silence, and hoped that Irvine would remember that he, the poet, too, was an editor, and that poems as good as that don't grow on trees. He might, he said, take issue on one matter, if he felt that discussion of anything besides pure questions of technique were not hopelessly presumptuous and beside the point. He referred, of course, to the disturbing hint in lines 4-7 that Irvine was beginning perhaps to take a polite interest in God. That way, the poet begged leave to advise, madness lay, in his humble opinion—though one could if one liked (and indeed must, whether one liked or not) remember Dante and, if you insist, Eliot. But for a truly contemporary man, such as Irvine? But he would say no more. And it was in every important respect a welcome and truly superb poem. He looked forward to a resumption of their old bouts, "when this indecent mess is over."

He was just as glad he had destroyed the other four— though one, anyhow, was probably a better poem anyway than The Nativity. And he was not at all sorry that he hadn't bothered to answer the letter—though it did embarrass him to remember his embarrassment over that, the evening they met.

He had no interest in talking about poetry, and very little
interest in reading it—or anything else, for that matter, of contemporary work anyhow. Some of it was good, he supposed, a
damn sight better, anyhow, than *he* had ever done. But he had
no trust in it—or to put it more simply, no interest whatever.
He detected in this lack of interest some aliment of jealousy, of
self-pity; though he had long ago pretty thoroughly given up the
idea that he was a writer. Or had he? If I haven't, he thought,
it's high time I did. Like so many of the others, he realized, he
had just been one of the overliterate "sensitive" middle-class
boys with a great deal of adolescent excitement and a certain fa-
cility of the senses and with words and forms. Of most of them
he couldn't see that they were anything more than this. The difference was, simply, that they had kept on producing. Maybe the
difference was, that essentially it was they who had remained
adolescent, that it was he, comparatively (oh *very* comparatively) speaking, who had grown up. In any case he saw nothing
in their work (what little of it, he took care to remind himself,
I've read), that could convince him that any one of them, except
unquestionably Auden, was in the least what he meant by being
a good artist. Smooth craftsman, adroit—well *fairly* adroit—
intellectuals, experienced manipulators of images that came too
easily; producers of no doubt perfectly creditable work that didn't
have an ounce wit to the ton, of even the most modest, minor
art. Certainly it was impossible to regret not being one of them.
The thing to regret was: was he not something more than that?
He could not entirely, or permanently anyhow, get over the feeling that he was. And this feeling persisted even though he realized, thinking back over the writing he had done, that nothing
existed in that writing—or at best very little and very debatable—
to indicate it. It settled nothing either, to remind himself that no
matter how glib the non-artists were, a good artist too is a man
who constantly produces.

Why did that make no difference?

Melville? Coleridge?

He caught himself in shame: the old, adolescent has it.

He realized that each of these producers whom he held,
yes, more or less in contempt, must certainly have in themselves that confidence that they at least, no matter about the
others, were true artists, which for all his own years-long stultifi-
cation, he could not get rid of.

So what, he thought. And suddenly, with incredible sadness, he remembered a morning out at the shore, when, though the paper was soft with dampness, he had sat on through lunch (eating the sandwiches his mother brought), until he had finished the story of the girls and boys and of the rat—so tired that several times he put his forehead down on to the paper and stayed there several minutes, and nauseated with chain smoking (it was his first summer of being open with tobacco), but during the six and a half hours the job had taken, not once getting out of the chair except to go to the bathroom. Towards the end he had felt almost irresistible haste to finish so that he could read it to his mother; and had successfully resisted the haste and finished it as it ought to be finished; in spite of the speed, it had been a really carefully written story. And how proudly and unexpectedly he realized, once it was done, that for the first time in his life he felt very well in control of his eagerness to read it to his mother or to anyone else—in fact, it became clear to him that he really had no desire to read it, to anyone except himself, and that very likely he would not bother to read to her, either, the things he had brought along from school, that hadn't been printed yet. He read the story over, coldly, correcting and recasting with a feeling of perfect professionalism, and at the same time with the coldness and the resourceful proficiency, felt complete enjoyment and satisfaction. He clipped it, transferred the spring's work to a lower drawer, and laid the manuscript carefully into the empty, upper left-hand drawer. He stood up, stiff, slightly dazed, swollen with self-delight, and walked quietly back into the kitchen to the gin bottle. He was already allowed to drink, moderately, and might with impunity have made himself a highball, but he felt for some reason, doubtless connected with the lack of need to read the story to his mother, more triumphant in deceit. He poured an inch into a tumbler, added a little water, and drank it down rather quickly. Then he put ice and ginger ale into a glass and, his head swimming quietly, went out onto the screened front porch. He cranked up the portable, put on *West Side Blues*, sat down and looked around him through the three screens, feeling like a king.

It was going to be a wonderful summer.

He heard the delicate, passionate music through, now, in a strange state of mind: perfectly, fiber by fiber, in cold and helpless regret; perfectly at the same time, recalling, re-experiencing, the best that he had ever heard in it. The record had been new to him that spring, and he had first heard it at a perfect time to hear it, when his delight in jazz music was experienced but still fresh, in opening bloom. The record had seemed to him the best that need ever be asked for, of jazz, or of any other music. He had tried to use it to prove to his mother and father that jazz is as pure a lyric art as can exist, and that it can reach, among several men at once, improvising at that, great subtlety of mood, and beautiful development and integrity within that mood—as thorough and as good, he insisted, as anything in Mozart, and as distinct in everyway, not a chance missed or soft pedaled, not a superfluous note. His father grinned and said he agreed there was nothing soft-pedaled about it anyhow, and sipped his highball. He replied, with astonishment and almost with rage, as to someone who sneers comfortably at one's close friend, that at least half of that record was played mezzo-piano or still more quietly, as anyone who had any ears could hear. His father, sorry for having sneered, answered this affront gently, saying that he guessed he just didn't have the right kind of ear for jazz, though he thought it was pleasant enough to listen to. Disheartened, and ashamed of his vehemence, Irvine then avoided asking his mother for her comment; but at the first rebalancing of feelings that seemed to her appropriate (and she had a fairly careful though far from adequate intuition for this) she said, also gently, that while perhaps she liked it better than Irvine's father, and thought it very pretty and pleasing indeed, and in places really *talented*, she could perfectly well see what Irvine meant about the lyricism, she certainly couldn't feel that it was possible to compare it with *Mozart*, or really that you could call it an art, perhaps. Irvine said quietly, all but interrupting her that he hadn't at all meant an out-and-out, all-round comparison with Mozart, and also he didn't mean "art," at all the way she said, that the worse thing that could happen to jazz would be, if people got to thinking of it as an "art," and he hated to think what any jazz musician would feel about anyone who said so—not that he knew any—but all the same in its own entirely distinct way it obviously *was* an art, with very strong and distinct disciplines of its own, and one that could be very eloquent and accurate about emotions and states of mind, too, like the one he had just played, and—. She interrupted, again gently, to say that though very likely, in the special sense he meant, it was an art, she supposed the real trouble, the real reason she wasn't as appreciative of it as she'd like to be, was a difference in generations. He asked, again too quietly, what kind of really good music she thought that could be said of: Mozart? And she replied, trying not to be rough or complacent in her triumph, that that was exactly the difference she meant, between Louis Armstrong and Mozart. "For East is East and West is West," Irvine's father said, smiling in a friendly way. And he hastened to add that he had said this not to make a comparison, to the disadvantage of either musician (here he could not wholly restrain his slight but not malevolent amusement), it simply came into his head anent the differences between the generations. ("Anent," a word which amused him, did not amuse his son.) The conversation then became general, as both parents remembered popular songs they had liked, which had not been enjoyed by their parents, and songs their parents had liked, which had seemed, at best, prettily old-fashioned to them. They began to hum and sing these songs, some of which interested and pleased Irvine, and before long, regretting that he had laid himself open, and had been so talkative (for his new motto was "silence, exile and cunning"), he decided not to try to bring it up again, listened with real pleasure to their singing, and even joined in, where he could.

The music had developed in him a distinct image of a place he had never known. When he tried to take the image apart, he realized that nothing much like it was, for that matter, likely to exist. But in the course of taking it apart, and imagining what was likely in it and what was not so likely, he only made it the less likely, and was satisfied that his changes were improvements. It was not a large room, and was not decorated. It had a quality of semi-legality.

It was very late. Nearly everyone had gone home. Those who stayed were those who were there for the night. They were nearly all around thirty—on Irvine's scale of age, neither young nor old. Most of them were negroes. Most of them were also poor people, working people, but not of a kind to work any harder than was absolutely necessary; not of a kind, in fact, to work for security. Though they were of an age when most people, of whatever degree of wealth or poverty, have become responsible, and careful, it had never occurred to them to live for anything other than enjoyment, and it probably never would. In a sense they were as unquestionably dedicated as the musicians themselves—who would now, like them, soon be quitting for the night. Those who had to, musicians and listeners alike, would go straight on from here to their day's work. Those who could afford to would soon be asleep.

Now they were all at the most beautiful time of the night, and in the most beautiful of states of being: full of gin, but no longer at all drunk; deeply tired, and quiet; completely gentle. Some kept on drinking gin; others drank black coffee; the place was never at its worst very professional, except when the un-liked type of white came in; now it was as filled with easy fond-ness, and a lack of commercialism as the best kind of love. Faces which more normally might be sharp, clownish, brutal, de-manding, suspicious, were all perfected, now: responsive as drumbeats; yet as peaceful as sleep. The waiter, bringing more drinks and more coffee, walked in perfect silence; the drinking too was silent: not one noise of china. Some watched the musi-cians, or lifted their eyes and watched, smiling slightly, during the best moments. Most were looking at nothing; they were simply listening. A girl moved softly against the man she sat with; he put his hand along the side of her head and brought her head against his chest. The singer and the clarinetist, both low, sank lower, through chromatic minor thirds; the pianist picked it up. Two simple chords, a strong bass note; a bass tenth and the swung chord, against descending lacework, sharply, softly played. Now the tenths descending, the right hand rising—and in both hands, a sudden few chords of chisel-like energy, dissolving into tremolos. The bass again, squaring it out for the steep run down, to the low melting of the hands; then a climb of arpeggio chords, major, and the trumpeter takes it off the last, flatted note, lifting, a half tone, another, a third high, the note held, the trombone gathered beneath that, and the clarinet, and the guitar, and the brushes, and the piano at its most elementary, while the held note holds, intensifies, enlarges, shines, in the pulsing of the other instruments, a full eight beats: to burst open at length into a rapturously gentle, spasmic figure, built on that high note and down from it, five times repeated, then climbing a full tone and down again, down, well into the low register and flaring up again, and down, an octave—to the piano's bell-like left hand, deep, and ringing right, five octaves up, flaring its chords out of its shaking heart, descending with each, shading over into minor, imitating the trumpet's opening salute as it comes into middle voice, flatting: a held breath, and the trumpet's imitation of the imitation, at the most simple possible, as simple as falling at last to sleep.

The window shades were drawn; daylight came through the cracks in them. There was dew on the rails of the track and on the weeds, and now that the music was over, you could hear roosters crowing.

The cornetist had drained his horn. Now he wrapped it in an old silk scarf and snapped it into its case.

It was time to go to work, but nobody was moving yet.

He cranked the machine, and started again with the piano solo, and sat back again. He had never been to a place like the one he imagined, yet it was more familiar to him than any place he had ever known. He tried taking it apart again, and realized, as he had often before, that it was not likely that there was any place like it. [But that did not impress him.] Musicians as good as those earned their living by it; even when they played for pleasure, even if they were Negroes, they probably never played in a place so poor. Or even if they did, it was not situated as this was, in a great field at the edge of the city, near the tracks; a field of dump-heaps, rusty iron, wild grasses and rough flowers, great lonely signboards, a few mysteriously flashing stalks of corn. You did not look out through the shade into the shining morning and watch hundreds of men, along the tracks, and the paths invisible along the great field, on their way to work. You did not see, so clearly, like the most beautiful closeup, the dew on the shine and oily rust of a section of rail and frogplate, the gravelly cinders and the oak tie, the dew on the spikey, flowering weed. Nor was it likely, in the Southern city he was thinking of—New Orleans? Algiers?—that whites and Negroes, however fond of the same music, would be so thoroughly at ease together as this. And if such an outlandish outsider as he should find his way there, would he ever be allowed to come in? Or if allowed, wouldn't he manage to destroy the spirit, quality and ease of everything?

But none of these doubts made any difference. With each critical repetition, in fact, he only added further detail to the reality of the place—a calendar against the wall, the picture of a girl in a great red hat; a cockroach on the electric light wire; the subdued sound of eggs frying back in the little kitchen; the cook leaning his face at his window, during the final solo; the way it sounded to a man on his way to work, a quarter of a mile up the track, and the fleck of steam above the starting locomotive, far down at the roundhouse. You could see a little of the river from there, like moving putty, but guess its grandeur mainly by the smallness of everything on the far side. If it didn't exist, it ought to, and that suited him. But of course it did exist, and so did ten thousand other things as good, in just this kind of music.

He turned back the pickup and put the record back in its folder.

There was no chance, for him at least, he knew, of ever being a hundredth as good as that, in the art he worked at, and hoped to practice; but today, and still at his age in general, his own confidence was untroubled, even by such knowledge. He was glad there were such musicians in the world, and hoped he might learn something from them, and felt no fear for himself; only great sureness and pleasure.

He leaned back once more in the noisy wicker chair and looked through the three screened sides of the porch at the screened, shingled cottages along the irregular shore. Salt had made patterns on the screen on the sea side; there was already a little sand along the porch. It was a dull, cool dry, and the cottages too looked dull—even boring, he supposed; but he liked the way they looked, and the silly caps and suits hung out in the back.

It was going to be a wonderful summer.

He thought of the new story he had finished earlier in the afternoon, secure in its otherwise empty drawer, the first work of the vacation—very possibly his best so far, the first day. He felt too pleased and too mature even to reread it. He thought of the gin in the kitchen cupboard, and the whiskey hidden (not too secretively) in the sideboard; he felt too well even to take another drink.

He went upstairs and changed into his bathing suit.

Like most of the beaches along this rough section of the shore, the one just below Irvine's cottage, to which he came now, was a makeshift, hundred-foot crescent along which sand had been dumped. The sand was renewed every spring, and stayed fairly well, but even by this time of year, late June, you could feel the rocks under foot and see them working through. A small sign freshly painted each spring, appealed to the bathers as gentlemen and ladies with the single word: PLEASE! and on the whole the beach was kept quite tidy. A life-preserver, also freshly painted, hung from a T-shaped oak stand; by the preceding summer, it had begun to appeal to Irvine as an esoteric emblem. Except at high tide it was necessary to wade on rocks and to get off your feet as soon as the water would hold you. This in turn, was uncomfortable, except for the proudly brash, for even in sunny weather the water was cold. Those who intended to spend much time swimming and sun bathing went to the Yacht Club float, a quarter of a mile downshore, or drove three miles upshore, in their bathing suits, to the broad public beach; or those few who knew the wealthier families of the neighborhood well enough, used their small, expensively developed private beaches, taking care not to invite themselves too often. But for casual swimming, everybody was used to and even rather fond of the deficiencies of these small semi-public ledges of discouraged sand which, like the small neat yacht clubs, were maintained by and for the cottage owners of the middle class.

There was practically nobody out on this cloudy afternoon, and Irvine was glad; the first few days of vacation always involved many exchanges of senseless courtesies, and the longer they were put off the better. His family had been spending summers here since he was five, among other equally stable cottage-owners. Everyone knew everyone else, amiably enough but in general, quiet avoidance, without interest or fondness. For as Irvine had only lately begun to realize, most people of his parents' generation cared for privacy almost as thoroughly as he did, and made these crowded vacation compromises chiefly because they could afford nothing better—though he was still unable to understand how they could endure the uses they made of such privacy and leisure as they had. Mrs. Dart and her son Eddie and her daughter Anna were on the beach, and Irvine said hello to them, and talked with them, emptily but pleasantly enough, while he smoked half a cigarette; then excused himself, put it out, and made for the water a little sooner than he wanted to.

It was even colder than he had expected. He swam out as fast as he could until he was winded, turned over and floated, and looked back at the shore. The Darts, to his satisfaction, were picking their way up to the duckboard between the high rocks. He watched Eddie help his heavy Mother over a difficult place. It was a natural enough courtesy, and he would have done it himself without a second or even a first thought; but it had a look of unquestioned servility and of tedium, which he disliked.

He watched Anna's too-short, dabbing steps in her white rubber bathing suits [*sic*]. He could not feel the least interest in her, either, though he reflected now that she had developed a good deal, over the winter, and had watched him surreptitiously, while he talked with her brother and mother, in a way which would have made the coming summer look exciting, if she had been any girl less dull. For the first time he felt restive and uneasy, almost imprisoned, in the prospect of a whole summer in this place.

He warmed himself by swimming some more, and lay over and looked back again. Now he could see the whole range of middle-sized, somewhat too closely crowded cottages, stepped up-and-down, back-and-forth, along the rock bluffs; and, down to the left, the compact, rather intricate yacht club, with its staring coat of new paint. Under this clouded light the brown and gray shingled cottages, and the brown and gray rocks, and the vegetation, were particularly drab, whereas the white on the water and on the clubhouse and the intense perfect ring of the life-preserver on his beach, glowed like white cloths at dusk. He saw a sedan turn in from the highway. George Helms was gassing his launch. Jordan Reid was already mooring; the main sail, weltering, sank without a sound. Four people whom he could not quite recognize, but knew were no strangers, lolled rather disconsolately on the float. Far behind his floating head, like a lost cowbell, a buoy drizzled its warnings. Down between the rocks, along the section of duck board, came two more people to his empty beach.

Both were female; and even at this distance, he knew they were strangers. He wanted to swim to shore as quickly as possible. Though he was suddenly very cold, he waited, while they laid aside their robes and walked cautiously into the water. One, in dark blue, was a mature body; the other, he was sure now, was young. Her bathing suit was the color of cedar. As soon as they were sufficiently absorbed in swimming not to notice him, he hurried in, dried himself, lighted a cigarette, and carefully examined a barnacle cut in his heel. By the time he was able to taste the tobacco, they were coming in. They looked studiously into the water as if they were trying not to admit that they were dismayed to have committed themselves to such a place for the summer. Irvine suddenly realized that the life-preserver was badly corroded; a bottle, emptied of sun tan oil, leaned against a rock. The older woman had a hard well-kept body and a hard well-kept face which were unpleasantly masculine. Irvine did his best not to look either at the girl, or too pointedly away from her; but their eyes met, on her part cooly, he could see, on his, in a frightening spasm of hopeless joy. Instantly, proudly, yet gently, and he suspected, contemptuously, she looked away. He looked as quickly away; he felt as if she had slapped him.

He knew he must be calm, and courteous; he took care to catch the older woman's eye. "How do you do," he said, smiling gravely, and bowing his head, he realized too late, with a much too presumptuous graciousness. Her eyes were knowing and impersonal. "How do you do," she said, and turned from him to pick up her towel. She and the girl dried themselves in vigorous silence, put on their robes and sat down, their backs to him, a little ahead of him and to the right. The line of the girl's cheek and her [ ]* rubber cap, were very cold and remote as she looked away at the water. Then as she drew up one knee and, putting both hands beneath her left ear unfastened the chin-strap, he saw the subtly vigilent turning of the older woman's head. But the woman said nothing, and the girl removed her cap and, her fingers spread from the nape, shook the damp hair loose. It was fine, flowerlike, full of golden light, the color of brown sugar. Irvine felt again, but more gently, the incredulous fear and kindliness of the moment when their eyes met. He knew by their voices that, so long as he remained, they were able only to make conversation. He put on his sneakers and laced them, carefully took apart and scattered his cigarette, caped his towel over his shoulders, and started towards the duckboard, stooping as he walked, to pick up the empty oil bottle. As he passed behind them he murmured, "good afternoon," in the inflection appropriate to withdrawal. The woman replied in the same tone, but when, a second later, the girl said it, the words had become a salutation, to which he felt, as he climbed the duckboard, the back of his neck burning, he should have replied.

Normally, showering after a swim, he merely rinsed off the brine. Now he used soap as well, and was more than usually interested in his body; and as he combed his hair, he watched himself carefully in the mirror. But his mind was so absorbed in her image, as she came out of the water, that he hardly saw himself. It was awkward and unpleasant, wading on rocks which

---

*Adjectives illegible.

were not only sharp but unfamiliar; but her awkwardness continually suggested her grace. For all her restraint, her breath was
shakey and her teeth rattled. Her chilled lips were almost the
color of her eyes. She had the kind of delicate skin which shows
cold readily, and beautifully; her thighs were a mulled, marbled
net of rose and azure. Tight with cold, and caught small in the
gray-gold bathing-cap, her features, and her head were at once
nun-like and saurian. Her breasts were also tightened with the
cold, and he tried hard not to either remember them, or imagine
them.

But even better was the moment in which she had shown
her hair.

Had she known? Or done it unconsciously, because unconsciously she was attracted to him? Or was she unconscious of
his existence? Or had she done this in deliberate contempt?

She had spoken to him; he remembered her voice; it was
as startling as her eyes, and as impossible to deduce.

Don't be a fool, he kept warning himself. Take your time.
Don't ask questions, or give yourself away. Don't try to force
yourself on her. It's a long summer. You'll know her, soon
enough.

But it was even harder to keep to himself a matter of such
importance, than it would have been to betray himself. All during supper he was as silent, and as secret, as if he had just committed murder, and as elegant as if he were dining among
princes. He gathered that his father honestly did not notice it,
and saw that his mother was doing her best not to show that she
did, was trying, even, to restrain her private curiosity; but it was
as obvious and painful to him as if he were shouting about it,
and he found that his efforts to appear casual were even more
stupid. He even began to realize, with something of the helpless
shame which one feels in dreams of nakedness, that he had
dressed for this purely domestic meal, almost as scrupulously as
if he were going to a party. He began to resent the girl, to try at
least to reduce her to what she really was. There was nothing,
actually, at all remarkable about her. It was a perfectly ordinary
voice, when he remembered it with any detachment. This idea
that she was unusually graceful was just so much adolescent illusion (but then he remembered the moment in which, in one
motion, she had drawn up her left knee and loosed her chin
strap; even the elbows alone, were very graceful, there was no
use doubting that). That kind of skin, in a way, which got so

mottled with cold, was actually rather ugly, under those conditions, anyhow (but under other conditions, he had to admit, it
might not be so ugly; in fact it was very attractive, perhaps even
beautiful, under any conditions at all, so far as he was concerned). He did not at all like the way she had looked away from
him; after all, they were in a sense neighbors already as she must
have realized, and there had certainly been no possible grounds
for showing contempt; it suggested that she was a cold, prim,
narrow sort of girl—very much the kind, in fact, you might expect of that kind of mother. One thing was clear enough, anyway; he did not like the mother, anymore than the mother liked
him. He did not like the strong line of muscle down the outside
of her thigh, or her dark face, which looked almost shaven, or
that cold, hard, dark eye. There was no reason for that kind of
coldness. It was perfectly true that he had overdone the kind of
grand-seigneur act, the old whatsitact business! when he spoke
to her, but was he not expected to speak to her at all? There was
such a thing as courtesy, after all, and it seemed very much his
place to speak and to speak first, since they were new here; also,
he had taken natural care to address the older woman, and even
more care not to seem to demand any further conversation by
doing so. So why would it have hurt her, to say a little more
than that cold how do you do in return—the absolute minimum
required of her? Why couldn't she have at least given an opening for something more he might say himself? Or at least have
smiled? And come to think of it, why had the girl said nothing?
If either of them knew even the elements of common courtesy,
they would realize that when he was addressing the older of the
two he was addressing both of them; that in fact he had no right
to address the younger one directly, in the presence of the older
one, but certainly meant it to be for both of them. Then what
was one to make of that silence, on the part of the one he was really interested in, and that coldness, on the part of the other?
One had to make just this of it: that they were either people of
no kind of breeding at all, or snobs. Well, it wasn't exactly a
period of history where snobbery was appreciated. It—

Don't be a fool, he insisted again. You're making a mountain out of a molehill. She's just another girl; she may be a very
nice one, she may stink. You'll find out.

Within half an hour after the meal he heard himself say,
in a voice at which he wanted to shout his ridicule: "Some new
people down at the beach, this afternoon." His mother looked at

him. He detested himself. "Woman and her daughter." He felt
himself blushing and quickly got up, to be above the line of the
light. "At least I suppose it was her daughter," he said.

"New people?," his mother said, taking care not to watch
him. "Who would they be, Burt?"

His father paused. "Must be the Parkers," he said, "Linton
T. Parker. Rented the Fowler's cottage. Only new people *I've*
heard of.

"Then the Fowlers *did* go abroad?"

"I don't know whether they went abroad. I know they
rented their cottage."

"They were talking about it so much, last summer."

His father looked at her sharply, and grinned. "Don't
worry," he said, "We'll go one of these days. Might as well wait
until Irvine is old enough to get the most out of it.

"I think I'll go over to Ed's," Irvine said.

"Don't stay out too late," his mother called, as the screen
door shut.

His father shook his head at her. "Don't nag at him," he
said. "He's not a baby anymore."

Irvine's cottage was set high, quartered towards the sea
and overlooking the Yacht Club. The Fowler's cottage was further from the shore, near the bottom of an opposite slope.
Irvine could see its lights as he shut the porch door, and they
were as startling among all the other lights he could see, and as
quietly handsome as his name had been when he had first seen
it in print in his school's literary magazine.

Don't be completely childish, he told himself, and started
walking towards the lights. Even when the time came to choose
the path to the Dart's cottage, he made no effort to choose, but,
repeating, for God's sake don't be *utterly* childish, kept on towards the lights, the pit of his stomach cold.

Before he got near enough possibly to be seen, he cut off to
the right, behind several cottages, and approached the Fowler
cottage from the rear, which was dark. It was the front room
which was lighted. The girl sat on a wicker couch with her feet
drawn up and her skirt tucked carefully around her knees. The
woman sat in another wicker chair next one of the Fowler's
bridge-lamps. A man sat with his back to Irvine, in a morris-
chair. He was reading The Boston Herald and smoking a cigar,
and Irvine could see only his cheek, which looked square, beefy,
and truculent. The mother was playing Canfield and letting

cigarette smoke through her nostrils like a quiet oath. The girl was reading; he could not see what. Taking care to stay out of the light, he came closer. She read in a way that fascinated and satisfied him, detachedly, yet in complete absorption. Each time she turned a page, it was like watching someone take another mouthful of food, with perfect elegance. Then, with the same elegance, she put her finger tip into one nostril, and worked, patiently, without interrupting her reading, until she had extracted the annoyance. Still reading, she rolled it between the tips of her forefinger and thumb, until it was dry, smelled of it, and flicked it to the jute carpet. God, Irvine thought: she's wonderful! He felt ashamed of himself; for now he waited, hoping that she would do this or something like it again; and when he became sufficiently aware of his shame, he withdrew, to past the rear of the cottage. There on the line, he could see bathing suits. He struck a match so that he might enjoy the cedar color. Suddenly we [sic] wanted to smell the suit. What sort of a Peeping Tom am I, he said to himself, touched it—it was a fine silk-wool—and walked away.

He remembered the school word: Furter. Runs around smelling girl's bicycle-saddles.

"Nice going," he said scornfully, aloud.

So he sat and played bridge with the Darts, as a form of penance and because he could think of no better way to pass the time; but he left early, afraid he might already be too late, and ran all the way to the rear of the Fowlers'—Parkers'—cottage. He was too late. Mr. and Mrs. Parker were still up, but the girl was nowhere in sight, and there were no lights on upstairs.

It serves me right, he thought.

The bathing suit smelled of its own fabric and of the sea, and again he remembered the delicate discoloration of her thighs.

She is like the sea herself, he thought.

> Where I waited, listlessly,
> On Summer's unportentuous brink,
> You stepped up out of the sea.
> Now I can no longer think
>
> Of any idle dream on earth
> Which once beguiled my wasted days.

When the quiet sea gave you birth,
I too was born, to sing your praise.
Born for that, and that alone.
Here for all time I dedicate
Heart and mind, and blood and bone,
Wholly to our mutual fate.

Like a wild creature of the sea,
Colored like the sea at dawn,
So you first appeared to me:
Just so, would I see you drawn,

Had I the knowledge and the art
A hundredth, toward that peerless task.
Dear, I have neither, but my heart
Is wholly yours; you've but to ask.

Nuts, he said to himself.

He changed *idleness* to *idle dreams,* and back to *idleness; peerless* to *matchless.*

"*You've but to ask;*" he thought, "Who's doing the asking around here anyway!"

He had seldom written a worse poem. But he did not destroy it. Instead, he gave it the title *On First Watching a Young Woman Come Out of the Sea,* and went to bed. Five minutes later he turned on the light, deleted this title, wrote *Sea Piece,* changed *a hundredth* to *one thousandth,* and again shut off the light.

It was nearly four o'clock.

"Dream Sequence"

"Dream Sequence"

This unusual dream is the first step of Agee's "journey" back into what he could remember or infer about his earliest childhood. A beautiful, but frightening, story, which seems to have been written during the beginning of the composition of *A Death in the Family*, it is the true introduction to that unfinished novel. It may also be seen as evidence that *A Death in the Family* was closer to being finished than has often been thought, insofar as one of the reasons for writing it—to recall things remembered or inferred about the father—had been achieved.

The narrator of "Dream Sequence" (Agee?) states that he must write about the years of his childhood. Some of the same phrases which appear in *A Death in the Family* are employed in this "dream" also. The implication of the "dream" is something Agee was at that time discovering: for the writer to return to memories which yield material for art, other interests have to be ignored. For the artist to retain his integrity, he must concentrate on writing. This is also the only way he can retain his dignity.

Like "1928 Story" which precedes it in this Agee volume, "Dream Sequence" is a personal remembrance; but in the "dream," images of childhood are fused with the horror of contemporary times. The near surrealistic method of its style is reminiscent of Céline. A scene can suddenly shift from broiling heat to freezing cold, or people on a busy city street can go about their business ignoring the grotesque. The phraseology of the "dream," especially near its beginning, is much like the opening of "1928 Story." But the horror of the time is only hinted at there. In this manuscript, by contrast, the present becomes a hideous nightmare and is fused with earliest childhood. The death, the absence, and the "betrayal" of the father all seem to be related to the disappointments of the dreamer with the contemporary world, yet it is impossible for him to understand how past and present are related. As the "dream" is read, however, it becomes clearer and clearer that the only action which has any meaning is the individual act of integrity.

After the nightmare has been suffered, it is clear to the dreamer/narrator that he must "go back" into the years of his childhood. When that "journey" is honestly undertaken, some peace of mind may be found, even though the chaos of the contemporary world remains. Thus, Agee seems to have realized as he began writing his last book that it was much more important for him to perform the individual artistic act, "a simple act of veneration," than it was to remain worried about the problems of a mass society.

The "Dream Sequence" is an explicit expression of Agee's realization that something like the clarity of earlier times can be achieved by art. It was excluded from use as introduction to *A Death in the Family* because editors felt that "Knoxville: Summer, 1915" (actually written in 1936) seemed a more pleasant, appropriate opening for the novel. However, this intended beginning to Agee's novel about family strikes many chords which suggest both the writer's dissatisfaction as a writer, and his ability to demonstrate that he could successfully build on frustrations.

"Dream Sequence"
(An unused passage possibly intended as
introduction to *A Death in the Family*)

It was about noon, the lunch hour for clerks and for men in
overalls, and for that hour the city, crowded as it was, was be-
mused and slack; a softly rattling, almost Sunday stillness. The
sun bore straight down without shadows. It was so hot that the
air was a gunmetal haze, smelling of soft coal, live steam, and
exhausts. In the shapeless part of town where he walked, there
were more open yards than buildings, and the yards were full of
old iron of used and derelict cars; above them, the heat, like curling just visible flame. Many were sitting, eating, in weak little
edges of shade; nobody was walking who could help it, and those
who walked went slowly.

He had thought that it was one of the streets of Chattanooga between the two depots, but now he began to realize that
he was back home, in Knoxville, for he could see that the broken
street thickened, far ahead of him, into the busiest blocks of Gay
Street. He was both happy to be home, and wary, for he liked the
Southerners who had never gone North but he knew if they
knew his mind they would hate him. Two blocks ahead a crowd
was doing some terrible piece of violence, and the pit of his
stomach went cold, yet now he felt really at home. He kept on
walking towards it at his same pace, the loose stride inherited
from the mountains, but a little more briskly than Southerners
walked. He was pretty sure that the violence would be over, and
the crowd drifted, by the time he got there; if it isn't, he thought,
and they turn on me, that's all right to [*sic*]. Not just exactly, but
the way it was meant to be. He took care not to slow down, and
not to hurry, for it was not his business to try to alter fate; and
sure enough, by the time he was half a block away, the crowd
was releasing like a fist undoing, and the hunched men in shirt
sleeves and in undershirts were moving away, and now he
could see the man they had attacked, naked across the sidewalk,

and even before he came up to him he knew that he was dead. He knew, too, that this man had stood in the street with furious eyes and had dared to shout into the noon hour, for everyone to hear, the truths and self-deceptions and the passionate beliefs and commitments which must certainly and always mean great danger to him and sooner or later, now at last, death. For just as he had begun to suspect, this was indeed John the Baptist. It was the first time he had seen him face to face but he knew him.

The whole time, everywhere, was bursting with woe and fear and injustice and with this kind of passion and cruelty, and he was no longer of any side, no longer capable of any sufficient conviction except in the heroism, and meanness of soul, and blind hopelessness, of the whole gnashing machinery: one who could truly love liberty and honor must know that all those who tried to advance either, destroyed both. His most hopeful belief had been the belief for which John had died, and echoes of that hope and devotion returned to him now, quite hopelessly, as echoes of religious faith sometimes haunted him. He stood and looked down at the killed man and smiled, remembering, and cried quietly inside, dry crying, which hardly touched him. The old loudmouth, he thought with affection; the old ranter. He knew by heart the bawling cheapness, and the fierce-eyed frenzy, part real, part put-on, and he felt as much respect for it as dislike. It was from *way* back. Way back in the country, and in time, and in the human race. A stubborn, intrepid, archaic, insanely bigoted man, begging for trouble, begging for violence and for death until finally they gave it to him. A hero, not a neutral. Neutrals can die too, he reminded himself; caught in the crossfire from all the convinced ones; they are despised by all the convinced ones, and by each other, and by themselves; and sooner or later that will happen. You have no more choice about neutrality, he told himself, than about partisanship. The only possible faithfulness is faithfulness to the best you can understand at the time. Nevertheless he could only think ill of himself for his inevitable but convenient lack of convictions, as he looked down at the dead man; and this perhaps gave him more courage than he might otherwise have had. For even as he looked down he could see out of the ends of his eyes that the brutal and light-triggered nucleus of the crowd still lingered, not far away, and watched him, and even if he had not seen, he would have felt their eyes on him, and he knew very well the qualities which are uniquely to be feared in the eyes of the men of his part of the country; such still eyes, watching, with that terrifying whiteness increasing in them. The sons of bitches, he said to himself. The damned scum. The Common Man. It isn't enough to set on a man and beat him to death in the street (however obnoxiously he insulted them into martyring him); you strip him naked and you leave him where he lies as you wouldn't even leave a dead dog. No sense of honor towards a brave enemy. No sense of honor towards the dead. O sure I know, he reflected quickly; his crowd is no better than yours; and he thought of Mussolini and his girl, hung up like hogs at the filling station, and the falsely libertarian faces, goggling, he would have loved to have spit in. Nearly all, of every side, are just so many apes and cowards and vindictive swine, he thought; my own kind included; but on every side too there is devotion and the absolute honor that is in absolute courage: and this is how they recognize it and honor it. What they loathe and fear most of all. They beg so for the contempt of brave men that as a matter of fact they beg the brave crazy ones to beg them to kill them. To show one flicker of sympathy, he realized, is quite possibly just as dangerous as ranting. Hogs. Fools. Cowardly bullying bastards. He straightened up and looked cooly around into one pair of eyes and then the next and at all of them, and they were all watching him and waiting for what he might do, and he did not lower his eyes or even blink, dry as his eyes were getting, and neither did they. He looked down again at the dead man and his heart spread and he loved the brave old bellower misled and misleading. Come on, John, he whispered, smiling again. We're going to find you a better place to rest than this. We're going to find you a place where you can lie out in the open, but in honor and in state. Laid out decently as a dead man ought to be. Where everyone who goes by can know you for a dead man and a hero. He squatted down and put his arms under the shoulders and under the knees and picked him up and carried him like a baby, but with the killed head lolling deep and heavy. The place you want to be, he whispered, as he started walking; and instantly he knew where that place was, and how to get there, though it was so many years now since he had been in Knoxville. He was pleased that he could remember the way so well. It was a certain corner, a vacant lot; he could already see it vividly in his mind's eye. That was where John wanted to lie for a while before burial and that was where he would bring him.

He crossed the street at his own pace through the traffic, and he looked into the eyes of those who lingered with cool arrogance. He could feel their eyes on him after he had passed and, knowing their kind, he knew that now quite possibly somebody would throw a rock or a tire-iron to jolt him or bring him down or even that some ex-football star might clip him. He was braced for it, and he knew that he could not get rid of the dread of violence and of pain, but he was quietly happy to realize, all the same, how little he really cared what would happen to him; and he began looking forward to how much damage he might be able to do them before they should make that impossible. From the hips on up his back felt cold and tight, waiting. He came near the corner he should turn into, to take the corpse where it belonged; he knew the eyes were all still on him, but still nothing happened. Again he took care neither to slow down nor to speed up, thinking, it's not my business to tamper with it, and realizing, somewhat less clearly, that to keep the same pace was also the safest thing to do. A few steps from the corner he was tempted to keep on straight down the same street, to show them his contempt, but again he thought, my only business is John, it isn't my business to meddle; and turned west into the new street; and as he turned, realized, that thus to vanish might also be the thing which would bring them into action, or might be the safest thing; and kept on, taking care not to meddle. After a few seconds he could feel their eyes again, but after a few seconds more he became sure that they were only standing there; nobody was following, and nobody was going to throw anything or do anything. He was tempted to look back because he was sure that would insult and challenge them, or make them believe he was afraid; and because he was curious to satisfy and increase his contempt for them by seeing them gangling there, but he knew that it would be beneath the dignity of his action which, after all, needed all the dignity he could retain for it by now: for evidently there had been no danger after all, or at best it only required a show of courage and contempt to make them put their tails between their legs, or possibly the mere sight of respect for the dead, and for courage, had awakened what little capacity for shame and for honor might perhaps be left in even the meanest of spirit; anyhow he was certainly no hero in what he had done and was doing; very likely his neutrality stuck out all over him; possibly even the corpse they had made was a shield behind which he was hiding. All right, he thought. All right. Let it be.

All it is at best is a simple act of veneration for the dead who died bravely, a simple act of contempt for those who killed him and stuffed him and let him lie where he fell. And he continued to look cooly into the eyes which met his, eyes of strangers to the action and to the meaning of what he was doing. There was clearly no further danger. His concern now was guardianship. To guard this violated man and to guard the meaning of both of them. He was contemptuous of all curiosity, and conjecture, and failure to understand, which he saw in these new eyes, and then he was contemptuous of his own contempt for how should they know, better than they happened to know, and it was, of course, an unlikely sight, even preposterous, possibly shocking. He began to feel almost kindly towards their innocence, and suddenly he became aware that in all this while since he had begun to carry him, he had been thinking only of himself and of the others, not of John at all. He was filled with shame. He found that the body had sagged clumsily during his carelessness, and he readjusted his hold, to carry it more decently, and looked down at the ruined body and down across his elbow at the head which hung so heavily, so deeply sunken into this death only a few minutes old, that he could see only the arched throat and the plowlike underside of the jaw and the chin through the pointed beard which stood straight upward like a spike. He shook his own head as he walked, continuing to gaze at that derangement of throat and jaw, and a certain darkness and stillness clouded his heart, yet chiefly he felt a kind of amused and reverent tenderness and whispered repeatedly to the yawing head, "Poor old boy. Poor old boy." He was watching his burden so constantly now that he gave no heed to where he was going but he was sure he knew the way; without even seeing, he could see along his right the dying exquisite houses of the middle nineteenth century, furnished rooms, doctors' offices, and along his left a cold unhappy stillness, the hush gray stone of the church in which he had been confirmed; on the feast of the conversion of St. Paul, he reflected idly. Then more of those intricate houses, on both sides an occasional face of limestone tricked with sooty marble; a few shade trees, few people, the silence of parked cars, the silent heat: God how it all came back. And now the second corner and the turn to the left and there was the corner he had in mind, exactly as he had remembered and foreseen it, thought it must be twenty years; and as he came nearer that empty corner he knew that it was not the right one after all, and in the same instant he knew the one which was right. He was equally amused by his stupidity and by his instant and now unquestionable knowledge of the somewhat similar corner he had really meant. Yes. Back down that street and across the other viaduct, not Clinch, Asylum; on the far side: and again he could see it clearly, and all the streets between. He laid John down gently and in order, and took a breather. He had become quite heavy, the last block or so.

But when he bent low to lift him again the smell had become so sickening that he had immediately to straighten up into the clear air. He stood there a few seconds and thought about it, with his stomach knocking and his mouth flooding saliva. He knew that it was going to be more than he could do, to carry him now. The whole body had softened and was streaked with brown, and it seemed that the stench became still worse with every second.

But when he leaned down low to take him up in his arms again, the corpse stank so that he had immediately to straighten up into the clean air. He stood there for a few seconds and tried to brace himself up to what he had to do, but his stomach kept knocking, and his mouth flooded saliva, the very hands with which he had just touched the body, felt nausea. The whole body had softened and was streaked with brown; he could see the brown streaks extend and widen even while he watched, and the stench became still more rotten with every second. To carry him now, decently and kindly, as he ought to be carried, was just more than he could do. For a little while he could not quite bring himself to do what he had to do; then abruptly, turning his face away and holding his breath, he reached down with his right hand and caught the sharp bones of both ankles between his knuckles as if he were handling a baby, and turned his back, and began slowly to drag the body along the pavement like a sled. He tried to drag it respectfully, but one backward glance was enough to convince him that in what he was doing, there could be no respect. Again he wondered whether he could possibly carry him; but even as it was, the smell was as much as he could endure. It's all I can do under the circumstances, that's all, he thought. It's a hell of a way to treat anyone, but it'll have to do. And he set himself the modest goals of dragging the body gently, so as to hurt and bump it as little as possible, and of keeping his face clear of any show of disgust or even of doing anything out of the ordinary; and in the effort to look sober and stolid, he began to feel sober and stolid. The town had certainly changed. It wasn't as he remembered it from childhood, nor did he like its looks as well as his memories of it, nor was it as he remembered it from the middle thirties; he didn't like its looks even as well as that; it was a blend of the two. And for every old sight which touched him and made him happy and lonely, there was something new which he disliked. Even the heat and sunlight of the weather was different, it was the weather of a bigger, worse, more proud and foolish city: ignored, as if it were possible to ignore, and complained about, as if proper legislation might improve it; and there was something else altered and odd about it. The light of the noon sun was as white as snow on the pavement and looking down, he saw that in fact it was snow and that his feet were numb with cold, and with good reason, for they were bare; and not only his feet, he was as naked as the man he dragged. Well I guess that's as it should be, he thought, accepting the new turn of fate with calm amusement; and again he became aware of the people in the streets, meeting their eyes with calm, and with a challenge behind the calm; but they took no special notice. He came down the little hill across from the Asylum and turned left into Asylum Avenue and he could see where the viaduct angled ahead, just as his earliest memories of it, and now he was on the viaduct; and the pain in his feet, which by now were bleeding as well as frozen, gave him back a sense of courage, difficulty, and dignity, so that he felt gravely cheerful, and knew there was a smile on his face. There were quite a few people along the viaduct and he was intensely interested in them because they were so uninterested in what they saw. It wasn't as if they did not see at all; without exception they saw this naked man dragging this naked corpse through the thin snow; they looked with some interest; they even stopped in their tracks and looked after. But their interest was so strangely out of ratio to the thing they were looking at. It was about as if he were fully dressed, he realized, and was carrying something slightly outlandish, unwrapped say, one of those fancy bridge lamps with a lot of beaded fringe, or maybe a watercloset bowl: something which might slightly amuse and interest you to see carried in the open through the streets, but you would subdue your interest and amusement out of a sort of amused sympathy for the man who had to carry it. Or of course, the times being what they were, very likely this weird mildness of curiosity was a measure of the commonness, by now, of just such things, mob murders, corpses of heroes dragged through the streets, the callousness, the anesthesia, which must have developed during the plagues of the Middle Ages. But these were all such well-meaning, comfortable, nominally safe and civilized people, and that was what made their casualness so amazing and so amusing. He became more and more fond of them as they passed, and more and more amused by them and by the whole matter and by the world they all lived in, so touched, and so amused, by his sense of the absolute corruption of spirit and by his knowledge of doom, that suddenly he heard his soul exclaim in silence within him, delighted, sad, and in some way proud, "This could only happen in Alexandria!" But instantly he was aware that it was better even than that: for it was happening in Knoxville, in East Tennessee, in the middle of a day towards the middle of the twentieth century, and if this could only happen in Alexandria, then this was Alexandria now.

Without pausing in his walking he looked back to see how John was holding up: the snow had helped. There were blue streaks now as big as the brown, and they meant that the flesh was frozen, and would keep at least for a little while. The only trouble was the head. Through some kind of interplay between freezing and corruption, much of the head had become a kind of transparent gristle, yellowish and rubbery. He could see the thin dirty snow and the thin blue ice straight through it and, through the ice, the yellow and brown sand colors of the pavement, and all these colors of snow and ice and pavement were streaked by the movement of the dragging into straight graying streaks, and the trail the body had left in the snow was blue and brown. The head was not lasting at all well, it was only a question of time. He looked ahead to see how far they might still go, not far, he could remember, and sure enough he could see it, with a flinching deep within him of tenderness and joy and melancholy and great loneliness, he could see it, the very corner, the same outcrop of wrinkled limestone, like a lump of dirty laundry, the same tree even, and the tree had not even grown an inch. So shabby and sad; it had been waiting there all this time, and it had never changed, not a bit. So patient, and aloofly welcoming. Well. So you came back. His cold heart lifted in love and he walked more quickly, so quickly that a thud, striking him like a light blow in the stomach, just reminded him that he had neglected to jostle the body from the curb just opposite its corner; the head had struck hard, and looking back he could see, with sickness and grief, that now it hung to the body only by translucent shreds: and even as he looked, not yet having presence of mind to stop his dragging, the last shred broke and the head rolled clear, in a half circle, to a wobbling stop, cradling quietly in the middle of the street, so that with a groan of pity and shame he dropped the stony ankles and hurried to it and squatted to pick it up and saw it curling swiftly upon itself like a jellyfish, an armadillo, with a shape roughly like a catcher's mitt, and twitch away from his reaching hand. He could not endure to chase and corner and trap it as if it were some frightened animal but gently, sharing its escape with both hands, trying by the gentleness of his hands, without speaking, to assure it that it need not fear him, slid both hands beneath it and lifted its cold and gritty weight as if it were a Grail. By its withdrawal into itself it was no longer a head. It was a heavy rondure of tough jelly and of hair and beard and the hair sprang wild and radiant from his center where, meeting his eye, was one again, so disfigured that it was impossible to know whether it was a bloody glaring eye, or a mutely roaring mouth.

Waking, he felt none of the wise, sad amusement which had pervaded so much of his dream. His whole substance had become only horror and the coldest sorrow, so heavy and so still that when at last when he was able to reflect, it was only to wonder, without caring, whether he could ever lift himself up from the bed or move again. Then slowly he began to realize a few of the things which, during the dream, had wholly evaded his notice. The church was the church of St. John the Baptist. The Asylum was the Asylum for the Deaf and Dumb. John: St. John: had not been killed by beheading; the head had come off just short of the corner, and it was he who was responsible. The corner was where he used to sit with his father and it was there of all times and places that he had known best that his father loved him, and had known not only that he loved him but that he was glad of his existence and that he thought well of him. And his father had come out of the wilderness, and it was there that the Son had best known his homesickness for the wilderness.

So I suppose I'm Christ, he thought with self-loathing.
But which was John?

I've betrayed my father, he realized. Or myself. Or both of us.

How?

He thought of his father in his grave, over seven hundred miles away, and how many years. If he could only talk with him. But he knew that even if they could talk, they could never come at it between them, what the betrayal was.

He thought of the dream. He had no doubt of the terrifying magnitude of the dream, or that its meaning was the meaning he sought, but he doubted so thoroughly that the true meaning of any dream could ever be known, that he suspected that every effort to interpret a dream serves only to obscure and to distort what little of the true meaning may ultimately suggest itself.

He thought of all he could remember about his father and about his own direct relations with him. He could see nothing which even faintly illuminated his darkness, nor did he expect ever to see anything, yet if he could be sure of anything except betrayal and horror, he could be sure that that was where the dream indicated that he should go. He should go back into those years. As far as he could remember; and everything he could remember; nothing he had learned or done since; nothing except (so well as he could remember) what his father had been as he had known him, and what he had been as he had known himself, and what he had seen with his own eyes, and supposed with his own mind.

The more he thought of it the surer he became that there was nothing he could hope to understand out of it which was not already obvious to him. All the same, he could make the journey, as he had dreamed the dream, for its own sake, without trying to interpret; and if the journey was made with sufficient courage and care, very likely that of itself would be as near the answer as he would ever hope to get.

My father, he thought, not quite whispering the words, "My father," he whispered. And for a few moments it was as if his father were there in the room, not visible but clearly visible to the imagination, and his presence much more than imagination, a silent but almost unendurable power and aliveness: and he was not as the son could remember him, but was as he would have become by that time, by that morning of awakening from the dream: a strong, brave, sad old man, who also knew the dream, and no more knew or hoped ever to know its meaning, than the son. And even if they could have talked, there was not much they could have said to each other; but that was no great matter, for at last all was well. All his life, as he had begun during recent years to realize, had been shaped above all else by his father and by his father's absence. All his life he had fiercely loathed authority and had as fiercely loved courage and mastery. In every older man, constantly, he had looked for a father, or fought him, or both. And here he was, and all was well at last, and even though he was more rapidly fading, and most likely would never return, that was all right too. It might never be fully understood, but would be all right from now on. From now on it was going to be all right. Thank you for coming, he said in silence. Goodbye. God keep you. Or whatever it is that keeps you.

His father did not say goodbye, anymore than the other time, but he knew of his brief smile, much as it had always been, and then he was gone.

He was alone again now, but that was no harm, for in a way in which he had been alone for so many years, he knew that he would never be alone again.

"Surprise"

"Surprise"

This is an excluded chapter from the working manuscript for *A Death in the Family*. It demonstrates how Agee allowed his mind to work over materials from his childhood. Had editors chosen to include it in the posthumous book it would have necessitated omissions in the inter-chapters of the book, the other flashback sections. Yet it stands as an excellent example of the ability Agee had developed as a writer. In some ways this unused chapter is more interesting than the one which it parallels in the book because it provides a more detailed picture of Rufus. That detailed picture also suggests considerably wider meaning.

In one of the notes for *A Death in the Family*, Agee recalled that on the day of his father's funeral he and his sister were taught how to read the comic papers—on their stomachs, legs up, elbows just so. In a related note he commented: ". . . 'comic strip' people doing and being archetypal things & unaware of it."[1] Agee realized that actions such as comic-reading, or seeing a baby sister for the first time, if delineated properly would stand for more than just particular events recalled. They would be in the fullest sense archetypal actions. This realization suggests an important facet of *A Death in the Family*. A particular memory, or inference, carefully written about, yields universal meaning.

Note

[1] Agee, *A Death in the Family*: "Notes 1909-1916" and autograph miscellaneous pages. Harry Ransom Humanities Research Center, The University of Texas at Austin.

"Surprise"
(An unused chapter for *A Death in the Family*)

One day his mother gave him a bath all over right in the middle of the morning and put new white stockings on him and the shining, crackling thing she called his white peakay, and while she dressed him she told him that soon now Aunt Paula was going to come and take him down to Granma and Granpa's for a nice visit, two or three days maybe, and when he came home again there was going to be the most wonderful surprise. He thought he knew what a surprise was but to make sure he asked, and sure enough, she said it was like at Christmas when Santy brings us all presents, you remember don't you Rufus?, and he could vaguely remember; only, his mother said, this was going to be even more wonderful than Christmas. When asked what is it she said, Now if I told you it wouldn't be a surprise anymore, now would it? And no matter how he begged, she wouldn't tell him. It'll be so much more fun, she said, if you *wait* and find out. I just want to see your little face, she said, when you *see* it.

Then Aunt Paula came and his mother told her that everyone must keep the surprise a deep-dark, ess ee see are—now isn't that silly of me: *secret*! And they both laughed. Before he left she took him to the bathroom for one last try, and even washed his hand for him though he knew how, and then she said come here a moment Rufus, and sat on the creaking dirty clothes hamper and took him between her knees. She looked into his eyes very closely and began to smile. "Little Rufus," she said, and her head tilted to one side and she still looked at him, still smiling. "Now be a good boy," she said, "And Rufus, Try your *very* best not to wet the bed. Will you?" He nodded. "Don't drink *anything* for supper or from *then on*. And be sure you try one last time. *Just* before you go to bed. Will you?" He nodded. He knew all this by heart and he knew there was no use in it. "And the *minute* you feel you want to go in the night just *rush* out of bed and use the potty. Don't wait one *single* minute! Will you?" He nodded. She put her long warm hand along his cheek and he leaned his head against it. He could see the little orange freckles dancing in her eyes. She did not speak. Her face looked almost frightened. For a moment a strange feeling came over him as if they were both moving very fast. "Goodbye my darling," she whispered finally, and he wondered whether she was going to cry, though her eyes were dry and very bright. "Mother loves you *so dearly*," she whispered, and hugged him hard.

But she didn't tell him what the surprise was, and during all the three days he stayed at Grandma and Granpa's, nobody else would tell him either. When he heard that it was still a secret Grampa grunted and said "the fait accompli," and then he made that noise with his lips that Mama didn't like. "Personally," he said, "I think it's a lot of damn nonsense. But if Poll wants it that way, that's all there is to it." He ate a few bites. "Ours not to reason why," he said. He ate a few bites more. "Betcha dollars to doughnuts she'll tell him it came from heaven," he said. "*God* did it, not us: God." And again he made the noise. "Well what would *you* say Papa?" Hugh asked. "Fair question," Grampa said. He ate some more. "Well I wouldn't take him on a tour of the interior," he said. Uncle Hugh laughed. "Papa," Aunt Paula said, and laughed and blushed. "None of his business," Grampa went on. "But at least I'd let him know what's up. And I'd leave *God* where he belongs." Grandma was looking polite with her trumpet stuck out and now Uncle Hugh told her what they were talking about. "Yes," Grandma said. "So Paula told me." And she laughed merrily and politely, all by herself. "I think perhaps we'd better not discuss it, before him," she said. "So do I," Uncle Hugh said. "Consider me squelched," Grampa said. "Eat your vittles: stop your mouth." And he said no more about it.

The next day his father didn't come to see him, though he had promised to. "He has other fish to fry," Grampa said. "He means he's so busy he can't come," Uncle Hugh explained. But the next afternoon he did come, looking very tired and cheerful and somehow sheepish, and he brought candy for Rufus and ice cream for Rufus to give everybody else. "That surprise is home now," he said, "and tomorrow you'll come home and see it."

And instantly his curiosity which had been uncomfortable but hopeless, became almost more than he could stand. "O goody goody," he hollered, "What *is* it! What *is* it daddy what *is* it!" His father looked annoyed for a moment and then shook his head and smiled kindly, still looking annoyed. "I oughtn't even told you its come," he said. "Dog *gone* it." And for a moment Rufus was sure he was going to tell. But he shook his head again and said, "Son if I told you she'd snatch me baldheaded." Rufus looked at his father very seriously imagining his mother grabbing him by the hair and yanking it off so he had just a shining bald head like Grampa. It would be awful. His father looked into his worried eyes and laughed. "*Honey* I don't mean she *really* would," he said. "That's just a way of talking. Just a joke. I just mean mama'd be awful sorry, and mad. She'd feel just *awful* bad if she didn't get to tell you herself. She'd cry. Now you don't want to make mommer *cry* do you." "Oh *no*!" "Then you just be a good boy and wait just one more day. Huh?" "He's been just simply *swell* about it Jay." Hugh said. "If he could control his bladder the way he does his curiosity he'd be a champion, take it from me." "Sure he's a champion," his father said, "He's my *boy*." And he roughed his head against his thigh, and although Rufus was blushing about the wet bed, he felt wonderful. "All right then Rufus?" his father asked. He nodded. "All right then," he said. "Now kiss me goodbye and I'll see you on tomorrow." And he stopped and Rufus came to him and suddenly was sweeping next the ceiling and looked down into his father's dark, exhausted, happy face, and his father shook him so hard that he screamed with pleasure. Then he set him down and said "Well I gotta make tracks—fast," and hurried out the back door while they all called "Love to Laura," and he called back, grinning, "I sure will," and he hurried with long strides up the hill; and as he watched him get smaller along the hill Rufus realized that he wanted so much to be home with the surprise that he hadn't even waited for the ice cream which just now, even though it wasn't long till supper, Granma brought in on a shining silver tray, in special dishes, with cookies, and iced tea, and little lace napkins. She was beaming and looking mischievous, and Rufus could see that she was surprised and disappointed that his father had already gone away, but she pretended that she wasn't and said gaily, "Well even if our guest of honor can't be with us I think it's a very suitable occasion to spoil our appetites." And a little later, after seeming to wait for Grampa to do something, she raised her frosty glass and said "To Jay and dear Laura and the darling little—" She seemed to catch herself and she looked at Rufus and laughed mischievously. "The little *surprise!*" she said. "And little *Rufus* too!" Then they all drank iced tea. Grampa grunted, but he drank too. And she kept saying to Rufus, "Is there still room in that little breadbasket for one more cookie?" So he ate all the cookies and ice cream he wanted, and even in spite of the bed she gave him a second glass of iced cambric tea. "Afloat in the forest," Granpa said as Rufus shyly accepted it, and Uncle Hugh and Aunt Paula burst out laughing, though Rufus couldn't imagine why; and the more puzzled he looked, the harder they laughed. "*In the forest* is good," Uncle Hugh said, looking at his bewilderment. "Me retrroveye donze oona selve oscoorrrah." And they kept laughing. "Aww *pore* little Roofis," Uncle Hugh finally said. "He looks *soo* hacked." "We're not laughing at *you*," Aunt Paula said gaily, and that made him feel less uneasy, though they certainly did seem to be laughing at him; so he began to grin shyly himself, and at that they all laughed more, but he could see they were laughing kindly. "Something amusing?" Granma asked; and suddenly they all realized that all this time she had been smiling courteously, with her trumpet ready. "Oh poor Mama," Uncle Hugh said, and Granpa leaned close to her trumpet and said: "Nothing much, Emmah. It's just—too com—pli—cated—to repeat." She nodded smiling with each word. "Sorry," he said. "Thank you," Granma said, smiling; "no matter." And she laid her trumpet down and sat smiling with her scarred hands in her lap; but now they all took care to talk to her.

That night he wet the bed so hard it even went off the oil cloth and soaked his pillow too, but Granma was just as nice about it as ever. "Some people simply learn more slowly than others, she said. "But you'll learn, and how nice that will be. Won't it." "Yes, Granma," he shouted earnestly and he could almost imagine how nice that would be. But not that he would ever learn.

Next day right after his nap Granma said, "And now little Rufus is going home." She washed him all over and helped him into his white pekay. To Aunt Paula she said, "Give dear Laura all my love and ask her, if she feels up to it, say we'd all like to pay a little call, late this afternoon." To Rufus she said, "Granma has been so happy to have you for this lovely little visit and she hopes that Rufus has enjoyed it too." She waited

a moment. "Has he?" She said sweetly. "O yes Granma," he
called, and they kissed. "Strong little back," Granma croaked,
and she rubbed and patted it hard. "Tell Mama that Granma says
you've been *very good* and it was a joy to have you," she said.
"Yes Granma."

Now every step he took brought him nearer and nearer
and nearer knowing what the surprise was, and he could not
imagine what it was going to be. "Is it ice cream?" he asked
Aunt Paula; but even before she smiled and said "no" he was
sure it was something even nicer. "Is it chocolate candy?" But
he knew it was better than that. "No." "Is it a vuh, a vuh,
vuhl—" "Velocipede?" Aunt Paula asked. "Is it?" It must be for
she had said it, and that *would* be a wonderful surprise. "No
Rufus," she said, "you'll have to be a little bit bigger for that. But
you just wait and see. It's a nice surprise." It couldn't be as nice
as a vuh, vuhl, he thought. Unless—he turned and looked up at
her with his eyes shining, "Oh Aunt *Paula*," he said, almost
breathless with joy. "*Is it pants that flap open in front?*"
"*Awww*," she said, "No it *isn't* Roofis. But I know it's something you're going to like, just *ever* so much. I promise you."
But now he could not think of anything else that could be good
enough; and soon they turned a corner and down the bright
street in the twinkling shade he could see home. "*Run* Aunt
Paula," he gasped, and he started running as fast as he could, and
she trotted laughing beside him.

When he turned in from the sidewalk, and raced straight
for the front porch it was even more exciting, for the porch and
the front door looked strangely still, as if nobody was inside, and
they got big as he ran towards them, and when he heard his feet
on the front steps and hollow on the porch floor his scalp began
to prickle and he knew that in almost no time now he would
know. And as he came, he could see through the screen door
how something large and white came rushing through the dark
hall getting bigger and bigger, and the screen door burst open and
a great big fat old lady in blazing white, with such black skin, ran
out to him, stooping while she ran, and swept him up in her
arms, crying "Lord God how mah baby done *growed*!" She was
so big and she came so fast that she frightened him but as soon as
she took him in her arms she smelled so good that he wasn't
frightened anymore; mystified as he was, he pushed his forehead
against her warm neck and for a moment he felt almost sleepy.
She was droning and groaning happily, words he could not quite

hear, and now she took him by the shoulders and held him away, saying "Lemma git a good *look* at you chile; hello Miss Paula," she said over her shoulder, "You lookin *mighty* sweet," but she continued to look at him, through her little gold glasses, and as he looked back into the huge shining face and at the little glasses which perched on it like a butterfly, he liked her so much that he asked Aunt Paula, "is she the surprise?" "Why no Rufus," Aunt Paula said, "that's *Victoria*. Don't you remember *Victoria*? It's all a surprise to him," she explained to Victoria, "it's a secret." "Blus his lil hot," Victoria said. "Victoria took care of you when you were just a tiny baby," Aunt Paula said. "Bless his lil hot how *would* he remembuh," Victoria exclaimed. "He was still in didies when I seed him de las," She got up grunting. "Come on in Chile and see yo lil—" she laughed and moved inside. "You come an find out about dat lil surprise, honey." And she stood aside for him. "Ain't he a *darlin*," she said to Aunt Paula as they followed through the door. "Ain't he jist the *spittin image* of his *mama*?" "No, in heah, chile," she said, and turned ahead of him. "Mama's *downstairs* now;" and she led them back to the door of his room and rapped softly on the door. "Miss Laura?" she said in a low voice. "Mist Agee? He's done heah." "Come in," he heard his mother's voice. And Victoria opened the door.

And there she was. She was propped up on pillows in bed, smiling, and she looked weak and gray and pretty. "Come here darling," she said in a weak voice, and smiled even more. And there was Daddy. He was standing on the other side of the bed where it was almost dark and he looked shyly at his son, looking even more sheepish, and then he grinned and Rufus could see his white teeth in the shadow. "Come here," his mother said again, but he still hardly heard her. The shade was drawn more than half way down so that the room was faint and hot and there was stifling power and stillness all through the air and a delicate stifling smell, so that he stopped at the threshold without knowing he had stopped. Then he realized that she had said "Come here," twice, and he walked shyly over to her, looking into her smiling eyes. "Oh be *careful* dear," she gasped; and he was startled, and then he realized that he had knocked against a sort of basket by her bed. He stepped away from it and she took him in her arms. "Mother's little boy," she said. The delicate smell was much heavier now. It came from her and he wished he could put his head out the window but he suspected that she would not like it if he pulled away. "Mother's so happy to see him again," she said. "Paula?" "Hello Laura," and he felt her close behind him and stood aside, and Aunt Paula and his mother kissed. "Hello Daddy," Rufus said. "Hello there," his father whispered, and he grinned again. He was wearing his best suit, coat and all, and a white shirt, and he was sweating. "Rufus," he heard. It was his mother again. "See what's here." "Huh?" he said before he thought and expected her to say, "Don't say *huh* Rufus, say what *is* it?" But instead she said, "in the little basket, darling. Be very *quiet*," and she pointed, and it was quite a big basket, the one he knocked against; and standing on tiptoe to look in, he saw a baby there, smaller and redder than he had ever seen before. It was asleep and there were round bulges under the big eyelids. She smelled just like his mother did. He was very much interested and looked to his mother and then to his father to explain. They were watching him very closely and they were smiling. His father looked bashful and amused, but his mother said: "That's your little sister, Rufus, Little Emma. She's come to live with us and make us all happy." Behind him he could hear Victoria, laughing hard but inaudibly inside herself and murmuring, almost inaudibly, "Bless his lil hot; hee hee hee! Whoooooeee! Bless his lil hot! hee hee hee! Whoooooeee! Bless his lil hot." So that was who. He looked back at the baby. That was where the air was so strong and still. The netted shadow of the curtain lay on her round cheek. It scarcely moved, but it moved more than she did. There was a little hand, almost lost in its sleeve. The way the long eyelid closed its lashes across the bulge it looked like a baseball. He reached in with one stiff finger to see if he could make the eye open and heard his mother gasp "O Rufus Jay Victoria!" and when, startled, he looked up at her, she looked scared to death and looked at him with such sharp eyes that he was scared too, and his mother said "*He's trying* to put out her eyes!" And just as she said it a great black hand swept over his hand and pulled it gently away and he heard three people say "O *no*" and then his father laughing and saying "He just wanted her to open em up! Just want to see what they look like, don't you Rufus?" and he nodded uncertainly, and Victoria said, "he jes curious Miss Laura like his Daddy say, he ain't even ah seed his lil sistah befo, dat's all. He wouldn't hurt her, *would* he?" she said to Rufus. "He wouldn't harm a haih of her haid a purpose." That puzzled him a little because she had scarcely any hair *on* her head, but he knew he didn't want to hurt her, so he nodded. "Of *course* he wouldn't," his mother said, "He just scared me to death for a minute that was all. I guess I must be just sort of nerved up." "Sure darling," his father said. "But Rufus dear," his mother said, "You pay close attention now because there's something mother must tell you right now. Do you hear me?" "Yesm." "Tiny babies are very *very delicate* Rufus. They're very easy to hurt unless you know just how to take care of them. Do you see?" "Yesm." "So Rufus, you *look* at little Emma, all you *like*. We *know* you love her and want to see her. But don't *ever* touch her, dear, unless, we say you can. Because, Rufus," she made her voice very serious, "You might hurt her perfectly terribly Rufus, without meaning to. You see?" "Yesm." "Will you be sure to do that?" "Yesm." "Promise?" "Yesm." "Because if you don't Rufus, we might have to send little Emma away where you *couldn't* touch her, or ever *see* her. You wouldn't want us to do that, would you darling." "No mam." "Of course you wouldn't." "He thinks you're scoldin im Laura," his father said; and now that she took care she could see that he did look at least awfully unsure. "Why *darling*," she exclaimed, "Come here to Mother!" And he came and she took both his hands in hers. "Mother's not scolding," she said. "Not one bit in this world. Mother just wants you to know how very careful you must be with little Emma because she loves you *both so much*. See Rufus?" He nodded. "Yesm," he said. "Sit down by me a minute," his mother said. "*O no be careful,*" she gasped, for he almost sat on her. "There." She put her hand over his knees and then lifted it and smoothed back his hair. "Is my little Rufus glad to be home again?" she asked. "Mm-hm," he said. "Granma told me to tell you it was a joy to have me." He heard a kind of snicker from his father. "Well now isn't that *nice* of Granma." "Was he a good boy Paula? Why Paula! Why you haven't even seen the *baby* yet." "Why that's all right," Aunt Paula said, stepping over towards the basket. "I just didn't want to interrupt." She stood shyly in her summer dress and looked down at the baby with her hands folded. "My she's just darling," she said. "*Isn't* she," his mother said. "Just perfectly darling," Aunt Paula said. "What I can't get over," she said after a little while, "is those tiny hands." "I know," his mother said. "They're so, well so *complete*. To be so tiny." "I know." "Even little fingernails." "I know it seems just incredible, doesn't it." "Yes it does," Aunt Paula looked a little while longer without

saying anything, then she said, "Just darling," and stepped back.
"Mama's *so* happy about her name," Aunt Paula said. "*Is* she,"
his mother said, "Well I'm glad. I hoped she would be of course.
I only hope *little* Emma'll like it." "Why of course she will,"
Aunt Paula said, "Why wouldn't she?" "Well you never
know," his mother said, "I've never liked my name you know."
"Don't you," Aunt Paula said somewhat [   ]ly.* "Not that I care
much anymore but I used to simply hate it. Hugh doesn't like
his either." "I like yours all right," Aunt Paula said, "but I can't
stand mine." "Why Paula! Why! It's a *nice* name!" "I just
don't, that's all. But don't ever tell them." "Why Paula what a
shame. I always assumed you *liked* your name." Aunt Paula
laughed. "Always thought both of you did, too." His mother
laughed. "Well as I said you just never *know*, do you. You
mean so *well*, but the child may turn out to just hate it." "How
do you feel about your name Jay?" Aunt Paula asked. "Suits me
all right," his father said. "What about your other name, Hugh I
mean." "Well I don't use it but I ain't—I haven't anything
against it. Seems to me it suits Hugh fine." "It's a *nice* name
I think," his mother said. "I like *both* your names Jay." He
grinned. "Well you're pretty used to both of them," he said.
"Well that's true of course," she said, "But I think I like them
just for their *own merits* too. " She looked back and forth between his father and his aunt. "The only thing I feel a *little* sorry
about," she said,["] is not to have one of the Agee names in it.
Like Lamar or Margroves at least. No not Margroves, for a girl,
but Lamar. Jay's mother's maiden name, you know." "Oh yes,"
Aunt Paula said. "That'd be a *very* pretty middle name, why
didn't you use it?" "Well once we'd settled on Emma,"—"Well
anyhow! Just felt like doing all I could for Mama. Besides it just
sounds better, Emma Farrand. Emma Lamar. Just too many
ems don't you think?" "Why I don't know," Aunt Paula said.
"Emma Lamar. Emma Farrand. Emma Lamar Agee. No Laura I
kinda like it." "Me too," his father said. "I know dear. But then
people'd be so apt to call her *both* names. I know it's done a lot
dear, you don't mind it at all." "I kinda like it," he said, "But I
guess it's just too 'southern' for me to get used to, I'm sorry,
Emmer Larmar. Immer Lamaarr," she called. "Don't you see?"

---

*Adverb illegible.

she asked him. "Sounds all right to me," he said, "but why I don't want it is, *you* don't like it." "Aw, dear," she said, and took his hand. "I've been awfully selfish about it I'm afraid," she said. "And Jay's been just his own generous self." She squeezed his hand. "Jay wouldn't tell me which he hoped for," she told her sister, while his face darkened with a blush, "not til it was all over. Then he told me he'd *hoped* it would be a girl and he wanted to name it after his mother." She looked up at him. "Oh Jay, I'm embarrassing you!" "Naw that's allright." "I'm awfully sorry. I'll just shut my trap, as Papa would say." "Honey you started, you might as well go on ahead." "Dear," she said, and squeezed his hand again. "Well I spose you're right," she said, "Goly [*sic*] I shouldn't ever have started." Nobody spoke. "Well I—just *couldn't*," she said. "Much as I wanted to. I just couldn't give the name Jay wanted. Isn't that a shame Paula." "What is the name," her sister asked. "Actually its a perfectly nice name I guess and certainly as Jay's *mother's* name I like it because I do think the *world of her*. But it did seem too—well, *odd* a name, to give a tiny baby girl to grow up with. I jus—" His father broke in, smiling. "Laura's not goana get around to saying it if she talks all night," he said. "It's Moss," he said bashfully. "What?" "Just Moss. Like on a rock. Em Oh Ess Ess." "Moss," Aunt Paula said, carefully, "Moss, Why Laura I think that's a *nice* name. I *like* that. Moss. Moss Agee." "Then people'd call her, Mossy," his mother said, "and that I just couldn't stand for. Do you really!" "Why yes I do. Not Mossy but Moss. No I think that's nice." "Well for goodness sakes I'm glad you do. I'm glad you do like it. It must be something in *me* that I ought to—" "Laura dear," "I ought" "Laura, you know darn well you just don't like it and wouldn't even feel easy with it so honey please don't back track like that. Besides it's too late now. Think how your mother'd feel if you went and changed now. Besides it's bad luck to change a name. So let's not keep botherin our heads about it." "Wise," his mother said. "You certainly make me ashamed of myself to be so selfish but I guess you're right. It *is*, it would be a shame now that Mama knows. And they ought to be names we both like, not just one of us. You *do* like Emma, Jay? You weren't just pretending?" "Any name you like, Laura, I told you. Cep maybe Gweldolyn. I'd bring my foot down on that." They laughed. "Dear," she said, and she squeezed his hand and they smiled at each other.

"I don't want to stay too long," Aunt Paula said. "Why,

you're not Paula." "You need to rest. Besides, Mama." "Yes?" "Mama wanted me to tell you that if you feel up to it she'd like to come up a little while later this afternoon. Papa and Hugh, probably." "Why of *course* I feel up to it." "So maybe you ought to get a breathing spell, hum?" "Well actually I feel pretty fine considering, Paula, but I pretty soon do have to nurse her and it's true I guess I ought to lie quiet a little bef—" "Sure you ought." They kissed. "Mama sends you ever so much love," she said. "So do everybody. Clifford too. He wondered about later in the week, he'd—" "That would be fine." "he [*sic*] wanted to wait and give everybody plenty of time." "Later whenever. That would be fine. And my love to everybody."

Victoria was no longer in the room. Rufus now realized, and now that Aunt Paula pulled the door softly to behind her the room became breathlessly still, and they all just stayed in a quietness so deep that they could hear the baby breathing. His mother drew his father down by the hand and he sat on the edge of the bed, and Rufus looked from one of them to the other, and back, and again, and the two older people looked at each other and at him, smiling, and with very bright eyes, yet somehow very seriously, and the room seemed to lift quietly as a ship does when it is quietly lifted upon a long slow wave; and he saw how his father and mother now kept looking at each other, so gaily and yet so seriously, almost sadly, longer and longer, and how while they looked their smiles became so broad they tried to quiet them, and couldn't, and tried again, and just grinned, and how a tear ran out of his mother's eye and down across her smile, and she sniffed and smiled and looked at him and whispered, "Well, little Rufus," and, after a moment, "here we are." And his father nodded slowly, smiling, and stroked her wrist, and after a moment she whispered "Here's our family." And then for quite a while nobody said anything, and Rufus watched the light and shadow freckled in the barely breathing curtains. And as he watched he began to remember what in the confusion and all the talk he had forgotten, and turned with joy to his mother and asked: "Where's the surprise?"

APPENDIX

"Notes and Suggestions on the magazine . . ."
and Criticism of Culture

Agee's "Notes and Suggestions on the magazine under discussion . . ." remains in manuscript. That draft manuscript is an excellent example of how Agee went about criticizing his contemporary culture. Because it is not possible to reproduce this document, and because it should be studied in relation to Agee's other suggestions, such as his 1937 "Plans for Work," some representative quotations are edited here which relate to Agee's continuing plans for cultural study as a basic thrust in his development as writer.

Agee's most extended description of a method which might have been developed to incorporate many of his ideas about the criticism of popular culture is an eight-page statement written by him in the mid-1940's which outlines his proposed stance for a new type of journal. While admitting that the very highest critical standards should be maintained for the inclusion of fiction and satire, he admitted that if such standards were consistently followed, there would be an "apparent gap in materials available for inclusion." That gap could be filled "in a way that no magazine or other publication so far as he knew attempts to fill." His key words capsulize his hopes:

> It is the business of journalism to report; of comment and analysis it does very little. . . . Nominally editors, columnists, etc. make comment and analysis their business; but the results are almost without exception that the mere surface has been scraped. . . . I suggest that this proposed magazine could work a pincer-movement on experience or "reality," with journalism functioning very importantly as a part of the opposite arm of the pincers. We would use the findings of journalists, in other words, as they in turn use the findings of researchers; we can also supplement or extend their reporting by direct investigations. . . .
>
> This section of the magazine would be subdivided into many others, and would constitute a complete review, analysis and documentation of what has been happening in fields which are not, normally, under very strict review . . . our technique of review would be quite untraditional; we would, in fact, have to invent it. A best seller, for instance, should be reviewed not only on its "entertainment value": we would investigate

> the causes of that particular "value"; and we should
> treat it, chiefly, as the valuably suggestive anthropo-
> logical exhibit which it essentially is.[1]

Thus, a new kind of "criticism" would be developed, which might assist readers to understand why particular items in a culture are, or are not, held in esteem. In addition, an explanation of why, or how, taste changes at different times would become part of the analysis. A work under scrutiny would not be ana-lyzed just as a separate entity, but in relation to other aspects of the culture. Agee listed and sketched over a dozen separate categories or possible "depart-ments" for his proposed magazine. In some instances he even named specific persons whom he felt were best qualified for a particular kind of criticism. Ad-vertising, art and copy; moving pictures; music; books; public speeches; letters; records; art as well as rather more specialized areas like "sexual ethics" were included.

In these "Notes" he also included a category labeled "self-criticism." Self-attack and analysis and "disagreement among its editors" would be neces-sary if the enterprise was to be a success. Agee knew "it is hard enough for one man to hold to the standards we are presumably setting; far harder for a group to do so; the only possible development and continuance of health is in a wide-open self and mutual-criticism." One of the things which he hoped might be accomplished by such a magazine would have been "to undeceive readers of their own—and the editors'—conditioned reflexes." Agee added the qualifica-tion that, poorly run, such an endeavor could be "one of the most vicious things that has ever seen print." Essential to his doubts was the following question:

> whether "popularization" is intrinsically diseased and
> self-defeating[,] or extrinsically [diseased, because
> most popularizers are primarily interested in their
> pocketbooks]. It might be possible for instance to con-
> trive techniques for making clear to the most average
> reader—gradually—what is true and what is phoney
> in a photograph or a public speech or a letter; [sic]
> without sacrificing or in the long run simplifying any
> standard or perception we have. But if we judge it im-
> possible, then we must by no means try any "next-best
> thing"; for every next-best thing is worst.

Ultimately what he outlined in these notes was a very special kind of criticism which already, he said, a very small minority of sophisticated readers ("which . . . read *The Dial*, or *Criterion* or *Kenyon Review*") use to a small ex-tent in their conversation and in letters, but which "has been used in print little if at all." This many-faceted magazine which Agee dreamed of never materi-alized. Agee's many suggestions imply a need for a regular medium which would analyze all manner of things. Had he been able to develop some of his projects he would have approached these undertakings (given a prodigious amount of energy and minimum support) in the same "amateur" way he had al-ready approached the cinema.

Note

¹ "Notes and Suggestions on the magazine under discussion," typed carbon copy manuscript, Harry Ransom Humanities Research Center, The University of Texas Library at Austin.

"Scientists and Tramps"

Another example of Agee's response to problems caused by World War II is the screenplay plan he sketched for Charlie Chaplin. That working draft for "Scientists and Tramps" includes outlines for many scenes, but no more than notes were finished. While the draft runs to sixty-six holograph pages, it must be emphasized that just a sketch was actually completed. Limited quotations do suggest the nature of the project.

The prologue to this film was to be accompanied by a satirical speech embodying *the* American politician. While other dialogue was projected and several scenes were outlined, only the prologue was worked out in detail. This was to be made from newsreel clips and accompanied by a satiric speech. An opening harangue by the "Grand Old Man" of democracy is a beautiful example of the parody Agee relished. It suggests what can occur if people only pretend they are individuals when, in fact, they have become parts of the unthinking herd. The irony of the opening speech, which quickly gives way to pathos, is that the speaker apparently *believes* all of the things he says. His inability to examine what he is saying is glossed over by rhetoric. The speech, only partially reproduced below, is an amalgamation of all the clichés that Americans maintain. Earlier in the prologue the "Voice of Time" inquires, "Can man come of age in time to prevent his own destruction?" The speech, and the cheers with which it is accepted, indicate that Americans seemed to be incapable of deciding against the Bomb. This shocking preface was for a film which was conceived in the most deeply humane way. The repetitive speech of the Grand Old Man is directed at several groups. By harkening to the "Spirit of Individualism" the speaker plays upon the herd instinct of the masses to reveal an attitude about society.

As Agee began to write scenarios, his view of contemporary society, his abhorrence of the atomic bomb, his life-long admiration of Charlie Chaplin, and (perhaps) his fascination with Chaplin's *Verdoux* seem to have converged to suggest the tramp as an appropriate vehicle for a vision of a new society where the individual might again play a significant role. The projected screenplay "Scientists and Tramps" was sketched as a suggestion of what could happen should man trigger the "ultimate bomb." If our civilization, apparently on the brink of blowing itself up, did so, then the individualism embodied in Chaplin's tramp could serve as the symbol of a revitalizing force. Agee's notes for "Scientists and Tramps" indicate his fears about society following World War II. The horror of man's first use of atomic energy was an important aspect of his consciousness, a horror projected most forcefully in the satire "Dedication Day," a report of the commemoration ceremony for the monument erected in honor of the first historic use of atomic energy. There the humor is macabre. The victims of the holocaust are imagined as those given the "privilege" of tending an eternal flame which commemorates the occasion of man's first use of atomic power.[1] In the projected screenplay Agee imagines society reconstructing itself after the "ultimate bomb" had been dropped; but the mood of the projected film was to be without the bitterness of "Dedication Day." It is an attempt to suggest what might be possible for man if he could, again, act as an individual. The problem of individualism is at the core of Agee's concern in this scenario. Implied is a question: is it possible for an individual to retain dignity in a society where faith has been placed in science to the degree that men no longer are willing to assume the burden of thinking for themselves?

If an atomic bomb leveled the United States and a new civilization emerged from its ruins, Agee saw the individualism which Chaplin's tramp represented as an important symbol for hope. A film about the possibilities of reconstruction could be both a comedy which relied upon all of the skill Agee admired in Chaplin's work, and a commentary about contemporary America. The film was to take place following the nuclear destruction of much of the world. Parts of it were to be made in Manhattan, and near there the "Tramp's Community" was to be imaginatively established. The scientist's camp was to be not so far away, at Philadelphia. The story line began in the following manner: After "no more than five minutes" of "comic political-scientific prologue" the "ultimate Bomb" is dropped. Opening scenes were to be incorporated depicting the world-wide devastation. Then Chaplin does the first sequence as a "tremendous solo . . . wandering in a dead metropolis."[2] On the second day the tramp is piecing together "a way of living" when he discovers a baby, all but new born. On the following day he encounters still another survivor, a young woman, and the opening three-day sequence ends at nightfall "before they . . . realize their fortune, the wonder of being alive and of being a family." Glimpses were to be provided of other types who have also survived. "Diplomats, who were spotted in the prologue . . ., keep right on trying to be diplomats. Still more important, scientists keep right on trying to be scientists." The scientists would also, almost immediately, begin piecing together a new civilization. The reemergence of the two divergent ways of life would provide the basic development for the rest of the film.

The opening scenes would have been a combination of the best aspects of Chaplin's humanism combined with an implied criticism of the technocracy which produced the Bomb. It does not seem accidental that a policeman was chosen as the "first victim of the bomb." The tramp stumbles upon the blasted figure:

> He is a very irate and brutal cop, running right foot and
> night stick raised, on his face a glowing ferocity. The
> force, light and heat of the bomb have reduced and
> flattened him to a slightly distorted photograph
> against the stone wall of the building.

Agee saw that when such a bomb was dropped the "authorities" would have met their match. But he realized that they, and all the powers of science and government, would have been obliterated only for a little while. And the conclusion of the projected film certainly makes this clear. It ends with the scientists again very much in control.

Agee's sketch, in addition to the prologue and the opening scenes with the tramp and scientists, suggests how an alternation between the two camps would follow. The gradual ascension of the scientists once again to power would be a basic part of the film. The plans were for the film to alternate from the "Chaplinesque" to the scientific. Thus, there would have been shifts between "The Forces of Good ('maturity,' 'responsibility,' 'social-mindedness,' all the beliefs that have made civilization what it is), contrasted with simple child-like survival." Agee suggested the scientists would be "far gone" in abstraction. And this helps them to keep on "improving on the science of destruction" and to reestablish contact "with their kind all over the world." Finally:

> It is they who gather in the stragglers and the ec-
> centrics, including the whole of Chaplin's little civi-
> lization; and it is they who end the picture in triumph,
> with an even more terrible bomb up their sleeves and
> even more terrible destruction just around the corner
> from the last shots in the picture.

Other scene outlines indicate how the scientists would be portrayed during those hours after the detonation of the bomb when they were still unsure of its total effect. These men, with their immense scientific capabilities, are able to recover much of their original powers within a short span of time. Yet at the same time they remain unsure whether it would be prudent to touch their women. Always contrasted with such scenes is the fact that the Tramp is very calmly going about the business of reestablishing a community.

Some of the additional sketched scenes include moments when the scientists reveal their ineptitude, or selfishness, as contrasted with scenes about the other emergent group which reveal forgotten skills rediscovered because of love and care for other persons. The Tramps' community is altogether different from anything the modern world is used to: "The one concern is, does my own enjoyment deprive or hurt another; and that is also one of the few laws." Agee suggested that in this imaginary community

> it is found that nearly everybody prefers to work. . . .
> The wages are barter or work in exchange. . . . [And] it
> is explained that there is nothing intrinsically evil
> about machinery, synthetic substances, labor saving,
> etc., but that once they are admitted, chain reactions
> seem inevitably to set in which get far beyond human
> control. Plenty of people remember, wistfully, the
> pleasures of auto-driving, for instance. But the making
> of even one auto, and the use of power, involves too
> many people to be good in the long run . . . though ma-
> chines are neither good nor evil, much is lost when per-
> sonal skill and strength are lost.

How to dramatize all of this, and how to suggest that in a "Utopian" community all of the problems were not solved, was finally something Agee knew would be extremely difficult. The film was to be a satire and thus parts of it would be extremely funny. But at the same time he knew that "an all-important aspect of the picture [was] that utopias are not never-never lands;

that many of the sorrows and needs of individuals are never to be salved. . . ."

In view of what Agee felt about the projected film as a whole, the final sequence of the imagined picture is not really surprising. The care with which he sketches out its inevitability is an accomplishment. Here he combined the tragedy of a fate which must befall the individualism of the Tramp with irony which creates satire—amusing, and frightening at the same time. For there was no way for an individual such as a tramp to be tolerated in a society like the one being rebuilt. It was only a matter of time before he had to be eliminated. The final sequence was to include a confrontation between the two camps, described in general terms, in the following way:

> One by one they all move over to the scientists' camp. Some of the last few speak to him, take his hand. The burden of their explanation is that they are heartsick to say so (and they really are), but it is hopelessly impractical. If only all people felt as he did, of course.— But they *do*, the tramp insists, in their heart they do! If only they had the courage, the trust, ... [Finally the tramp] stands alone now. He bows silent to the Scientists, tips his hat to some woman and starts away. Two of the scientists . . . whispering (general idea: that man *could* be dangerous; radio the word along to pick him up when it won't be noticed).

> Old Glory climbs the remains of the Empire State, band plays the Star Spangled Banner, while all stand in solemn joy; we last see the Tramp walking west on the G. W. bridge. The anthem comes thinly through somebody's portable radio. He is alone, walking west into Sunset. Walking east, escorted by arm-banded Scientific policemen, is an extremely variegated representation of the whole human race, combed from the ruins, converging, hopefully upon the birth of the new world. The tramp smiles at them sportingly, they give him a black stare. By degrees these stares become hostile, and his whole demeanor becomes older and lovelier. At the same time, more and more like the old tramp—so that he picks up great gayety of life of his own as he moves out. As he changes, everyone sees him more and more as a rank and possibly dangerous outsider. One of the policemen picks up the scientist's message on his little radio. He gives the tramp the eye and speaks to another cop. The tramp eyes them back. They start after him, walking. He walks faster. They walk faster. He trots. They trot. He breaks into a headlong spring and disappears, off the end of the bridge with law and order in hot pursuit.

The only part of "Scientists and Tramps" which appears to be near complete is the introductory speech to be delivered by the "Grand Old Man" of democracy, but it sets the tone for everything which is to follow. This speech, which Agee wrote to be delivered against a buildup of film clips from newsreels, is a parody of American politics, and an indictment of the gullible American public. The speech runs to ten manuscript pages and in it the speaker insists that he respects the individualism that makes democracy great "in its place." The speech builds to a crescendo which makes it clear that no deviation from established patterns is to be tolerated at all. Respect for the individual hardly exists, and it becomes clear that much of what passes for democratic action is in reality the result of a fear that individual thinking may result in trouble for the masses. As parody this speech ranks with the best humor Agee wrote. The alternating voices of "Time" and "Individualism" prepare the way for the "Grand Old Man":

> *Voice of Time*
> . . . for better or for worse, civilization is knitted together by the cooperation of individuals in groups, of men and women who forget their little differences for the sake of the many. That is the meaning of democracy.
> *Voice of Individualism*
> The death knell of democracy, you mean!

As Agee conceived it, then, the beginning of the film would have been political satire which would have used as sound track a speech, a harangue, delivered by the voice of a caricatured politician. The words would have spun out in a verbal explosion at the beginning and combined with an explosion of still shots, newsreel clips, and acted scenes which would have established the mood of the world as it approached nuclear catastrophe. The lengthy speech, apparently complete, is a successful parody of a politician's way of speaking. But it is also an indictment of the many things which Americans are willing to accept without really thinking. It is, of course, that kind of non-thinking which places man on the brink of blowing himself off the earth.

"Scientists and Tramps," as projected, might well have been impossible to execute in a single film. This ambitious project would have combined an appreciation of the virtues of individualism with a celebration of the human soul, along with satire about the political foibles of twentieth-century America. Agee was convinced that modern man, so reliant upon science, had forgotten how to act as a separate person. In the exchange planned for the beginning of this film the "Voice of Individualism" laments: "We have forgotten how to think as single individuals, and how to feel moral responsibility as single individuals. We think and pass moral judgment in groups." However Agee is fully aware of the immense difficulties he confronted in finding a way of

> *dramatizing fully enough*, how [the tramp] has his strong influence on people. I am sure of it, that people coming slowly together out of the shock and horror and finding this childlike man, surviving bravely and well, could rediscover the childlikeness in themselves and live accordingly. . . .

Perhaps Agee's hopes for the film are best compared to those of utopian fiction. In times of cultural crises men tend to seek refuge in the past, in the future, or in various kinds of psychic withdrawal. Agee's projected film could be interpreted as a retreat from the horrors of the contemporary world. A similar pattern was followed by him in the conception and execution of his autobiographical novel, *A Death in the Family.* In fact, in all of his writing he celebrates moments of innocence as they are overshadowed by the complexities of living. Such is his accomplishment in *Let Us Now Praise Famous Men* where he chronicles the lives of tramp-like common tenant farmers. The sketch for "Scientists and Tramps" is only a beginning; yet its insight into the difficulty of maintaining one's integrity in a society such as ours remains important. Written over forty years ago, it is prophetic.

Notes

The materials included as Appendix are adapted from *Agee & Actuality* (Whitston Publishing Company, Troy, NY, 1991).

[1] "Dedication Day, rough sketch for a moving picture." *New Directions*, No. 10, ed. James Laughlin (New York: New Directions, 1948), 252-263.

[2] This manuscript is in the possession of Harry Ransom Humanities Research Center, The University of Texas Library at Austin and is catalogued as "Unidentified television or screenplay," autograph manuscript working draft with autograph revisions (c. 1948), 64pp.

Index